DIGITAL MARKETING:

Integrating Strategy and Tactics with Values

A Guidebook for Executives,
Managers, and Students

Routledge
Taylor & Francis Group
NEW YORK AND LONDON

Written By – Ira Kaufman & Chris Horton
Contributing Editor – Alyssa Adkins
Designer – Spencer Ploessl

First published 2015
by Routledge
711 Third Avenue, New York, NY 10017

and by Routledge
2 Park Square, Milton Park, Abingdon, Oxon OX14 4RN

Routledge is an imprint of the Taylor & Francis Group, an informa business

Library of Congress Cataloging-in-Publication Data
Kaufman, Ira Morton, 1947-
Digital marketing: integrating strategy and tactics with values / Ira Kaufman & Chris Horton.
pages cm
1. Internet marketing. 2. Marketing--Management. I. Horton, Chris (Marketing consultant) II. Title.
HF5415.1265.K386 2015
658.8'72--dc23
2014009856

ISBN: 978-0-415-71674-1 (hbk)
ISBN: 978-0-415-71675-8 (pbk)
ISBN: 978-1-315-87945-1 (ebk)

This book has been prepared from camera-ready copy provided by the authors.

DEDICATION

To my three visionary teachers:

J.E. Rash – for discovering the essence of my universal values and spiritual being

Philip Kotler – for guiding my understudying of marketing as a universal exchange of value

Eric Waldbaum – for refining my strategic thinking with excellence

To my family – Ashley, Diyaa, and Jelal, with whom I share love

Ira Kaufman

To the team at Synecore, for providing motivation and insight

To my family, for providing inspiration and meaning

Chris Horton

DIGITAL MARKETING:

Integrating Strategy and Tactics with Values

A Guidebook for Executives,
Managers, and Students

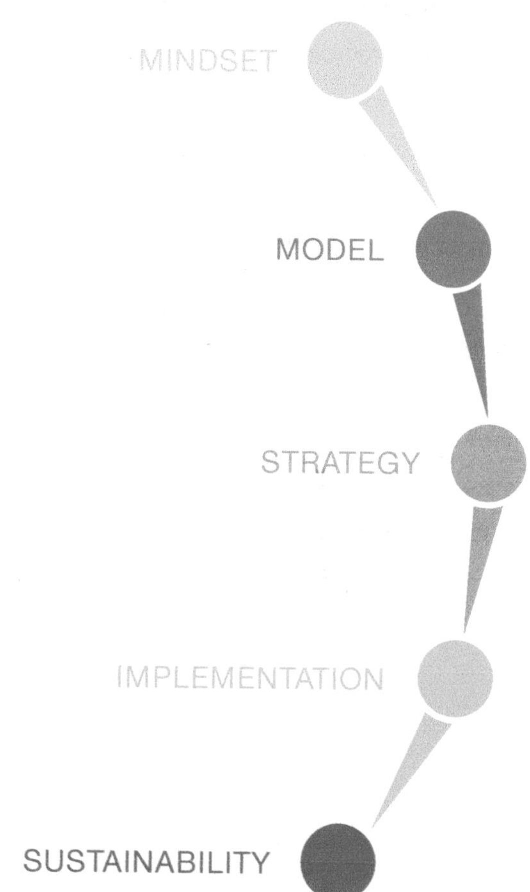

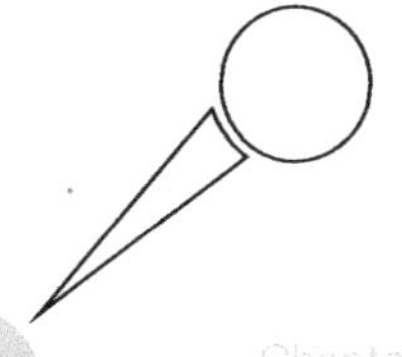

TABLE OF CONTENTS

FIGURES

ACKNOWLEDGEMENTS

The goal of this book is to prepare readers for the challenges and opportunities of marketing in the digital age.

To accomplish this, we drew from many different perspectives, collaborating with digital experts and novices, businesses and non-profits, Fortune 100 companies and SMBs, professors and students, and online magazines and research centers. Moreover, we realized it was important for us to "live digital" in terms of the book's design, content, and delivery.

First and foremost, we are grateful to John Szilagyi, former Business and Management Publisher at Routledge, who had the vision and courage to contract to publish this unique digital project. We are also appreciative of other members of the Routledge team, including Sharon Golan and Manjula Raman, who guided us through the publication process.

We sincerely appreciate the commitment and vision of Sean Royer and his team of digital natives at Synecore – a forward-thinking, integrated digital marketing agency – for the development and design of the book. As *Digital Marketing's* graphic designer, Spencer Ploessl was unceasingly dedicated to creating an attractive, digitally interactive book. Much of the content reflects the dedication and insightful work of Alyssa Adkins, as contributing editor, Craig Phillips, as program associate, and Derek Kegerreis and Erin Gough, as research associates. Web design diva Jacey Gulden conceived of and built the book's *Digital Marketing Resource Center*.

Ginger Conlon, Editor-in-Chief, Direct Marketing News, was very supportive of the project, providing content and ideas from the publication's executive contributors.

Professor Joe Turek, Dean of Lynchburg College School of Business and Economics, supported our vision of helping students take a strategic approach to digital marketing; the Lynchburg College students who tested the insights and refined the exercises provided invaluable input. Designing a book that would truly speak to and prepare executives, managers, and students for the digital age took two years of hard work and collaboration. Kip Knight, President, International and US Franchise Operations, H&R Block and former senior marketing executive, outlined the needs of the business community. Stef Nicovich, Professor at Lynchburg College, recognized the necessity for an easy-to-understand guidebook on digital marketing strategy, tactics, and tools. Debra Zahay-Blatz, Professor of Digital Marketing, Aurora University, helped frame the input on Internet marketing and broad data, while Renee Flutie, consultant and counselor, collaborated on editing and integrating the business and academic approaches. Some 15+ academic and trade reviewers encouraged the book's publication and made valuable inputs and criticisms to refine its concepts. Thank you all for your contributions to making this book a reality.

Finally, any mistakes or errors contained within the body of the manuscript or on its companion website are solely our own.

EMBRACE THE NEW DIGITAL MINDSET *[Foreword]*

I have been a long time marketing scholar and practitioner who helped launch modern marketing with my books on Marketing Management and Principles of Marketing. I drew together insights from other fields, such as economics, social science, organizational theory and analytics to build an integrated platform that companies could use for creating customer value, the objective of any company that wants to win.

Looking at the recent great revolutions in globalization, technology, and sustainability, I recognize that modern marketing must be reconstituted to move into the digital age. I applaud Ira Kaufman and Chris Horton's effort to advance marketing. In ***Digital Marketing: Integrating Strategy and Tactics with Values***, they stress the role and critical importance of a digital mindset in operating today's businesses. The old mindset of marketing products by developing expensive campaigns built around the 30-second TV commercial is rapidly becoming obsolete. Thirty-second TV commercials can still play an important role but they must be integrated with the newer information, communication and technology (ICT) vehicles that make up our digital world. Companies no longer have the only voice, or strongest voice in shaping and motivating our brand choices. A far larger role is played by the new media of Facebook, Google, Twitter, You Tube, LinkedIn, and other tools that enable search and messaging. Companies need to dive into the new "*Digital Tsunami*" if they want to survive and prosper.

Kaufman and Horton provide rich case studies and describe best practices to help companies and students master the new marketing on a strategic and tactical level. Their book shows how readers can learn and integrate digital into their current organizational environment. They illustrate how the digital world has transformed the 4P's (Product, Price, Place, and Promotion) and *CRM* (Customer Relationship Management) into the ***New Marketing Normal***.

Digital Marketing provides a hands-on road map to the most relevant digital tactics and tools and their operation and integration with existing channels. Using the latest mobile technology, this information is linked to dynamically updated content housed on the book's companion website.

Building on a values-driven approach, ***Digital Marketing*** will prepare executives, managers, owners, and students to integrate digital marketing strategies and tactics with core values and business goals to achieve unprecedented levels of efficiency and innovation. The result will deliver a sustainable and ethical competitive advantage to those who embrace the new digital mindset.

Philip Kotler

S.C. Johnson and Son Distinguished Professor of International Marketing, Kellogg School of Management, Northwestern University, USA

January 2014

MORE THAN NEW CHANNELS, IT'S A NEW PERSPECTIVE *[Foreword]*

The fundamental nature of marketing is shifting to one of customer centricity, massive micro-campaigns, and relentless focus on the customer decision journey. As a long-time advocate of this shift in marketing, I share Ira and Chris' belief that we need a new guidebook for marketing practitioners.

One that can bring the right levels of academic rigor and practicality, using the tools of digital interactivity to bring its examples to life. In particular, I find it refreshing that this book takes a perspective that goes all the way back to core values and the essence of what a brand, and a company, needs to be about. With the incredible transparency now cracked open by customers and employees being able to use social media, brands need to raise their game and flip their viewpoint to one of HELPING others achieve their goals. Those goals need to be addressed on an individual level, using information a marketer has about someone's context, by designing experiences that empower each user, and by being accessible through any device, all the time. Doing that is no simple feat.

But the key spin that I love here is that it is not all about the mechanics and operations of making this happen. Behind it all needs to be a culture and a strategy that informs all of a brand's action with the right guidelines for what they are trying to do. How do they learn about what different customers need? How do they learn what works and what does not? How do they change their organization to put the right roles in place that can enable a complete customer experience and bring deeper insights to bear about individual needs?

These are the types of questions Ira and Chris put forward, and it is about time they appeared alongside all of the details about becoming real-time, big-data capable, and omni-channel; the complexities in operations that marketers face is unprecedented. And finding ways to use technology and operations to address those challenges is a very important piece of the puzzle – one that Ira and Chris certainly cover. But it is the bigger strategic questions they raise that drew me into the material and the real issues about roles and goals that I loved. When your every move as a brand can be tweeted and exposed, what are your core values? How do you translate those into guidelines? These are the new questions I know we are helping our clients with, and it is good to see them raised amidst all the other important material about the hard skills needed to get things done digitally.

I think that balance of fresh perspective and deep capability building is what most companies are seeking, and I am energized to see a book that brings both to the fore so well.

I look forward to seeing the reactions that Ira and Chris inspire and am sure that those who read this book will come away ready to get to the heart of what really needs to change for their companies to become digitally-adroit leaders.

David Edelman
Partner & Co-Leader, Global Digital Marketing Strategy Practice, McKinsey & Company

January 2014

WHAT IS DIGITAL, AND WHY SHOULD I CARE? *[Preface]*

Better get ready, you're about to be hit by a tsunami. Not the watery kind, but rather a *Digital Tsunami* of 1's and 0's that will eventually spill over into every aspect of your business and personal life. Time will not abate or dissipate the impact of this unseen force; it is gathering strength and breadth with each passing day. You might already feel overwhelmed in the midst of its initial waves. In fact, this storm is just getting started. You had better prepare now – before it's too late.

Welcome to the digital age.

"Marketers are facing a dilemma: They aren't sure what's working, they're feeling underequipped to meet the challenges of digital, and they're having a tough time keeping up with the pace of change in the industry.… What's worse, no one hands you a playbook on how to make it all work."[1]

Ann Lewnes, Chief Marketing Officer, Adobe

Don't worry, you're not alone. Irrespective of our rank or station as executives, managers, junior professionals, consultants, students, or otherwise, we are all being swept up by this silent *Digital Tsunami*. However, many of us differ greatly in our understanding of and relationship to the various digital technologies, strategies, tactics, and tools used to navigate today's dynamically changing marketing landscape. Often, these differences reflect divisions in personal values and world view that impact our degree of alignment with the emerging digital culture and mindset. Digital adoption is not monolithic; virtually every organization the world over can point to a digital native, immigrant, alien, or integrator within their ranks. Some of us are challenged to learn new skill sets, while others of us struggle to apply our existing skills to develop engaging and integrated strategies.

"There are hundreds of thousands of people who were trained and mentored, and studied classical marketing, and they got good at it.... Unfortunately, the world has changed – and that education is no longer relevant." [7]

Clark Kokich, Former Chairman, Razorfish

- 66% of all marketers think their companies won't succeed unless they have a successful digital marketing approach.[2]
- Despite this, only approximately 15% of marketing budgets are allocated to digital.[3]
- 96% of brands surveyed said they will increase digital marketing budget allocation over the following 12 months.[4]
- Less than half of digital marketers feel proficient in digital marketing.[5]
- Just one-in-three marketers think their companies are highly proficient in digital marketing.[6]

THE DIGITAL SCREEN

Regardless of our degree of digital preparedness, we all share one thing – a daily interface with the digital screen, and an increasing reliance on digital technology.

In addition to its impact on our personal lives, the digital screen is transforming business and organizational landscapes. It is opening up access to global markets and communities of interest, uncovering new pricing models, revolutionizing the placement and distribution of products, transforming media, facilitating greater collaboration and efficiency within the organization, and empowering consumers to demand new, consumer-centric marketing models. As with any powerful evolutionary technology, however, the digital screen carries with it a darker side: information overload and chronic distraction; numbing de-personalization and de-humanization; the threat of privacy invasion by Internet predators and information control by global technology giants.

Perhaps most importantly, though, for good or ill, our increasing reliance on the digital screen is generating vast amounts of data.

As our interface with digital grows apace, many of us are already beginning to form intimate, almost organic relationships with the various manifestations of these technologies. Eventually, they will become seamless extensions of all of us, embedded in the very fabric of what we use, what we wear, even what we consume. In this way, digital will increasingly influence, and as such define, who we are and what we believe.

At this point we will have become immersed in the emerging global digital culture – we will have "gone digital." Over time, this digital culture will leave its imprimatur on all other cultures throughout the globe, each taking on, by varying degrees, its core values and fundamental attributes.

If this digital future sounds like science fiction, it's not. If it sounds threatening, we need to face the reality. Much of this has already happened or is on its way to happening in the coming years. Given the broad impact of the digital evolution on society as a whole, its impact on business is beyond dispute.

EVRYTHNG in 77 seconds

PLAY VIDEO

Figure P.1: EVRYTHNG in 77 seconds – Video[8]

"As the drive toward increased digitization continues, enterprises have to get a handle on its impact to the organization. Corporate C-levels will have to step up to the challenge and ask, 'Are we digitally ready?'" [9]

Peter Weill & Stephanie Woerner, Center for Information Systems Research, MIT Sloan School of Management

- ***But how did we get here?***
- ***And more importantly, what can we do about it?***
- ***How can individuals and businesses leverage digital to sustain and grow their organizations now and into the future?***

These are the principal questions this book seeks to address and resolve.

YOUR ROADMAP TO DIGITAL INTEGRATION *[Introduction]*

Digital is changing the business and marketing landscape quickly and dynamically. We are all, to some degree, students of the digital evolution – executives and non-profit managers, owners and entrepreneurs, professors and instructors, undergraduates and MBAs. Even though we each may have different experiences and responsibilities, we are all faced with the same overarching challenge: to prepare for the *Digital Tsunami* that is already reaching our shores, and learn how to effectively respond to the rapid transformation coming in its wake. Doing so requires that individuals and organizations have the confidence and understanding to make *digital integration a strategic imperative*.

Digital Marketing: Integrating Strategy and Tactics with Values is a game changer for practitioners and students alike. It delivers visionary but practical content through an interactive format. It is a primer for digital literacy, arming the reader with the tools needed to sift through the profusion of choices and data characteristic of today's ever-changing digital landscape. Foremost, it is VISUAL - an engaging and easy-to-use resource; a one-stop shop for digital marketing information, implementation, and transformation.

Digital Marketing is a guidebook; it provides grounding in digital vocabulary, a snapshot of how digital technologies impact strategy, and a comprehension of how to implement and measure widely available digital media tactics and tools, which are evaluated in terms of industry best practices and their ability to achieve strategic goals.

Digital Marketing Offers

- Preparation for executives and students to operate in a digital environment.
- Digital insight to help the reader translate digital trends into business opportunities.
- A digital marketing training manual for executives, managers, and students.
- Digital diagnostics to help the reader reflect on their organization's positioning.
- Case studies from companies experiencing digital integration firsthand.
- A *Digital Marketing Resource Center* to keep the reader current on the latest digital trends, strategies, tactics, and tools.
- Best practices for creating sustainable digital strategies and evaluating campaign ROI.
- How-to's for applying proven digital tactics and tools to your organization.
- Insight into how to restructure existing silos (marketing, IT, HR, customer service) and redefine the role of the CMO.
- A roadmap for creating a *Digitally Integrated Organization*.

YOUR JOURNEY BEGINS WITH A SIMPLE VALUE PROPOSITION

Digital Marketing: Integrating Strategy and Tactics with Values draws on the latest digital tactics and strategic insights to prepare individuals and organizations for sustainable growth through digital integration.

With a particular focus on the user experience, *Digital Marketing* prepares you to navigate the *Digital Tsunami*, helping you stay competitive, innovative, and responsive in a highly connected and rapidly evolving digital economy which is fundamentally altering many long-held business conventions:

- Channel control was an asset, now it is an impediment to customer relationships.
- Disruption was an obstacle, now it is a strategic opportunity.
- Silos were profit centers, now they are barriers to innovation and collaboration.
- 4P's were the standard, now the 6P's are the *New Marketing Normal*.
- Facebook and Twitter were for social conversations; now they are powerful business tools.
- Data was the focus of market research, now it drives decision making throughout the organization.
- Core values were things you reflected on during your holy day, now they are major inputs in marketing and organizational strategy.
- Transparency was a risk, now it's a necessity.
- Digital literacy was optional, now it's imperative for survival.
- Company chatter was relegated to water cooler gossip; now intra-organizational social inputs are integral to success.
- Selling was the focus, now it is about generating advocacy and managing the user experience.
- Hierarchy was the structure, now collaboration rules.
- Integration referred to bridging ethnic diversity, now it is the currency of organizational sustainability.

Organizations are faced with two competing forces in the digital age: chaos and integration.

- The chaos of the *Digital Tsunami* that threatens the marketing/business status quo, destroying existing paradigms and ushering in a business climate marked by constant flux.

- The integration of digital technologies with marketing strategy and core values to achieve efficiency and long-term sustainability for the organization. Integration is the calming force lessening the chaos brought on by the *Digital Tsunami*, allowing the organization to adroitly ride its waves and harness its abundant power for competitive advantage.

HOW IS *DIGITAL MARKETING* ORGANIZED?

Digital Marketing takes you, the reader, through an incremental journey along the five-step *Path to Digital Integration*. Each unit builds on the previous to provide you with a fundamental understanding of *Integrated Digital Marketing*, so you can effectively implement its strategies, tactics, tools, and best practices throughout your organization.

1

***Adopt a Digital** MINDSET* — Introduce the digital culture into the existing organizational culture.

2

***Embrace a new** MODEL* — Integrate the fundamentals of the *New Marketing Normal* into current marketing efforts.

3

***Formulate a new** STRATEGY* — Apply *Integrated Digital Marketing* tactics and tools to enhance marketing initiatives.

4

***Execute its** IMPLEMENTATION* — Incorporate *Integrated Digital Marketing* best practices to facilitate open communication and collaboration within and without the organization.

5

***Generate** SUSTAINABILITY* — Align the core values of the organization with its actions to create a *Digitally Integrated Organization*, which benefits customers, stakeholders, and the wider community.

PATH TO DIGITAL INTEGRATION

Though the five steps of the *Path to Digital Integration* are generally linear and progressive, they are not necessarily fixed. For example, the adoption of a digital mindset is based upon one's individual core values, and therefore may take time to manifest within the organization. Certain members of the executive team may have a high level of empathy, integrity, and openness, but because of organizational constraints, they cannot manifest these core values into digital strategy and action.

The following are a few other considerations that may affect the speed, extent, and nature of the *Path to Digital Integration* for any given organization:

External & Internal Influences – Digital mindset may evolve into full digital integration over time; however, the speed of this transformation may be influenced by various externalities, such as changes in the competitive landscape, digital technologies, customer experience, and overall business environment, as well as internalities such as business size and nature (larger business-to-business (B2B) organizations may be slower to change and adapt), and available talent within the organization.

Type of Organization – A traditional broadcast advertising company focused on TV and radio may realize the necessity of adopting a digital mindset, although their approach to designing an effective strategy would likely vary significantly from that of a digital-native tech startup that has been an innovator in digital integration.

Internal Structure – A company with a non-hierarchical organizational structure that encourages open communication, equality, and collaboration – such as the digital-native tech startup previously mentioned – is more likely to facilitate efficient digital implementation than, say, a traditionally oriented business-to-consumer (B2C) firm which may have to work hard to break down silos in order to foster the same.

Values Orientation – Finally, if an organization's core values are clearly laid out, and its adherents work hard to manifest these values in the company's daily actions, sustainability is easily achieved. By contrast, an organization that is not living its values will struggle to deliver on the integrity and transparency required of brands operating in the digital economy.

HOW TO USE THIS GUIDEBOOK

Much more than a stale repository of information, *Digital Marketing* is a dynamically updated guidebook and interactive learning resource. The book incorporates a number of specially designed features to help the reader address any questions and challenges quickly and easily:

Fast Facts provide current statistics and facts on the topic at hand.

Takeaways are bulleted points at the end of each chapter summarizing the highlights and best practices covered.

Case Studies offer real-world examples of applied digital marketing in small, mid-size, and large businesses and non-profits.

Expert Insights are brief 150-200 word impressions from experts relating their own experiences along the *Path to Digital Integration*.

Glossary provides detailed explanations of the digital vocabulary referenced throughout the book.

Shout Outs are comments by executives and managers reflecting the real-world challenges faced by many small, mid-size and large businesses. They serve as mini-case studies linking to articles with details on specific best practices.

Broad Learning Solutions (BLS) is a fictitious company going through the experience of digital transformation; references to its experiences are integrated throughout the book. The interactive dialogue between the BLS management team and its consultants provides the reader with a window into the common challenges organizations face along the *Path to Digital Integration*.

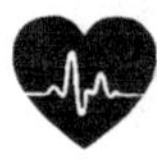

Digital Diagnostics are tools for self-reflection meant to help practitioners and executives ask the right questions as they face up to some of their old habits and conditioning. *Digital Diagnostics* are placed throughout the narrative so you can take an accurate snapshot of where your organization is on the *Path to Digital Integration*. Taking a digital snapshot of yourself and other members of your team takes some courage, but it is a necessary step to becoming a leader and innovator in the emerging digital culture.

The ***Discover More*** and ***Play Video*** icons leverage augmented reality technology from Zappar to connect you to expanded and updated content housed on our companion website, *Digital Marketing Resource Center,* via your smartphone or tablet. In addition, the ***Play Video*** icons utilize Vusay's point-in-time video commenting technology to enable interactive conversations alongside each video. These technologies come together to create a *Connected Digital Experience*.

How to use Zappar

Figure I.1: How to use Zappar – Video

Here's how to get started with Zappar:

- Download the free *Zappar* App in the Google Play or Apple App Store.
- Look for ***Discover More*** and ***Play Video*** icons. These are called *Zapcodes.*
- Open the *Zappar* App on your device.
- Point the camera on your device to the *Zapcode* and hover over it.
- Watch as the *Zappar* App reveals the expanded content.
- Interact with the content by touching the screen.
- Experience Zappar by hovering over the ***Play Video*** icon above to learn "*How to use Zappar.*"

Reading this book on your smartphone or tablet? We have conveniently hyperlinked all Zapcodes, allowing you to easily access ***Discover More*** and ***Play Video*** content with the touch of a finger!

WHO IS THIS BOOK WRITTEN FOR?

Digital Marketing prepares executives, managers, and students, whether more or less digitally savvy, to effectively navigate the current and future digital landscape.

- ***For Executives*** – Whether you are a member of the C-suite (CEO, CMO, CFO, CIO, etc.), an entrepreneur, or a business owner, it prepares you to
    - Anticipate digital opportunities to gain a strong competitive position.
    - Integrate digital strategies to increase performance and opportunity.
    - Initiate customer engagement throughout the organization.
    - Collaborate to implement broad data initiatives throughout the organization.
- ***For Managers*** – *Digital Marketing* will help you
    - Leverage digital marketing best practices, tactics, and tools to improve operational efficiency and customer experience.
- ***For Students and Instructors*** – *Digital Marketing* delivers easy-to-adopt, customizable digital course offerings, providing you
    - An opportunity to incorporate strategic applications into your facility with digital media.
    - An interactive, updated *Digital Marketing Resource Center* to improve the learning experience.
    - A Variety of undergraduate and MBA courses flexible to instructor's needs (varied levels of digital literacy).
    - Guidance and training to prepare you for future job opportunities.
    - Comprehensive instructor guidebook utilizing educational best practices and tools, including PowerPoints, case studies, exercises, and syllabi.

DISCOVER MORE

Digital Marketing reflects the real-world needs of each group, which we've tried to better understand by crowdsourcing questions and trends from a number of areas, including our own LinkedIn Group, *Digital Media Marketing*; online business publications such as *Direct Marketing News* and *CMO.com*; and soliciting feedback from executives, professors, and undergraduate and MBA students.

On another level, *Digital Marketing* explores the various tensions between the various sub-groups of the emerging digital culture, be they generational (Baby Boomers, Gen Xers, Millennials), organizational (executives vs staff), operational (strategic vs tactical; marketing vs tech), or demographic (digital native vs digital alien). Harmony within these sub-groups promotes integration, efficiency, innovation, and competitive advantage; disharmony engenders ineffective communication, inefficiency, stagnation, and marginal results.

WHAT IS ITS VALUE TO THE READER?

Above all, *Digital Marketing* is written to help you, the reader, prepare for the various trials and opportunities of marketing in the digital age. In this complex environment, organizations face a number of paradoxes that, if not addressed, threaten to stymy growth and handicap future sustainability:

- ***Content Paradox*** – The idea of transmitting digital content openly and transparently contrasts with the interests of the entrenched executive focused on controlling the message and its distribution.
- ***Literacy Paradox*** – Digital is being adopted at an exponential rate by consumers, but more than half of CMOs admit they are not technically or analytically prepared to address this opportunity.
- ***Marketing Paradox*** – Traditionally, marketing has operated in its own independent silo and has been focused on customer acquisition and engagement; now its functions and technologies are beginning to pervade all aspects of the organization.
- ***Organizational Paradox*** – Executives expect digital to transform their companies, but their organizations are not structurally or technologically prepared for the speed and complexity of this change.
- ***Sustainability Paradox*** – Some two-thirds of organizations consider sustainability a significant issue, yet a only small percentage have fully implemented sustainability initiatives; many more have not incorporated such initiatives into their strategic planning.
- ***Performance Paradox*** – As a rule, businesses with superior performance (in terms of sales or revenue) feel better prepared for digital transformation and have invested more resources in digital marketing than lower performers.

Solutions to these paradoxes are suggested throughout the book; their resolution is vital to the competitiveness and sustainability of current and future organizations.

Make no mistake, the Digital Tsunami is coming. ***Digital Marketing*** *will provide the insight and tools to navigate your way through it.*

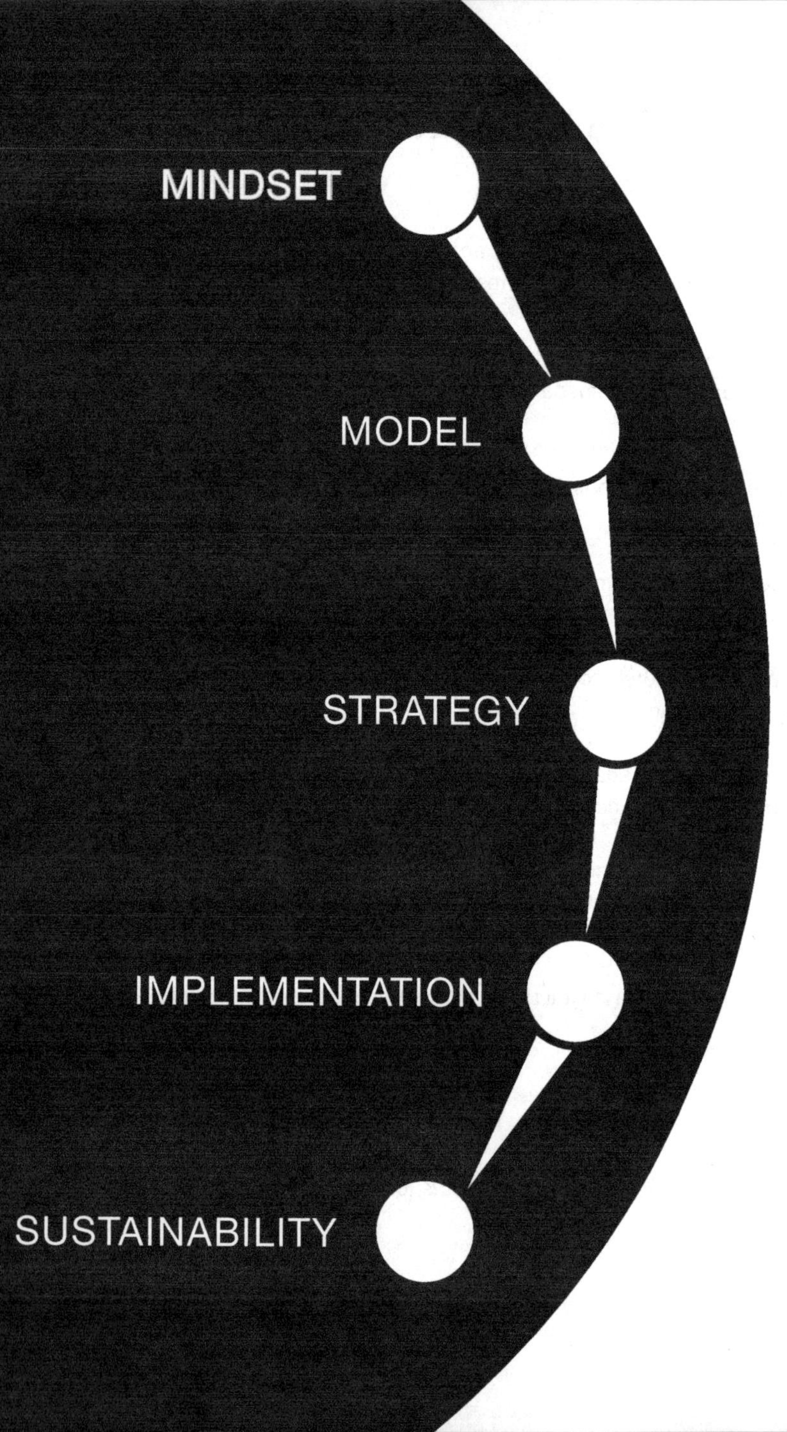

MINDSET

MODEL

STRATEGY

IMPLEMENTATION

SUSTAINABILITY

As the *Digital Tsunami* gains force and extends its reach, executives need to develop a strategic approach to address the impact that digital will have on their organization. They must develop a mindset that provides a strategic context for their management team to process the challenges and opportunities presented by the changing digital marketplace.

In chapter 1, we outline how the core values and fundamental attributes of the digital culture and related digital mindset come together to lay the the foundation for digital transformation. In chapter 2, we meet our fictional case study, Broad Learning Solutions (BLS), a digitally challenged enterprise just beginning its journey down the *Path to Digital Integration*. In chapter 3, we examine the fundamental drivers of change and emerging trends which are bringing forth digital transformation.

As a reminder, you can access in-depth information, videos, and updates from our *Digital Marketing Resource Center* (www.dmresourcecenter.org) wherever you see this icon.

CHAPTER 1: TRANSFORMING FROM TRADITIONAL TO DIGITAL VALUES

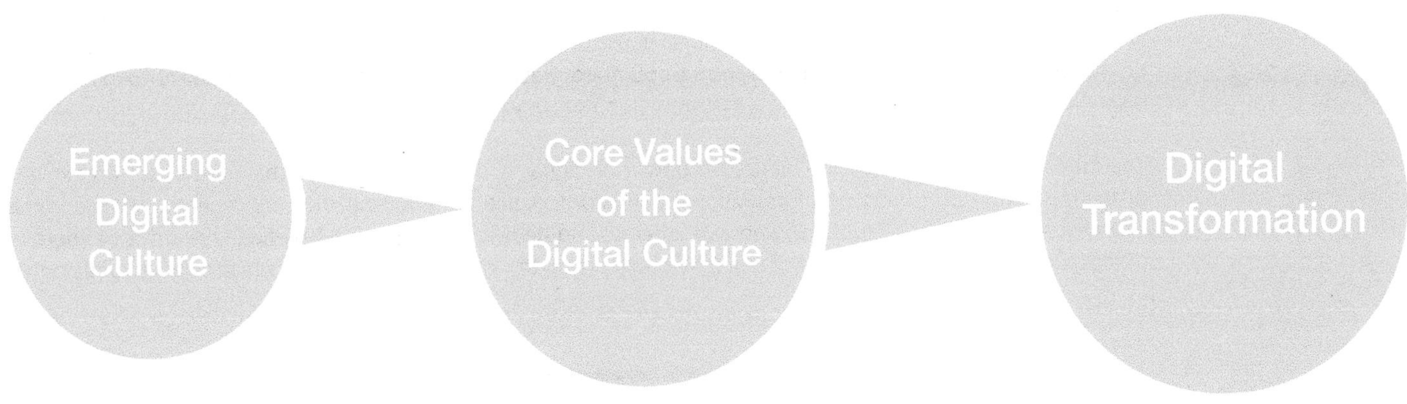

Since the dawn of our existence, we humans have been social creatures, using any means at our disposal to communicate our thoughts, ideas, visions, opinions, and values to all who would listen. We've used our hands and our voices to speak and write, paint and shape, mold and design – to express ourselves in order to bring about change. In doing so, we've often relied on an intermediary, whether ochre, cuneiform tablet, papyrus, or parchment, to transmit our thoughts and visions onto a physical medium that would store them for later observation, review, or sharing.

Communications media, though always with us, have grown in both sophistication and impact over time. Inventions such as the printing press, phonograph, magnetic tape recorder, and motion picture paved the way for broad-based social connection on an exponential level, allowing a single person or small group to share their thoughts and vision with millions across the globe.

Indeed it is fair to say that communications media have always played a role in shaping human cultural mores, although their relative influence has been largely dependent on external factors such as geography and technology. From the great religious doctrines of the East and West to the soaring artistic masterpieces of Michelangelo and Beethoven; from the brilliant treatises of Aristotle and Averroes to the seminal writings of Shakespeare and Sun Tzu; all have eventually become iconic treasures recognized and enjoyed the world over. But it often took time – in some cases decades, centuries, or even millennia – before their full impact was realized. This is because, until recently, these great works, and countless others like them, have been dependent on an analog distillation process often controlled by a select group of intermediaries and constrained by the limitations of geographical distance and existing technology to reach their greatest cultural import.

THE EMERGING DIGITAL CULTURE

The digital interface has changed all of that. Digital technology may very well prove to be the most profound innovation in human history. It is the great leveler, allowing average citizens from all walks of life and all corners of the planet to impact the greater world in countless ways, endowing them with the ability to publish and disseminate ideas and innovations in a matter of minutes, or even seconds.

The indelible footprint left by the disruptive power of digital is far more pervasive than its impact on business or technology. In part because of its exponential nature, digital is reshaping the very trajectory of the human experience, fundamentally redefining how we interact and develop as a species. The nearly seamless integration of digital into virtually every aspect of our daily lives earns it the right to be regarded in its proper cultural context.

#Socialnomics

Figure 1.1: #Socialnomics – Video[1]

In our world there now exists a nascent digital culture, full of its own values and mores, expressing itself both online and offline in countless ways each day; in a real sense, this digital culture represents the first truly global culture the human race has ever known.

The very notion of digital culture is inextricably linked to the fundamental essence or defining principle of digital: the language of the computer, the digital parlance of 1s and 0s. In simplest terms, a device or thing can be said to be digital if it ultimately relies on this language of 1s and 0s to exist or operate.

But does such a culture truly exist? If so, does the digital culture come with a distinctive mindset that is characteristic or representative of most or all of its adherents?

- *Why would having such a digital mindset be critical to the management team?*
- *How would it affect the sustainability of the enterprise?*

To answer these important questions, it's useful to look a bit deeper into how culture influences mindset in a general sense.

Culture is the cumulative deposit of knowledge, experience, beliefs, attitudes, meanings, and hierarchies of a particular society or group. One's culture informs the relationship a person has with both the environment and the people around him or her. In this sense, culture acts as a potent force in defining one's core values.

Core values, in turn, work in a collective sense to shape one's mindset, or day-to-day perspective on things. In this way, mindset drives a person's strategic objectives and tactical actions.

Mindset, then, can be understood as the extent of one's integration into a particular culture – in this case, the digital culture.

What is a Digital Mindset?

Figure 1.2: What is a Digital Mindset? – Video[2]

WHAT IS DIGITAL, ANYWAY?

One hears the term "digital" expressed all the time, often paired with nearly every conceivable device and action of daily life. But what exactly does it mean? What is digital, anyway? After all, isn't the very notion of the digital culture largely dependent on our conception of the term "digital" itself?

Perhaps the best way to understand digital is to compare it with its opposite – in this case, analog.

Analog can be described as a device or system that represents changing values as continuously variable physical quantities. Humans generally experience the world from an analog perspective. For example, vision, with its infinite gradations of shapes and colors, can be regarded as an analog experience.

Digital, on the other hand, is non-variable and finite. It utilizes discrete data points that are either on or off, ones or zeros. For years, the discipline of computer science has been largely focused on combining these discrete data points, or bits, in ever more complex ways to simulate, and in some cases augment, our analog reality through a myriad of devices.[3]

CORE VALUES OF THE DIGITAL CULTURE

Given this understanding of culture, mindset, and digital, it is possible to point to a specific set of core values and fundamental attributes which, when taken together, are reflective of an emerging digital culture and attendant digital mindset.

Core Values	Fundamental Attributes
Creativity	Disruptive, experimental, innovative
Equality	Non-hierarchical, flat, democratic
Empathy	Responsive, receptive, adaptive
Integrity	Honest, trustworthy, consistent
Knowledge	Analytic, data-driven
Efficiency	Agile, proactive, purposeful
Openness	Transparent, collaborative, authentic
Unity	Integrated, holistic, socially responsible

Figure 1.3: Core Values and Fundamental Attributes of the Digital Culture

Broadly speaking, the digital culture has some unique characteristics. It transcends geographical proximity; it knows no physical boundaries; it recognizes no socio-economic, racial, or ethnic hierarchies or divisions. Rather, the digital culture is a virtual culture open to anyone with access to a computing device and an Internet connection.

Perhaps most importantly, the core values and fundamental attributes of the digital culture which give shape to the digital mindset apply to individuals and organizations alike, influencing decision making and strategy at all levels. In this way, the adoption of a digital mindset lies at the foundation of digital transformation.

DIGITAL TRANSFORMATION

For organizations to find lasting success in the emerging digital culture, executives need to adopt a digital mindset and integrate it into how they communicate and serve their employees, consumers, and the greater community. To be effective, this digital mindset must permeate from the individual executive to the entire enterprise, transforming its culture.

At the outset of this transformation, the executive team may feel out of control, overwhelmed and "on foreign soil." But digital transformation is a necessary paradigm shift critical to the survival and growth of the enterprise. As Rupert Murdock once said, "The digital native doesn't send a letter to the editor anymore. She goes online, and starts a blog.... What I worry about much more is our ability to make the necessary cultural changes to meet the new demands of the digital native."[4]

Reflecting on her own company's digital transformation, Adobe's Senior Vice President of Global Marketing, Anne Lewnes, noted: "In a few short years, we went from spending very little to spending 74% of our marketing budget on digital...that kind of transformation requires more than just a change in tactics, you have to get people to believe this is the right approach – it has to become cultural."[5]

Digital is a Way of Life

"Digital marketing should be seen more as a way of life, rather than a form of marketing. The 'mindset' of digital marketing is how we treat our customers and the way in which we conduct business. Businesses with a digital mindset are radically transparent with their customers and extremely responsive to their customers; they are brutally honest. They don't see their customers as mere numbers; rather, they see their customers as partners, as leaders. If a customer does not have a good experience with a company and has the courage to speak out against the company on a social network, the company does not delete the tweet, Facebook post, etc. Rather, the company engages with that person, and they look at that negative comment as an opportunity to improve. A company that adopts the digital mindset is authentic and caring."

Brandon Carroll, Vice President, Koofers
Campus Recruiter, USA

In the past, traditional organizational hierarchies and power centers have operated in silos and controlled information with a one-way communication flow. These silos (e.g. marketing, information technology, public relations, operations, human relations) are dissolving, as new media facilitates open dialogue and two-way communication up and down the organization. Information, feedback, and ideas are now often shared in real time. These changes are altering existing communications structures, influence flow, and access to critical data, encouraging collaboration and joint decision-making.

Blair Christie, Cisco's Chief Marketing Officer Worldwide, agrees. "Our customers expect real-time engagement. This means it impacts all of Cisco – HR, support, finance, etc. – not just marketing. For Cisco, social is not just 'a marketing exercise.'"[6]

> *"Digital business is among the most significant factors driving business and societal change worldwide. Digital innovations have led to the creation, destruction, and transformation of businesses, industries, and even governments. Yet few organizations are fully exploiting digital disruptions or innovations....*
> *Realizing breakthrough success in digital business requires not only forward-thinking strategies but also a transformation of the company's underlying functions and organizations."*
>
> AT Kearney on Digital Transformation[7]

Digital transformation is not a "one-shot deal:" rather, it is part of a continuous process that reveals new possibilities daily as relationships, data, and markets expand. Organization-wide adoption of a digital mindset fuels digital transformation, encouraging democratic participation in the enterprise's strategic decision making, continuous innovation in the design and implementation of products and services, and deeper connection with existing and future customers.

For additional insight into how digital transformation is impacting organizations -> DISCOVER MORE

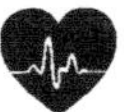

What questions does digital raise for business, government, and non-profit leaders?

- How is digital affecting my current organization?
- How might digital transformation impact its future?
- How will the demands of the emerging digital culture alter the strategies required to meet its short- and long-term business goals?

- Digital technology may very well prove to be the most profound innovation in human history. It is the great leveler, allowing average citizens globally to impact the greater world by publishing and disseminating ideas and innovations in a matter of minutes, or even seconds.

- The core values and fundamental attributes of the digital culture which give shape to the digital mindset apply to individuals and organizations alike. Thus the adoption of the digital mindset lies at the foundation of digital transformation for both individuals and organizations.

- To be successful in the digital world, executives need to adopt a digital mindset and integrate it into how they communicate and serve their employees, consumers, and the greater global community.

- Digital transformation is not a "one-shot deal:" rather, it is part of a continuous process that reveals new possibilities daily as relationships, data, and markets expand.

CHAPTER 2: A DIGITALLY CHALLENGED ENTERPRISE

Broad Learning Solutions (BLS)

The Digitally Integrated Organization

As we noted in the last chapter, digital transformation and its expanding cultural environment demands change in the business enterprise and non-profit organization. This change must necessarily begin with an acceptance of new technologies and a reexamination of the organization's core values and overarching business goals in light of digital.

By adopting a digital mindset, the executive team can begin to infuse new technologies and values into its strategic marketing decisions, taking the first critical steps down the *Path to Digital Integration*.

For many organizations, the *Path to Digital Integration* will not be an easy one, as sometimes decades-old processes, models, and mindsets are questioned, disrupted, and in some cases completely overturned. For the transition to be truly effective, however, everyone in the team must be involved, regardless of their skill or comfort with digital technology on an individual level.

To properly illustrate the various dynamics of digital transformation, we've crafted the following fictional business case study which features a group of characters (executives, managers, and staff) who reflect the prevailing archetypes of the digital culture: the digital native, the digital immigrant, the digital alien, and the digital integrator.

INTRODUCING BROAD LEARNING SOLUTIONS

Meet Broad Learning Solutions (BLS), a 30-year old, $50 million language training company in Fairfax, Virginia, that markets language learning resources through traditional educational wholesale distributors. To help transition to the digital age, the company recently purchased a state-of-the-art, cloud-based language training software application which has been designed to operate on virtually every kind of mobile device. Although internal market research has identified business to consumer (B2C) as the fastest growing segment of the online learning industry in which BLS now operates, there also looks to be reasonably strong demand from a number of corporate and educational institutions in the business-to-business (B2B) arena, as well as some interest from a select group of military and government institutions in the business-to-government (B2G) sector.

Given its existing structure and orientation, though, BLS will likely face many challenges as it works to design a marketing strategy for its new interactive language training software. The company traditionally has been a heavily sales-focused organization; as such, its employees do not have the expertise or preparedness to develop or launch a comprehensive digital marketing campaign.

The BLS team is multigenerational and multicultural, with one or more of its members representing each of the four digital archetypes: digital natives, digital immigrants, digital aliens, and digital integrators.

Engaging Digital Natives Means Throwing Out the Rulebook

I'm a millennial. It means that I've (almost) always had access to the Internet and technology; it's my way of life.

For brands, my generation poses a problem. Traditional methods no longer apply. Engaging us means throwing out the rulebook.

Why? We're cynical of advertising. Only 3% of millennials consider online advertising to be credible.[1]

To be engaged, we need to be entertained. This means brands have to become something that can be hard to do: Be human. Ditch the corporate brochures. Start tweeting. Hold social contests, invite us to share our stories and photos, and make sure your real-time social strategy means you're always there for us.

And, scrap the text-heavy sales pitches. Speak to us in the language of images and video. It's how we express ourselves, our emotions, and our dreams.

Millennials are a new animal. But, if brands can be authentic, entertain, and provide a stellar customer experience, it's a generation that could become their biggest brand advocates.

Kira Sparks, Digital Content Writer, Shoutlet.com

Let's briefly meet a representative member of each archetype to better understand how the BLS team can work together to address the company's current digital marketing needs and convert on future opportunities.

San – Digital Native

Meet San, a 21-year-old female marketing associate and recent business school graduate. Like many others of her Millennial generation (aka Generation Y), she was brought up in a fast-moving, urban, multicultural environment that is but one aspect of an interconnected world defined by rapid, systemic change. A digital native, San has an almost organic relationship with digital technology. San sees her smartphone, tablet, and the Internet as extensions of herself that allow San to communicate with others (both existing friends and those she has never met), learn, gather news and information, and search for things to do and to buy.

Real-time responsiveness, transparent dialogue, and openness to change are standards for San. Her world is filled with texting, social networks, mobile, and video. She uses digital technologies socially to interact, entertain, and co-exist. You could say San has intuitively adopted a digital mindset, and as such has unwittingly (or perhaps organically) taken the first step down the *Path to Digital Integration*.

However, San needs to be prepared to enter the business world and interact with colleagues at different points along this path. She needs to understand how to communicate and collaborate effectively. To do so, San must learn how to translate her proficiency with digital technologies into viable business strategies. San has to consider how the goals and objectives of each Tweet and Instagram post can support broader strategic marketing initiatives. She must realign her thinking to recognize the ways in which social communication can become touch points for specific audiences. She needs to learn how to effectively monitor and collect data to evaluate return on investment (ROI).

Despite living a digital mindset, the strategic opportunities that come with digital aren't obvious to San. She must essentially step outside of her daily experience with digital in order to translate it to relevant business applications; she must refocus her efforts on improving the customer experience rather than on sharing her own experiences; she must learn how to use digital best practices, tactics, and tools strategically. With the development of these skill sets, in time San will grow to become a digital integrator.

To learn how digital natives are changing the business landscape ->

Quincy – Digital Native

Quincy is an 18-year-old programmer, gamer, and digital entrepreneur. As a child, he was in love with video games and always tinkering with technology. He learned to program at 12 and won awards in high school for his science fair projects. While tutoring computer programming at a local Boys Club, he noted that many of the boys who spoke Spanish as their native language had problems with the language interface. He decided to work with them to create an interactive, fun Spanish-English software application, which they designed for desktop and mobile use. An early iteration of the app was offered free to local church members. They loved it and gave Quincy a lot of useful feedback as to how he could make the app more user-friendly.

A firm believer in open-source software development, Quincy crowdsourced the app's design; within a few weeks, he was contacted by San of Broad Learning Solutions. Quincy eventually sold the app to BLS and was brought on as a digital consultant upon graduation.

- Millennials will form 75% of the workforce by 2025 and, as such, are actively shaping corporate culture and expectations. Only 11% regard having a lot of money as a definition of success."[2]
- 84% say that helping to make a positive difference in the world is more important than professional recognition.[3]
- 92% believe that business success should be measured by more than profit.[4]
- 90% view entrepreneurship as a mindset "today" instead of the role of a business owner.[5]

"Digital Natives have an intuitive understanding of digital, but need to learn how to think strategically."

Samir – Digital Immigrant

Samir is a 40-year-old son of a restaurant owner. Raised in a middle class Washington DC suburb, Samir was brought up with a somewhat limited world view guided by family culture. Though his parents were digitally illiterate, he was introduced to a variety of computer technologies in high school and college.

As Broad Learning's Chief Marketing Officer (CMO), Samir realizes the importance of understanding how the application of digital technologies can improve cross-functional business processes. However, Samir has been with BLS since he graduated college, moving up the ladder in a traditional company operating out of separate silos. Largely because of this, he sees marketing as a set of discrete tools that can be added to or subtracted from the overall marketing mix.

Within his organization, Samir has always been considered pro-digital. He spearheaded the company's effort to hire a design firm to build a new company website, and continues to encourage his marketing team to use social media to broadcast company news and information. He dabbles in the latest tactics and tools, but has little time to learn how to design and implement a comprehensive, integrated digital strategy. Searching for answers and understanding himself, Samir struggles to lead his team into the digital age.

Samir clearly recognizes the value of digital marketing but needs to learn more about the strategies, tactics, and tools necessary for its effective implementation. He'll need guidance in order to fully adopt a digital mindset and seamlessly integrate digital throughout his company's marketing efforts.

For Samir and others on the BLS marketing team, an understanding of digital does not come naturally or innately, but is instead an ongoing learning process. To make any meaningful progress toward digital integration, he and his team must first learn a small number of digital marketing tactics and tools and then work to seamlessly integrate them into the company's marketing initiatives (both internally and externally). As Samir and his team's mastery of digital increases with time, they will be able to align the company's core values and business goals with its strategic marketing initiatives.

"Digital Immigrants recognize the value of digital, but need to learn the strategies, tactics, and tools for its successful implementation."

Bill – Digital Alien

Bill is 60-year-old son of a successful owner of a Mid-Atlantic bakery. Brought up in the family business, he left the organization after it was purchased by a Fortune 500 food products company. Bill then invested heavily in Broad Leaning Solutions, eventually serving as the company's Chairman and CEO.

Used to playing an active role in all operating decisions, Bill was schooled before "the existence of digital technology." In spite of this, Bill has managed to develop a basic skill set with computers and the Internet over the years, regularly using Word, Excel, email, and online search. In general, though, Bill has been slow to acknowledge the relevance of digital for business. He often stereotypes social media as "kids play" or "social chatter," and frequently challenges the notion that the digital revolution is here to stay. He's had an especially hard time coming to the reality that digital may have a profound impact on his company's bottom line.

Like many other digital aliens, Bill has never been fully convinced of the value of social media, and has been slow to support its adoption within his organization. Holding traditional and hierarchical values and never conditioned to rely on the voices of his employees or consumers, Bill's channels are largely closed to open dialogue or collaboration.

However, the increasing digitization of the educational marketplace, coupled with the BLS Board's decision to purchase the language training software application in response to the success of its competitors, has forced Bill to fundamentally rethink his marketing strategy. Partly out of annoyance, partly out of fear, he's hastily instructed his marketing team to "get an online presence" and "add a Facebook page" without himself having the perspective, knowledge, or commitment to make the transition to digital a company-wide reality.

At this point, Bill has become completely dependent on his marketing team to manage the company's transition to digital. Unfortunately, without any real expertise in doing so, BLS suffers from an incoherent marketing strategy throughout its various online and offline channels. The company has a brochure website that does not support its current business objectives. The marketing team has no real understanding of how to directly market to the online consumer or how to develop an integrated customer experience; they've never had to develop online content or design a coherent search marketing strategy. Though the company's social channels are set up, nobody within the organization knows how to effectively manage them. BLS is not employing any type of marketing automation software or other means to track and measure the results of their disjointed efforts.

Seeing this, but not fully understanding it all, for the first time Bill feels like he is losing control of his organization – a fearful prospect, indeed.

For Bill, the *Path to Digital Integration* is a long but necessary one. He will likely need to experience the value of digital marketing first-hand before he is able to fundamentally alter his traditionalist perspective and adopt a digital mindset. He must then obtain a high-level understanding of digital marketing strategies, tactics, and tools to ensure they are properly implemented within and without his organization.

By doing these things, Bill can transform himself and his business; he can move from digital alien to digital immigrant (and perhaps, eventually, to digital integrator), using digital marketing best practices to fully leverage the company's new language training app.

"Digital Aliens think strategically, but need to experience the value of digital."

NOTE: *It is not necessary for the digital alien to fully embrace each step of the Path to Digital Integration in order to find some success in the digital culture. The transformation from digital alien to integrator is a substantial one. Not every digital alien is actually going to want to or need to become a digital integrator. However, he or she must at least strive to become a digital immigrant, gaining a basic understanding of digital strategy, tactics, and tools and internalizing the core digital values that are relevant to his or her organization. In the short term, hiring a digital integrator as a part of the management team will help bridge the digital divide. Long-term sustainability, though, will require a fully integrated team to leverage the ongoing changes and opportunities of the digital era.*

Why I Think Digital

As a creative person, digital has let me take images to new places. Simple drawings could be shaped into things that looked more like photographs, and quickly I started animating them.

The animations turned into sharable content for people to send to friends. Later, they evolved into dynamic image creators that gave creative control to the masses. With that came complex interfaces with powerful creative design tools.

Eventually, Interface Design led to User Experience (UX) Design, allowing us to create truly unique brand experiences. These ranged from work-out videos on first-generation iPods to flash-based financial planning tools. We also learned that we could not just make it "great" for ourselves anymore. The world was watching.

The science of UX evolved and became the foundation of the agency philosophy. We digital weirdos started getting invited to agency pitches. We were working for Fortune 500 companies and were architects of enterprise systems that our clients depended on. How did drawing evolve into this?

Then came social media, the biggest step yet; we were tasked with creating and maintaining our clients' communities and trying to keep digital ecosystems the size of countries fed. In the anxiety, a whole new layer of inspiration showed up. I started out wanting to be an illustrator years ago; with social, I was an illustrator once again, creating ongoing content for clients and communities across an array of platforms, mapping the labyrinthine social sphere.

The digital interface has challenged me to learn, adapt, be thoughtful and enjoy creating small things and big things alike. For me, thinking digital is about staying curious and knowing that things are always going to evolve. It's the only thing you can count on.

Chris Henderson, Creative Lead/Founder, CYCL

Rosa – Digital Integrator

Rosa is a 40-year-old former Spanish Language teacher with an MBA in Marketing. After spending the majority of her twenties teaching, she returned to school to earn her MBA, after which time she went on to work in the marketing department of a global B2B software giant. She was recently hired as Director of Digital Marketing at BLS, where she is responsible for helping the company develop a truly integrated digital marketing strategy.

Rosa has been living and breathing the Internet since its early days when she was an undergraduate. She began as a digital immigrant but quickly evolved into that rare bred we call the digital integrator.

Over time, Rosa has grown to recognize the importance of aligning her understanding of strategic marketing with her core values through the power of digital technology. She finds herself translating these values into both her business and personal life – often there is no boundary. As such, Rosa is in the vanguard of the new digital culture, a culture whose adherents live their values through their actions.

Ranging in age from Millennials to Boomers, integrators are the innovators and early adopters of the digital mindset. Some began as digital natives, others as digital immigrants. Many are consultants, designers, journalists, instructors, and marketing executives. Regardless of their vocation, they are living embodiments of the digital culture. They are strategists designing applications across silos and integrating them with existing marketing efforts. They are communicators fostering consumer engagement and sustainable relationships. They are teachers helping digital natives, immigrants, and aliens to develop a digital mindset and implement cutting-edge digital strategies. More than anything, integrators understand the real value of digital technology and use it to seek out opportunities to make an impact within and without their organizations.

Such is the case with Rosa. She is living her values, innovating strategically with the help of digital technology. When digital integrators like Rosa live their digital culture, they begin to alter the very DNA of the organizations they work for, forever changing how these organizations interact with their employees and customers.

Enter Rosa into the marketing challenges of Broad Learning Solutions. Bringing all the confidence and digital savvy of a forward-looking Fortune 100 company, Rosa is walking into a political quagmire. Bill is looking for somebody to "lead the digital charge" on the new software product launch, although he doesn't have a clear understanding of what this entails. As CMO, Samir is receptive to Rosa's knowledge but leads a marketing department with little experience in digital; he must ensure his entire sales and marketing team transitions to digital as quickly as possible to assure Bill as well as the CFO, who has concerns about the ROI of digital marketing.

Like other digital integrators, Rosa has adopted a digital mindset, infusing her core values and facility with various digital technologies into integrated marketing strategies that enrich and nurture the customer experience. At BLS, Rosa needs to become an inspiring leader, living by example to help the team adopt a digital mindset and integrate the company's core values with its strategic decisions. At times she will be disruptive of the current norm, experimenting with new ideas and tactics and then testing and refining them. Beginning with the language training app, she must work with Samir to gain his buy-in and develop an integrated digital marketing plan that produces results. Step-by-step, Rosa must earn the approval and support of the team.

"Marketing departments need to have a balance of team members with both analytical (data-driven) and creative skills. Those rare individuals who are adept in both areas are set to inherit the digital earth."[6]

Based on the work of Ashley Friedlein, CEO, Econsultancy 

The tale of Rosa and Broad Learning Solutions is a metaphor, a hypothetical reflection of the experiences millions of businesses and non-profits face as they grapple with the demands of the digital age. It introduces the four digital archetypes in a real-world setting to help illustrate the part each plays in the organization's *Path to Digital Integration*.

The BLS story and its archetypes is not intended to present a rigid orthodoxy, but rather to serve as a tool for executives and their staffs to better appreciate the individual perspectives of various team members, and how each relates to the organization's overall state of digital preparedness. Given that digital integration is fast becoming a key determinant of future sustainability, visionary leaders will strive to draw digital integrators into their organizations to facilitate and accelerate digital transformation.

"Digital Integrators have an expert command of digital and its strategic implementation."

The challenge, then, for both BLS and its real-life counterparts is to evolve, by degrees, into a Digitally Integrated Organization (DIO). But what does this mean for the organization and its future marketing efforts?

THE DIGITALLY INTEGRATED ORGANIZATION

As digital integrators continue to live their core values of the digital culture (creativity, equality, empathy, integrity, knowledge, efficiency, openness, unity), they cannot help but impact the organizations of which they are a part. With an unwavering focus on the customer experience, digital integrators (much like Rosa in our example above) will teach digital immigrants and natives to leverage digital strategies, tactics, and tools to their greatest effect, and will help digital aliens find value in the same. By doing so, over time the organization will hit a tipping point where the core values and business goals of the preponderance of its individuals are in harmonious alignment with those of the organization in which they are involved.

Thus is born the *Digitally Integrated Organization (DIO)*.

When viewed as a macro-entity or corporation in the truest sense of the word, both the *DIO*, and the digital integrators who comprise it, are living their values, forming a symbiotic circle which consistently adds abundance to the fertile ecosystem that is the digital culture.

Digital Integration

In the broadest sense, "digital integration" has been defined solely in its technological context, i.e. as "data on any given electronic device that can be read or manipulated by another device"[7]

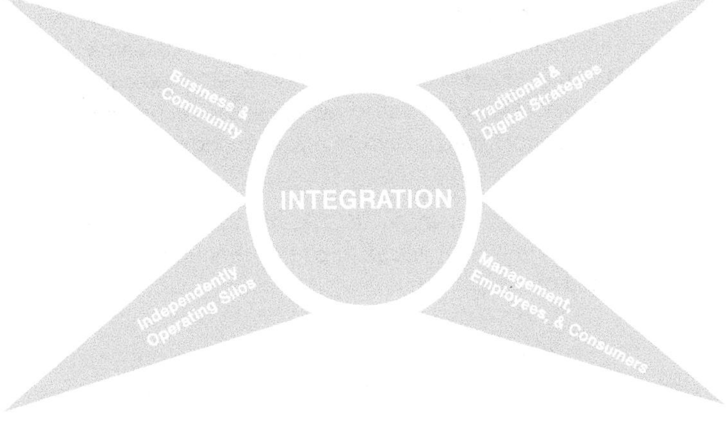

Figure 2.1: Digital Integration

However, in the context of the digital culture, we recognize that digital has impacted and integrated virtually all aspects of our personal, social, and professional lives. Given this, we define digital integration as the leveraging of the broad capabilities and vast efficiencies of digital technology and media by organizations to provide consumers relevance and value, thereby enhancing the customer experience.

With a clear understanding that the Internet, social, and mobile technologies have forever shifted the balance in favor of the consumer, the customer experience is the focus of the *DIO*. Accepting this fundamental reality of the digital age frees up the *DIO*, allowing the organization's aspirational values to align with those of its consumer base.

> *"We have to manage the reputation of the brand in the context of the vulnerability caused by the new digital world, by being honest, transparent and genuine."*[8]
>
> Dev Amritesh, President and CEO, Dunkin' Donuts (India), Jubilant FoodWorks Limited
> *From Stretched to Strengthened*: IBM Global CMO Study

Importantly, doing so has the effect of realigning the organization's functional character:

- Trust replaces fear.
- Openness trumps control.
- Communication and innovation is fostered between management and employees.
- Integrated applications and cross-functional teams tear down independent silos.
- Direct connections occur between C-suite executives and end consumers.
- Sharing and collaboration replaces proprietary control and information coveting.
- The bottom line changes to reflect engagement, relationships, and advocacy.

More than just a social business, the *Digitally Integrated Organization* combines digital technology and digital marketing with core human values to generate abundance for all stakeholders – its shareholders, employees, customers, and community.

> *"The most proactive CMOs are responding to these challenges by trying to understand individuals as well as markets. They are focusing on relationships, not just transactions. Outperformers are also committed to developing a clear "corporate character."*[9]
>
> *From Stretched to Strengthened*: IBM Global CMO Study

Benchmark MINDSET of the Digitally Integrated Organization

Measurable – The explosion of consumer data aggregation and behavioral analytics makes it easier for organizations great and small to measure real-time cause and effect and make immediate adjustments to digital marketing initiatives.

Integrated – Consumer sophistication is growing apace with digital innovation, creating a new class of highly-social, always-mobile, and ever-demanding consumers who want what they want, when and where they want it. When interacting with brands, today's digital mavens are demanding value-added experiences that are simple and convenient. To deliver, organizations must seamlessly integrate all digital channels efficiently and cost-effectively.

Nimble – Taking a fully integrated approach to digital increases business efficiency and productivity, creating agile organizations that can nimbly react to the unceasing stream of innovations characteristic of the digital age.

Disruptive – In the face of the continuous change of digital, change that may at times resemble total chaos, businesses must operate with dynamism and flexibility. Dynamic organizations learn to embrace change rather than be overwhelmed by it. Distruption and dynamism supplant regularity and rigidity.

Strategic – The speed of digital innovation requires executives to have an overarching strategic vision flexible enough to survive the constant experimentation with and implementation of new digital technologies.

Engaged – Mass consumer adoption of the Internet, social, and mobile has shifted the power from the producer to the consumer. To thrive in today's digital environment, organizations must take an interactive and synergistic approach. This involves an often real-time value exchange of information and insight between the organization and its consumers, where the organization utilizes consumer input to constantly improve its product and service offerings.

Transparent – More than anything, digital consumers expect utter transparency from the brands with whom they engage. Businesses can take advantage of this trend to build trust, form deeper connections with prospects and consumers, and foster long-term brand loyalty.

TAKEAWAYS

- Digital natives have an intuitive understanding of digital, but need to learn how to think strategically.
- Digital immigrants recognize the value of digital, but need to learn the strategies, tactics, and tools for its successful implementation.
- Digital aliens think strategically, but need to experience the value of digital.
- Digital integrators have an expert command of digital and its strategic implementation.
- With an unwavering focus on the customer experience, digital integrators help guide executives and staff to leverage digital strategies to their greatest effect.
- The *Digitally Integrated Organization* combines digital technology and digital marketing with core human values to generate abundance for all stakeholders – its shareholders, employees, customers, and community.
- The *Digitally Integrated Organization* is born when the core values and business goals of the preponderance of the individuals in the organization are in harmonious alignment with those of the organization itself.

CHAPTER 3: DRIVERS OF CHANGE

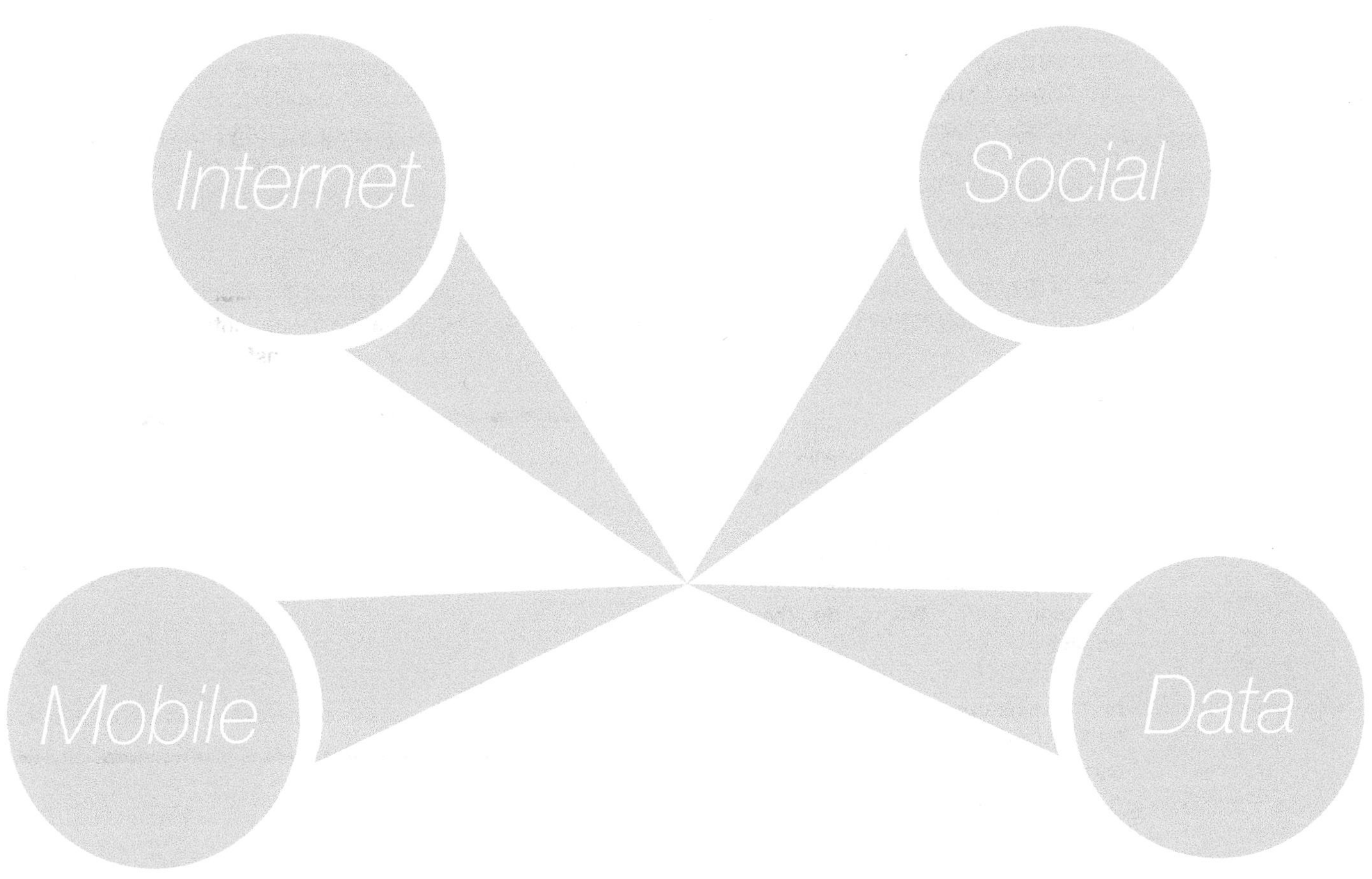

As we noted in the introduction, the *Digital Tsunami* represents a fundamental sea change in business and marketing, bringing forth a continued state of disruption in its wake. But how can you find order in the chaos? To properly operationalize digital marketing, you must first understand the fundamental drivers of change and current trends that are fueling rapid digital transformation. Doing so will help you gain a measure of ***"Digital Insight"*** into how these drivers and trends will impact your organization, both now and in the future – information which may prove vital for competitive advantage. It will also provide much needed context to your transformational journey along the *Path to Digital Integration*.

At a 2013 symposium on the future of digital technologies, Gartner Senior VP and Head of Research, Peter Sondergaard, suggested, "Many of the vendors on top of the IT world today – namely Cisco, Oracle, and Microsoft – will likely not be the IT leaders of tomorrow in the Digital Industrial Economy." Why? Because, Sondergaard noted, these companies have antiquated channel strategies, sales force, out of tune partner ecosystems and changing customer business models. Even today's leading technology companies are not immune to the challenges posed by digital transformation.[1]

One of the biggest challenges lies in the inherently exponential nature of digital transformation. This brief video (Figure 3.1) produced by Capgemini Group does a great job of capturing the fundamental reality that, even with all of the drastic changes in recent years, we are still in the early days of digital transformation.

Clearly, digital transformation is a major challenge for small- and medium-sized enterprises (SMEs) and major corporations alike. **How do organizations anticipate and plan for such a fundamental paradigm shift. Where do they begin?**

Digital Transformation

Figure 3.1: Digital Transformation – We Haven't Seen Anything Yet – Video[2]

In this chapter, we will take the following approach when analyzing each driver of change (Internet, Social, Mobile, and Data):

- *Driver of Change* – a brief overview of each driver.
- *Sub Driver* – an overview of the key micro drivers shaping digital marketing best practices.
- *Trending* – a review of the critical trends worth integrating into your digital marketing strategy.

Driver of the Digital Enterprise

Several key drivers have positioned the next decade to deliver a staggering – perhaps unprecedented – amount of change as the next-generation enterprise is on the horizon. The first of these indicators is the level of ***societal change*** *impacting everything from business to war. In the business world, the implications of this change can be seen in our employees, where for the first time in history, four generations of workers are in our work force. The associated challenges are coming into focus, as some of these workers are digital natives, but the vast majorities are digital immigrants. With customers, the shift of power to the individual has changed their role forever and placed them at the center of the company ecosystem. Other indicators include an* ***intense focus on growth****, which increasingly requires collaboration within and outside the four walls of the Enterprise. This growth agenda drives a new type of value ecosystem, enabling growth that in many cases is outside a company's traditional business.*

The ***search for effectiveness*** *is an emerging indicator that promises to drive many future initiatives. Whereas the goal of efficiency is doing things right, effectiveness will focus on doing the right things. In parallel, and after hitting an efficiency wall, companies will focus on creating next-generation efficiencies. The maturation and* ***convergence of Digital Technologies*** *(Social, Mobile, Analytics, Big Data, Cloud and the Internet of Things) will be key enablers. As commoditization across industries accelerates, companies will differentiate by creating consumer-like experiences, specializing, and effectively using insights.*

Perhaps the biggest indicator is the realization that future success is tied to ***Digital DNA*** *– or those characteristics that enable companies to operate in a rapidly changing business environment. Internet Companies and start-ups have the DNA advantage and the barriers for new market entrants continue to collapse. But most companies are traditional companies and have a considerable gap to close. To do this, enshrined organizational policies, practices, processes and structures that inhibit Digital DNA will change. When we look back, this structural change will be viewed as the catalyst that enabled next-generation enterprises.*

Frank Diana, Principal, Digital Enterprise Solutions, Tata Consultancy Services

How is your organization developing digital insight to anticipate the exponential digital transformation contemplated in *Figure 3.1*?

- How are you planning to leverage these technologies, both internally and externally, to better position your company in the future?

DRIVER OF CHANGE: INTERNET

Depending on who you ask, the roots of the Internet go back to the 1960s or even the 1950s. Regardless of its date of origin, few would dispute the Internet's role as the primary driver of change in marketing; its impact on business communication and commerce is far reaching, and growing with each passing day. If information is power, the Internet reigns supreme. It has fundamentally changed how we distribute, classify, seek out, and act on information. Indeed, the Internet has become the information superhighway of the digital culture.

Of all the elements that make up the complex Internet ecosystem, three in particular have greatly impacted the marketing function in the digital age – search, brand websites, and e-commerce sites.

Search

It all begins with the need for information – SEARCH. By providing an easy way to navigate its vast expanses, search engines have greatly enhanced the day-to-day functionality of the Internet. The ability of search engines to find and distribute virtually limitless information in a matter of seconds has transformed how consumers interact with brands, greatly increasing business efficiency.

Keyword-initiated queries have been a mainstay of search since its inception; however, exponentially faster processing speeds and storage capacities are now enabling us to take a more sophisticated approach to search. For example, a user can now easily execute a voice-activated or visual search query that taps into his or her search history and current location to provide highly contextualized search results.

- Google processes over 100 billion search queries each month.[3]
- On a daily basis, 15% of these queries (500 million) are new to Google.[4]
- Google crawls 20 billion websites each day in search of new data for query results.[5]

For years now, digital marketers have been optimizing web-based content for keyword-initiated search queries (e.g. the words the user places in the search bar) and then carefully tracking the results of their efforts. Indeed, search engine optimization (SEO) has been an indispensable tool for driving web traffic, leads, and sales. In October of 2011 this began to change, as Google first announced it would start implementing HTTPS/SSL encryption on all searches of logged in Google users; in September of 2013, the company announced it would expand HTTPS/SSL search encryption to all users of its search engine.

The move rocked the digital marketing world, as encrypted search made individual keyword tracking impossible, effectively rendering moot much traditional SEO analysis. To be clear, HTTPS encryption did not kill organic (unpaid) search itself, but rather the ability of website owners to track the results of organic search queries to their site. Although a big deal for businesses and marketers at the time, in a larger sense, HTTPS encryption served to underscore Google's steady move to a more sophisticated semantic search paradigm.

Throughout this period, technological advancement, coupled with the widespread consumer adoption of social and mobile platforms, has dramatically altered the face of search, overturning the accepted conventions of SEO. Thanks to faster processing capabilities and advancements in machine learning, search engines are finally moving away from static keyword strings to a more dynamic world of semantic understanding and higher-order entity recognition, by which search engines are able to recognize user intent – to understand *why* a user is asking something.

The roots of semantic search go back to May of 2012, when Google rolled out its Knowledge Graph, an artificial intelligence (AI)-like semantic search engine that forever shifted the search paradigm by focusing on "things not strings." With Knowledge Graph, search evolved from a static system that understood search queries as groups of keyword "strings" to a more dynamic, context based system that could recognize and understand references to actual "things," such as ideas or entities. At the time of writing, Knowledge Graph had more than 570 million entities and over 18 billion facts about connections between them.[6]

It should be noted, semantic technology is not limited to external search engines like Google or Bing, but is also being used in social media. Graph Search is Facebook's internal social search engine that operates in a similar fashion to Google's Knowledge Graph, further blurring the lines between search and social.

From here it is a short leap to the anticipatory recommendation engine – once a search engine is able to consistently recognize (and to some extent comprehend) why you are asking something, it can begin to anticipate what you are likely to ask next, and then act proactively to serve up customized recommendations. In short, search engines are beginning to think and act like humans.

Anticipatory Recommendations

Advancements in cloud computing, context-based search engines, and data aggregation are generating unprecedented levels of raw information; the difficulty lies in drawing useful meaning out of it all. Complex machine learning algorithms are now enabling computer programs to analyze real-time conversations to derive user intent. With time, and enough listening, these programs can even anticipate information that will guide user action, obviating the need for "search" altogether.

The anticipatory recommendation engine represents the perfect convergence of three emerging technologies: mobile, voice recognition, and big data. When programs are able to access tons of Internet, social, mobile, and geolocational data (aka proactive information discovery), and then filter and categorize it, they can predict, or perhaps more accurately anticipate, future actions.

Just like the archetypal English butler Jeeves, the longer the anticipatory recommendation engine observes and listens, the better it is able to anticipate your wants and needs – often before you do. Companies like Expect Labs and Nuance, whose voice recognition software powers voice recognition systems Google Now and Siri, are early players in the emerging anticipatory computing arena.

For deeper insight into the present and future of anticipatory recommendations ->

DISCOVER MORE

Brand Websites

So where do search engines drive traffic? Gone are the days of the brochure website with little or no practical functionality. As we continue to integrate digital into our daily lives, brand websites have become the primary go-to source of information for prospects and consumers, supporting, replacing, and in some cases improving upon many of the business functions of their bricks-and-mortar counterparts. Acting as an organization's virtual storefront, information repository, and online distribution hub, today's brand websites must convert on a number of levels, enticing would-be prospects, nurturing new leads, and servicing existing customers.

Virtually every day new research comes out underscoring the rapid consumer shift to mobile; there's a surfeit of online chatter about the importance of building mobile marketing campaigns and the need for "mobile first" marketing strategies.

It's important to remember that the term "mobile" refers to a set of devices, not a movement or a culture. As we argued in the first chapter, the term "digital" has sufficient breadth to be regarded as a cultural movement or a new way of thinking. The term "mobile," on the other hand, refers to an enabling technology or access point to the digital realm – a world in which the fundamental anchor is the Internet, and the primary focal point is the brand website.

Further, the proliferation and convergence of Internet-enabled devices (smartphones are getting bigger, tablets smaller, laptops with touchscreen capabilities, etc.), weakens our ability to classify based on device, "mobile" or otherwise. Instead, we are facing a new integrated digital reality that is user-focused and device agnostic.

Responsive Web Design (RWD)

In today's complex, consumer-centric techonomy, brands must be able to ensure that prospects and customers can easily access their website from anywhere and enjoy a seamless user experience regardless of the device and platform they are on.

Responsive web design accomplishes this, resolving a number of issues for businesses. Designing responsively eliminates the need to create a separate mobile site, saving time and money. It also provides users with a seamless experience across devices, offering the same information no matter how they access a brand's website. With RWD, organizations are able to maintain brand integrity by delivering consistent messaging to any web user. They can integrate mobile into their online presence to create a truly cohesive user experience, an experience focused on people rather than on devices.

E-Commerce

Sub-Driver

As a complement to brand websites, e-commerce sites have added functional depth to the Internet economy, providing users a highly convenient way to research, compare, and purchase goods and services from anywhere, anytime. Anecdotal evidence from the US Department of Commerce (Figure 3.2) suggests the e-commerce sector is experiencing far more rapid growth than the retail sector as a whole.[7]

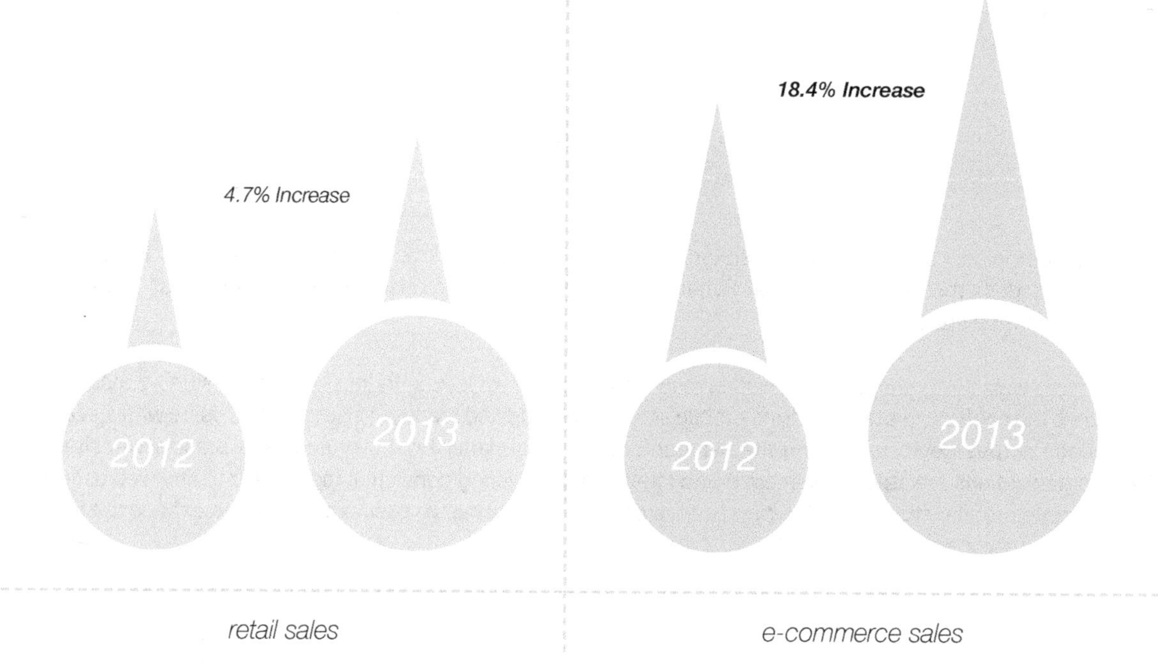

Figure 3.2: The Growth of E-Commerce

Admittedly, e-commerce is still in early days; US e-commerce sales in the 1st quarter of 2014 accounted for just 6.2 percent of total retail sales, making it much easier for e-commerce sales to show robust incremental growth.[8] However you slice the numbers, though, the trend is unmistakable.

Today's sophisticated online shoppers are looking for integrated, relevant, transparent, and convenient user experiences. In this climate, brands must ensure their e-commerce platforms do more than just support their websites, but also integrate in-store, social, and mobile channels into one unified experience. Brands with a physical presence must go one step further, providing prospects and customers an integrated online and offline, or "clicks-and-mortar," experience.

Highly visual sites that allow users to search for preferred goods, easily compare actual products and prices without much time investment, and provide a simple check-out process that offers a number of secure payment options tend to fare the best. Easily accessible customer testimonials and reviews help establish brand trust and relevance.

E-Commerce Spending by Generation

Contrary to popular assumption, e-commerce spending is not isolated to younger, tech-savvy digital natives. Baby Boomers are integrating digital media into their daily lives, and quickly.

For more information about the generational impact on e-commerce spending ->

M-Commerce (Mobile Commerce)

Given the meteoric rise in the consumer adoption of smartphones and tablets, the future of e-commerce seems invariably tied to m-commerce; in the US alone in 2014, sales from consumers shopping on mobile phones are projected to reach $38 billion, while sales from tablets will increase to $76 billion.[9] Tomorrow's m-commerce users will come to expect highly personalized and convenient experiences that organically integrate with their daily lives.

For businesses, this means preparing for total consumer engagement over multiple screens simultaneously (using more than one device at the same time) or sequentially (moving from one device to another), as consumers move to and from their PCs, smartphones, and tablets to research and purchase goods and services. For clicks-and-mortar retailers, this means the practice of "consumer show-rooming" (consumers using mobile devices to confirm features and compare reviews and prices on in-store merchandise) is not going away, but instead will become the norm.

- 81% of all smartphone purchases are spontaneous.[10]
- 88% of people agree that having a mobile device with real-time information makes them more spontaneous with shopping.[11]
- 51% of consumers expect transactions to be easier on mobile than they are offline.[12]

Instead of trying to fight a losing battle, smart retailers will capitalize on this trend by fitting their stores with near-field communication (NFC) technology, which supports data transfer over short distances, to encourage shoppers to purchase in-store merchandise online with a simple wave of their smartphones. Technologies like NFC allow brands to tap into the inherent spontaneity of the mobile consumer to transform the retail experience.

For examples of brands using NFC to enhance the retail experience ->

As brands gather more data on consumers, allowing for more sophisticated profiling, they will utilize algorithmic recommendations to deliver ever more personalized experiences to end users, providing tailor-made purchase suggestions by culling previous consumer behavioral data from numerous online channels. In the future, m-commerce will serve to blur the lines between the physical and the virtual worlds, quickening the inevitable convergence of Internet and retail in support of a fully integrated, omnichannel shopping experience.

Social networking connects people and communities, allowing them to share and transfer messages in real time. Much like our analog forebearers exchanging information and ideas in the ancient Roman Forum or the traditional town square, social media can be regarded as the virtual marketplace of online communication and engagement for the digital culture.

- 27% of all time spent online is on social networking.[13]
- 70% of B2C companies said they acquired a customer through social media channels.[14]

Unlike many forms of traditional marketing, whose reach tends to be linear, the power of social media lies in its exponential nature. Social media amplifies brand reach, empowering companies to leverage their content and messaging more efficiently than other marketing channels.

Here's an example. Let us say our fictional company, Broad Learning Solutions (BLS), shares a piece of content, such as its latest blog post, on Twitter (as a side note, keep in mind that every social follower of BLS has his or her own followers, be they five, 50, 500, or 5,000-strong). Now let's say a fan of BLS with 5,000 Twitter followers re-tweets, or shares, the blog post with his or her followers. BLS' blog is instantly exposed to 5,000 additional people who weren't directly following the brand. Moreover, any one of these people may, in turn, decide to share the blog post with their followers, and so on.

In this way, social media can provide brands of all sizes exposure on a truly massive scale.

Social Engagement

Exposure is one thing; effective social engagement is another altogether. Digital technology has given organizations an unprecedented opportunity to interact in a meaningful way with new prospects and existing customers – to connect more deeply and fluidly with those who have affinity for their brand. In today's digital culture, companies must go beyond social exposure to foster meaningful social engagement as a means of cultivating brand affinity.

Sounds logical; but how is it done? To resolve the "how of engagement," the Google Think Insights team created The Engagement Project to reflect on the movement from exposure to engagement as the driver of messages, user choice, interaction, sharing, and conversion. Here's how they summarize their strategy on social engagement:

"In the accelerating swirl of chaos, excitement, and yes, sometimes fear, the brands that win will prioritize engagement over exposure. They will flip the traditional approach of using mass reach to connect with the subset of people who matter on its head. They will super-serve the most important people for their brand first and use the resulting insights and advocacy to then broaden their reach and make the entire media and marketing plan work harder."[15]

They propose to transform the old sales funnel, based on reaching or broadcasting to as many people as possible, to the Engagement Pyramid concentrating on the 5% that really care about and have affinity for your brand, and using their networks to grow a strong, loyal following. Popular social brands (e.g. Starbucks, Amazon, Warby Parker) use this approach (refer to the *Digital Involvement Cycle* on page 83).

Social Advocacy and Engagement: The New Marketing Reality

Marketers are being squeezed between two forces that are literally reshaping markets: social advocacy – consumers' desire to create, curate and consume social content - and social engagement - the relative capability on the part of brands to respond and build on social advocacy. The need to respond effectively and timely has raised the bar on identifying, connecting with and tapping brand advocates, the superfans whose posts on social networks can influence purchase decisions.

What does this mean for marketers? It means shifting from a message-centric role into operational areas, especially customer service where the majority of brand-consumer interactions take place. Customer care is the new advocacy engine, and savvy marketers are revving it up. The result? A new emphasis in Marketing on understanding and managing digital involvement and the processes by which consumers are transformed into brand advocates

Taken together, the combination of the forces acting on markets – ubiquitous social behavior and the need to stretch marketing into customer care – and the absolute need for strong brand advocates makes understanding and actively managing digital involvement a fundamental best practice for marketers. Build your strategy around this new model and you'll benefit as superfans take up your cause on the social web.

Dave Evans, author, Social Media One Hour a Day; Vice President of Social Strategy, Lithium Technologies

Trending

Social Consumer Advocacy

The characteristic power shift to the consumer in the digital age has empowered them to publish and advocate their position through social media. Social consumer advocacy is reflective of how the digital consumer interacts with the organization. Social media gives the consumer power, control, access, and authority – all elements which were formerly in the hands of the organization. Social media has now leveled the playing field, forcing an ethos of transparency and accountability onto brands.

Social media is a catalyst for equality. As such, social advocacy is not only reflective of the core values of the digital culture; it's an example of the actionable nature of the core value of democracy in action.

- 90% of consumers would recommend a brand to others after interacting with them on social media.[16]
- 83% of consumers say user reviews often or sometimes impact their purchase decisions.[17]
- 80% of consumers have changed their mind about buying a product after reading a negative online review.[18]

What is special about social consumer advocacy is that it is organic, growing from within rather than being imposed from the outside. Brands can adapt to this truly customer-centric approach, making it the standard across their organizations. Product excellence, customer care, user-generated content, and consumer loyalty and advocacy programs are all inputs transforming the way social brands are marketed. With social advocacy, the consumer has the opportunity to influence their peers in a way that the brand cannot through advertising or other means.

To learn how brands are leveraging social consumer advocacy to connect with their audience -> DISCOVER MORE

"Engagement is often pigeonholed as just social, but we broaden that definition, because true engagement is anytime your target is choosing to interact with the brand, on everything from email to coupons. Now, we talk more about relationships. Marketing is not one-sided, and brands don't control the conversation anymore. In the '90s, brands could just put out their message. Now, they need to be having those conversations with their targets."[19]

Flora Caputo, VP and executive creative director at Jacobs Agency

Crowdsourcing

Similar to cloud computing but leveraging crowds of humans instead of servers, the essence of crowdsourcing lies in tapping into interconnecting networks of people to more efficiently address challenges and solve complex problems. From brainstorming new ideas to financing specific projects and initiatives (known as "crowdfunding"), crowdsourcing has become a social and business phenomenon. In fact, crowdsourcing is driving new business models; individuals and organizations are using crowdsourcing to tackle new ideas more efficiently and cost-effectively, bringing more competitive products and services to market.

Crowdsourcing is even impacting the publishing world. Walter Isaacson, author of the bestselling biography of Steve Jobs, is turning to crowdsourcing to edit his latest book about modern innovations. At the time of writing, Isaacson had posted chapters of his untitled book online for people to read, comment, and critique.[20]

By digitally aggregating the commonality of peoples' interests and capabilities to provide inexpensive, effective solutions, crowdsourcing is a tool with unlimited potential.

For additional insight into how brands are using crowdsourcing to drive business -> DISCOVER MORE

MOOCs

Massive Open Online Courses (MOOCs) are using crowdsourcing to transform the business model of higher education.

The traditional higher education model is all about "pushing" learning out to students (much like the old broadcast advertising model), compelling them to pay increasingly higher prices to follow pre-ordained curricula. The new online learning model encourages free interaction and open exchange of information, recognizing that the power is ultimately in the hands of the students, not the institutions. MOOCs often are more efficient, collaborative, and cost-effective, offering the proposition of a better education to students at a lower cost. Aside from their impact on education, the ascendancy of MOOCs has obvious implications for business, both in the short and long term.

To cite an example, organizations can capitalize on the remotely accessible, high-quality educational format of various MOOCs to offer ongoing training to employees at a fraction of the cost of physically sending them to university-based continuing education programs. Through MOOCs, employees have unprecedented access to leading professors and staff from a host of leading universities; employers can work with employees to create customized curriculum plans that most efficiently advance the goals of the individual and organization. Many of the leading MOOC providers – organizations such as Coursera, Udacity, edX, and Khan Academy – encourage their students to engage socially and leverage the collaborative spirit of the digital culture to foster deeper learning.

A number of top universities have already formed partnerships with leading MOOC providers. This is not surprising, as the MOOC model may offer a window into the future of higher education, giving universities the opportunity to more clearly define who they want to be, to carve out specializations without the need of offering buffet-style course offerings for fear of alienating students and losing out on revenues. In the future, collaboration with MOOCs may allow universities to run leaner, meaner operations that spend more time doing what they do best: educating.

Like social advocacy and crowdsourcing, MOOCs are living proof of the core values of the digital culture in action.

For an in-depth discussion of the impact of MOOCs on business and education ->

DISCOVER MORE

DRIVER OF CHANGE: MOBILE

More than just a device, mobile implies proximity (be it geolocational or online) in action. Think of mobile as the real-time enabler of the digital culture.

Given that mobile devices are ultimately toted around by humans occupying a physical (and virtual) space, the future of mobile is inextricably linked with social media and local proximity.

- A 2013 Interactive Advertising Bureau (IAB) survey found that the average person uses some form of "connected device" 34 times a day.[21]
- The same study found 52% of respondents prefer to check their smartphone if they have any "downtime" rather than just sit and think. Among 18-30 year olds, the figure rises to 62%.[22]
- India is the most mobile-centric country in the world, with 61% of its Internet traffic coming via mobile devices.[23]

In the past, a company's social, local, and mobile (*SoLoMo*) marketing efforts have been siloed. Organizations had separate social media marketing campaigns, geolocational marketing initiatives (usually offline) and mobile marketing, the latter being largely comprised of SMS text messaging.

However, the widespread consumer adoption of smartphones and tablets has changed all of this forever. One obvious but fundamental point many of us fail to fully comprehend is that smartphones and tablets are essentially pint-sized mini-computers. In fact, many mobile devices have processing speeds and advanced capabilities that eclipse many a desktop or laptop still in use today.

The advanced functionality of smartphones and tablets provides the on-the-go consumer numerous options and capabilities, empowering them as never before. In this way, while the ascendancy of high-tech mobile devices can be seen as a cornucopia for consumers, it can be viewed as a bit of a Pandora's Box for businesses and marketers. The latter must contend with the ever-increasing expectations and demands of sophisticated mobile users who, with smartphone or tablet in hand, want what they want when – and where – they want it.

The rapid advancement of mobile technology – with its integration of social media and expanding geolocational capabilities – has elevated the concept of contextual relevance in digital marketing; mobile users now expect businesses to provide contextually relevant online resources that inform, entertain, and/or resolve. In short, *SoLoMo* has shifted power to the consumers, and they know it.

SoLoMo (Localization)

SoLoMo reflects the convergence of social media, local proximity, and mobile devices. An example of *SoLoMo* convergence would be a smart phone app that can determine a consumer's location, suggest businesses close by, provide ratings and reviews of those businesses, and allow the consumer to post his or her own ratings, reviews, comments, and pictures onto the social networking site of their choice.

SoLoMo represents the growing marketing trend of targeting mobile consumers based on their current location with content or promotions designed to be shared via social networks.

Underpinning *SoLoMo* is the growing connection between social and mobile. According to the Adobe 2013 Mobile Consumer Survey, 71% of respondents reported using their mobile device to access social media. This deep connection between social and mobile should come as no surprise when you consider that mobile users prefer visual, concise, and contextually relevant content.[24]

Contextual relevance is where the "local" in *SoLoMo* comes into play. In the aforementioned Adobe study, 70% of respondents reported using their mobile device to search for local information such as event times, maps, and reviews. Almost a third of respondents have checked in via a location service on their mobile device, and 30% of those people said they received an incentive to check in.[25]

The importance of contextual relevance in *SoLoMo* is further underscored by the findings of a 2012 Nielson study on smartphone shopper activities, which found that 78% of mobile shoppers turn to their smartphones to find a store, 63% to check prices online, and 22% to comment on a purchase. These data anecdotally suggest that "*SoLoMo*" apps providing user-generated reviews and location-based offers have a significant influence on mobile consumers.

Moreover, companies with a bricks-and-mortar presence need to ensure they are easily accessible when prospects are nearby. Whether it's SMS text marketing, local SEO, local discounts and offers, or location-specific daily deals, proximity creates top-of-mind awareness and drives conversion. Each of these geolocational marketing techniques is most effective when executed with a *SoLoMo* mindset.

To learn how *SoLoMo* is redefining marketing ->

Location Recognition

Further evidence of the paradigm shift to *SoLoMo* can be found in the proliferation of social apps focused on location recognition. Location is so important to social media because it provides geospatial context. With the widespread use of mobile devices, social is moving beyond who and what to where, seamlessly integrating into our daily lives. Given this, many social apps are now created with the following objective in mind: to keep users engaged in-app for as long as possible in order to mine data from them (data which can be used to further improve the user experience and to generate ad revenue).

Many social apps are using geotagging (pinpointing the location of social media users) and geofencing (establishing a virtual perimeter around real-world geographical areas) to keep users connected anywhere, anytime. Social media giants like Twitter, Facebook, and Instagram rely on location tagging to connect users to each other and to nearby places.

Extreme SoLoMo: Geofeedia

Geofeedia, an American social media company, is taking social geotagging and geofencing to a whole new level. It maintains a series of patents that allow the desktop and mobile developer to pinpoint and track social media posts from Twitter, Instagram, Google's Picasa, Flickr, and YouTube in a customized space. Using sophisticated geotagging and geofencing capabilities, the company's software can draw a fence around a stadium or city block and the system will show every public social media post from users who have location services turned on. At the time of writing, Geofeedia is only available to qualified government institutions, businesses, and news outlets. Businesses are using Geofeedia for market research and for mining data from publicly available information posted by users in real-time.[26]

The pervasiveness of social/mobile location recognition technology is raising privacy concerns among individuals, businesses, and government. In 2013, US Senator Charles Schumer, working together with location analytics companies and privacy groups, introduced a new code of conduct so shoppers will clearly know when they are being tracked through their phones in stores; it also provides them with instructions for how to opt out.[27]

Mobile Apps

As mobile device usage continues to proliferate, users are increasingly reliant on mobile search and discovery. According to Google, 94% of smartphone users search for location information.[28] Aside from social apps and local search apps, retail or merchant apps will become more ubiquitous in the coming years.

Anyone who has tried to perform a general web search on a mobile device knows that it is not a user-friendly process, often taking forever to type in a query and then sift through an endless stream of results; voice-activated queries improve the experience but do not fundamentally change it. Mobile apps, on the other hand, are better able to target specific actions, providing simpler and more-relevant user experiences. Data from Nielson's 2013 Mobile Consumer Report bears out this notion, showing that 53% of US mobile device users are utilizing shopping/retail apps.[29]

Research shows that apps are beginning to dominate the mobile ecosystem. In 2013, the US consumer spent an average of 2 hours and 38 minutes per day on smartphones and tablets. 80% of that time (2 hours and 7 minutes) was spent inside apps and 20% (31 minutes) was spent on the mobile web. Digital marketers currently obsessed with producing ever greater amounts of web-based content in an attempt capture consumer mindshare may wish to consider this and shift some resources into specific-use mobile app production.[30]

Mobile Payments

Though still in its infancy, mobile payments are widely popular with those who have made the transition. According to data from Adobe's Mobile Consumer Survey, of those who have used a mobile wallet (18% overall, 25% of the younger segment) to pay for a product or service, 83% said that the payment experience was easier than providing their credit card.[31]

Mobile payments offer two advantages to consumers: convenience and security. Consumers are able to pay for everything through the one device which is on their person at all times: their mobile phone. Moreover, with most mobile payment arrangements, the consumer's financial information is not stored on a physical card, but rather in the highly encrypted cloud.

Though there are many types of mobile payments on the market, here are some of the most popular:

SMS Payments – SMS remains a simple and widely popular method of paying for goods and services via mobile, especially in the developing markets. In this method, the user sends an SMS text to a short code, and the stipulated charges are applied to their phone bill. When the payment is made the seller is informed of the transaction.[32]

QR Codes – Businesses are just now beginning to experiment with QR codes for payment. QR codes can be scanned with a smartphone in order to direct customers to a mobile website or a checkout location within an app.

NFC – Near-field-communication chips are a standard feature in many newer smartphones. With such a chip, customers can simply wave their smartphone close to a merchant's NFC reader to make a purchase. Some cities are already using NFC payment systems in public transportation.[33] Google Wallet is an emerging player in the NFC mobile payment space.

Mobile Credit Card Readers – These handy devices allow merchants to accept credit card payments through a small credit card reader that attaches to a smartphone or tablet. Square and PayPal are two companies that currently offer popular solutions. Many smaller merchants find credit card readers to be a more cost-effective alternative to credit card terminals.

Virtual Prepaid Cards – Virtual cards are essentially digital versions of the traditional gift card, located within an app. When customers pay via a virtual card, the app issues a barcode which can be scanned to complete the purchase.

Sub-Driver

Augmented Reality (AR)

Today's marketers are intensely focused on enhancing the digital experience. Augmented reality doubles down on this idea, giving marketers the ability to produce real-world user experiences that literally become digital. According to data from Juniper Research, 60 million users across smartphones, tablets, and smart glasses will utilize augmented reality apps in 2014; this number is expected to more than treble to 200 million unique users by 2018.[34] With such a robust adoption curve, augmented reality is poised to impact the business mainstream.

The term "augmented reality" is often used interchangeably with its technological cousin, "virtual reality." This is an unfortunate misapplication, as each term represents a different track – one outward focused and one inward focused – that we as humans are headed down with respect to our interface with digital technology in the near and distant future.

Augmented reality blurs the lines between what is real and what is computer-generated; it links the real and virtual worlds, using digital technology to enhance a person's natural surroundings. In this way, augmented reality can be understood as an externally focused digital interface.

By contrast, virtual reality is a completely immersive, computer-generated environment. Advanced digital technologies allow the user to view, hear, touch, and even smell the computer-generated environment. Virtual reality is all about convincing the user they are in a place where they actually are not. In this way, virtual reality can be understood as an internally focused digital interface.

Lending to their external focus, almost all augmented reality tools are apps for mobile devices such as smartphones, tablets, or wearables. Augmented reality provides a digitally enhanced view (reality) of the world in which we live and interact on a daily basis. Doing so requires a filter or lens (i.e. a smartphone, tablet, or wearable) to properly distill, or view, this enhanced reality. Given this, it comes as no surprise that many augmented reality start-ups are creating apps for Google Glass.

This very Zapcode is an example of AR in action! To learn how brands like Zappar are using AR to enhance the digital experience ->

DRIVER OF CHANGE: DATA

Think of data (in its biggest and broadest and sense) as the functioning brain, the underlying intelligence that provides content and context to the digital culture.

The term "big data" refers to a collection of data sets that are so big that they are difficult to collect, analyze, visualize, and process using regular software. Moreover, these data are typically unstructured. A recent study indicates that unstructured data account for at least 80% of the world's data.[35] The biggest challenge "Big Data" poses for businesses and marketers is how to glean accurate, relevant, and actionable insight from the seemingly unending deluge of information.

All the way back in August of 2010, Google's Eric Schmidt provided the following insight, which perfectly summarizes the challenge posed by data and its exponential growth:

"Between the birth of the world and 2003, there were five exabytes of information created. We [now] create five exabytes every two days. See why it's so painful to operate in information markets?"[36]

An interesting article on the science of data published in FastCoLabs touches on this very issue. In the piece, author Ciara Byrne quotes data scientist Jake Kyamka as saying, "Data science is not just about number-crunching.... It's all about people. The data comes from what people are doing, great data scientists have an ability to understand people and the ideal result is something which is going to help people."[37]

As such, the devil is not in the data, but rather in how it is sliced and diced, how it is interpreted and relayed. In an era rife with data, the greatest challenge for businesses and marketers lies not in the data itself, but in its meaningful interpretation.

Advancements in technology and data aggregation allow marketers to track, review, and refine virtually every aspect of a digital campaign. The ability to quickly compare marketing initiatives with real-world results allows businesses to continually refine their brand message and marketing initiatives, using content and context to better connect with prospects and customers.

Cloud Computing

At the foundation of cloud computing is the larger concept of converged infrastructure and shared services.

Think of the cloud as an unaffiliated system of online co-ops that enables the more efficient operation of the digital culture.

The generally accepted definition of cloud computing comes from the National Institute of Standards and Technology (NIST). The actual definition runs several hundred words, but essentially says that cloud computing is a model for enabling convenient, on-demand network access to a shared pool of configurable computing resources (e.g. networks, servers, storage, applications, and services) that can be rapidly provisioned and released with minimal management effort or service provider interaction.[38]

However, perhaps the clearest definition of cloud computing comes from an article in PC Mag written by Eric Griffith:

"In the simplest terms, cloud computing means storing and accessing data and programs over the Internet instead of your computer's hard drive. The cloud is just a metaphor for the Internet. It goes back to the days of flowcharts and presentations that would represent the gigantic server-farm infrastructure of the Internet as nothing but a puffy, white cumulonimbus cloud, accepting connections and doling out information as it floats....For it to be considered 'cloud computing,' you need to access your data or your programs over the Internet, or at the very least, have that data synchronized with other information over the Net."[39]

For organizations, cloud computing provides the option of outsourcing IT management and infrastructure to third-party, offsite cloud hosting service providers. This gives organizations the prospect of greater operational efficiency (no need to internally house IT infrastructure and staff), 24/7 accessibility, and cutting-edge security, often at a lower cost than traditional on-site IT solutions.

- Corporate spending on third-party-managed and public-cloud environments will grow from $28 billion in 2011 to more than $70 billion in 2015, according to IDC.[40]
- 63% of business leaders surveyed agree that the cloud can make their entire organization more business agile and responsive.[41]
- In 2013, 80% of large North American institutions are planning or executing programs to make use of cloud environments to host critical applications.[42]

There are three broad categories of cloud computing services for business:

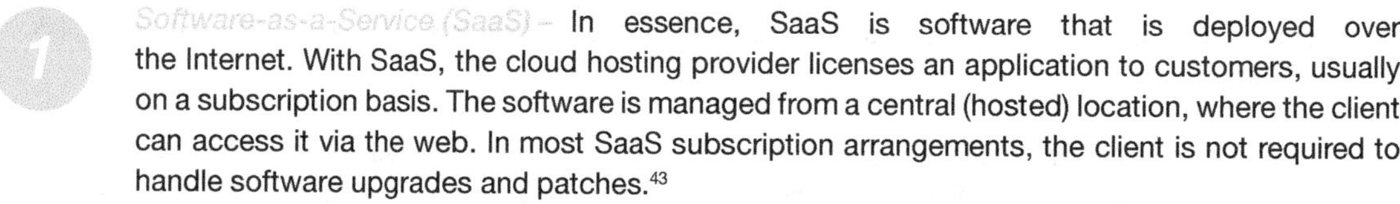

1. *Software-as-a-Service (SaaS)* – In essence, SaaS is software that is deployed over the Internet. With SaaS, the cloud hosting provider licenses an application to customers, usually on a subscription basis. The software is managed from a central (hosted) location, where the client can access it via the web. In most SaaS subscription arrangements, the client is not required to handle software upgrades and patches.[43]

2. *Platform-as-a-Service (PaaS)* – PaaS can be defined as a computing platform that allows the creation of web applications quickly, easily, and without the complexity of buying and maintaining the software and infrastructure that underpins it. PaaS is similar to SaaS except that, rather than being software delivered over the web, it provides a platform for the creation of software delivered over the web.[44]

3. *Infrastructure-as-a-Service (IaaS)* – IaaS provides cloud computing infrastructure (servers, storage, network and operating systems) as a fully outsourced, on-demand service. IaaS can be obtained as a public or private infrastructure or a combination of the two. “Public cloud” is considered infrastructure that consists of shared resources deployed on a self-service basis over the Internet; by contrast, “private cloud” is infrastructure that emulates various features of cloud computing, but on a private network. Some cloud hosting providers are beginning to offer a “hybrid cloud,” or a combination of traditional dedicated hosting alongside public and/or private cloud networks.[45]

Cloud computing confers many of the same benefits on individuals as businesses: 24/7 web-based access to innumerable products and services; inexpensive monthly subscription models (think Netflix streaming service); higher security (“cloud-based” online banking and other services utilize sophisticated encryption algorithms); and finally, lower hardware infrastructure costs. Consumers no longer need to invest in a rack of local servers to store pictures, videos, and other data; they can outsource data storage to cloud-based providers like Google, Amazon, Shutterfly, etc.

The growth of cloud computing infrastructure is not only revolutionizing business functions, it is re-ordering the very way in which we interface with technology. Nowhere is this more evident than in the emerging Internet of things.

Trending

The Internet of Things (IOT)

Perhaps the most impactful technology trend of the decade, the Internet of things (also known as the Internet of everything) is a world where virtually every thing (humans included) is imbued with one or more tiny computers or smart sensors, all transmitting an unending flow of data onto the Internet.

In the Internet of things, any natural or human-made object that can be assigned an IP address and given the ability to transmit data via a network is eligible – your tires, coffee maker, liver, underwear – pretty much everything. Thus far, the Internet of things has been confined to machine-to-machine (M2M) communications in larger industries such as manufacturing and utilities. However, the maturation of cloud computing will provide the converged infrastructure necessary to process the sheer volumes of data generated by the IOT in real time.

On a commercial level, the world of connected devices represents a boon for companies far and wide. As the world embraces the IOT, marketers may have to face the daunting prospect of having to create personalized web and social interactions not only for each segment of their target audience, but also for each audience's bevy of smart devices. Such is but one small implication of the emerging world of IOT.

As a side note, wearable is also considered part of the IOT ecosystem. From Google Glass to the Sony SmartWatch, wearable tech encompasses pretty much any smart, connected device you can wear.

Companies like IOT startup *Evrythng* plan on using the surfeit of sensor data from the objects around us to provide value to both consumers and businesses. In an interview with Econsultancy, Andy Hobsbawm, co-founder of *Evrythng*, boiled down the value-add of his company:

"Evrythng is a new service that creates active digital identities for products and other objects…. Evrythng helps organize the world's objects with an active digital identity for every thing."[46]

In an emerging IOT world that will see billions of devices constantly streaming data onto the Internet, the very notion of big data is about to get whole lot bigger.

For a more detailed discussion of how the IOT will impact society and business ->

DEVELOPING DIGITAL INSIGHT

Having been exposed to a plethora of innovative digital technologies (some quite overwhelming), how can an organization process all of the emerging trends to develop digital insight?

To help, we have designed the following six-step *Digital Insight Process* so that organizations can analyze each driver, sub-driver, and trend as a strategic opportunity rather than a cause for paralysis:

1. *Digital Trend Analysis* – Department teams are selected to use Figure 3.3 as a tool to benchmark each trend on nine dimensions in the context of adding value to the organization.

2. *Analyze Possibilities* – Representatives from each department meets as a group to brainstorm possibilities and determine best fit and potential contribution to the organization.

3. *Prioritize Trends* – A *Digital Innovation Unit* or other cross-functional team prioritizes the trends and make recommendations for applications (see page 221 for more detail on the *Digital Innovation Unit*).

4. *Pilot* – *Digital Innovation Unit* designs the pilot.

5. *Implement* – *Digital Innovation Unit* implements the pilot.

6. *Evaluate and Strategize* – *Digital Innovation Unit evaluates the results and compares them to goals, suggests adjustments, and proposes a strategy for the future.*

Note, after each team collaborates on this process a number of times with different trends, a pattern will emerge for the organization. Participants will become very efficient in filtering out best-use applications. Over time, the process will become a more refined tool for achieving digital insight.

Trend	Potential Internal Applications	Potential External Applications	Competitors' Use	Case Trials	Resources to Develop	Obstacles/ Risk	Time Frame	Access to Technology	Priority Level

Figure 3.3: Digital Trend Analysis

TRANSITION TO DIGITAL TRANSFORMATION

In 2013, MIT Sloan Management Review and Capgemini Consulting launched a global survey of 1500+ executives to benchmark digital transformation. In the survey, ***EMBRACING DIGITAL TECHNOLOGY: A New Strategic Imperative***, they defined digital transformation as the use of new digital technologies (social media, mobile, analytics or embedded devices) to enable major business improvements (such as enhancing customer experience, streamlining operations or creating new business models).[47]

Here are some key statistics from the survey:[48]

- According to 78% of respondents, achieving digital transformation will become critical to their organizations within the next two years.
- However, 63% said the pace of technological change in their organization is too slow.
- The most frequently cited obstacle to digital transformation was "lack of urgency."
- Only 38% of respondents said that digital transformation was a permanent fixture on their CEO's agenda.
- Where CEOs have shared their vision for digital transformation, 93% of employees feel that it is the right thing for the organization. However, a mere 36% of CEOs have shared such a vision.

Throughout this chapter, we have examined the drivers of change that are quickening digital transformation.

In a related blog post for Harvard Business Review, digital transformation expert Dr. Didier Bonnet summed up both the challenge and promise of digital for businesses:

"But here is the daunting and exciting thing: we're only at the very beginning of the next digital wave. Technology innovation is not slowing down or leveling off, but ramping up — and businesses will soon face a barrage of new digital possibilities. There is no time for complacency."[49]

How are executives relating to the challenges posed by digital transformation? Not well!

Executives, owners, and entrepreneurs need to look at new business models that will enable them to deftly manage the transition to digital, integrating their existing business strategy and structure with a new approach that will lead them step by step down the *Path to Digital Integration*. Digital transformation will impact the entire organization. It begins with a number of fundamental changes to the existing marketing function, which we collectively refer to as the *New Marketing Normal*. By degrees, it extends to the structural integration of digital throughout the enterprise, eventually leading to the creation of the *Digitally Integrated Organization*.

For an in-depth look at the challenges digital transformation poses for businesses ->

Beyond the numbers, the following two takeaways summarize the findings of the survey and provide insight for organizations considering digital transformation:[50]

- *"IT and digital is pervasive in people's lives now. So the advice I would give somebody starting it now is, think of yourself like a consumer technology company."* **Curt Garner, Chief Information Officer, Starbucks.**

- *"If you're an executive leading a company looking at these technologies, you need to lead the technology - don't let it lead you."* **George Westerman, Research Scientist, MIT Sloan's Center for Digital Business**

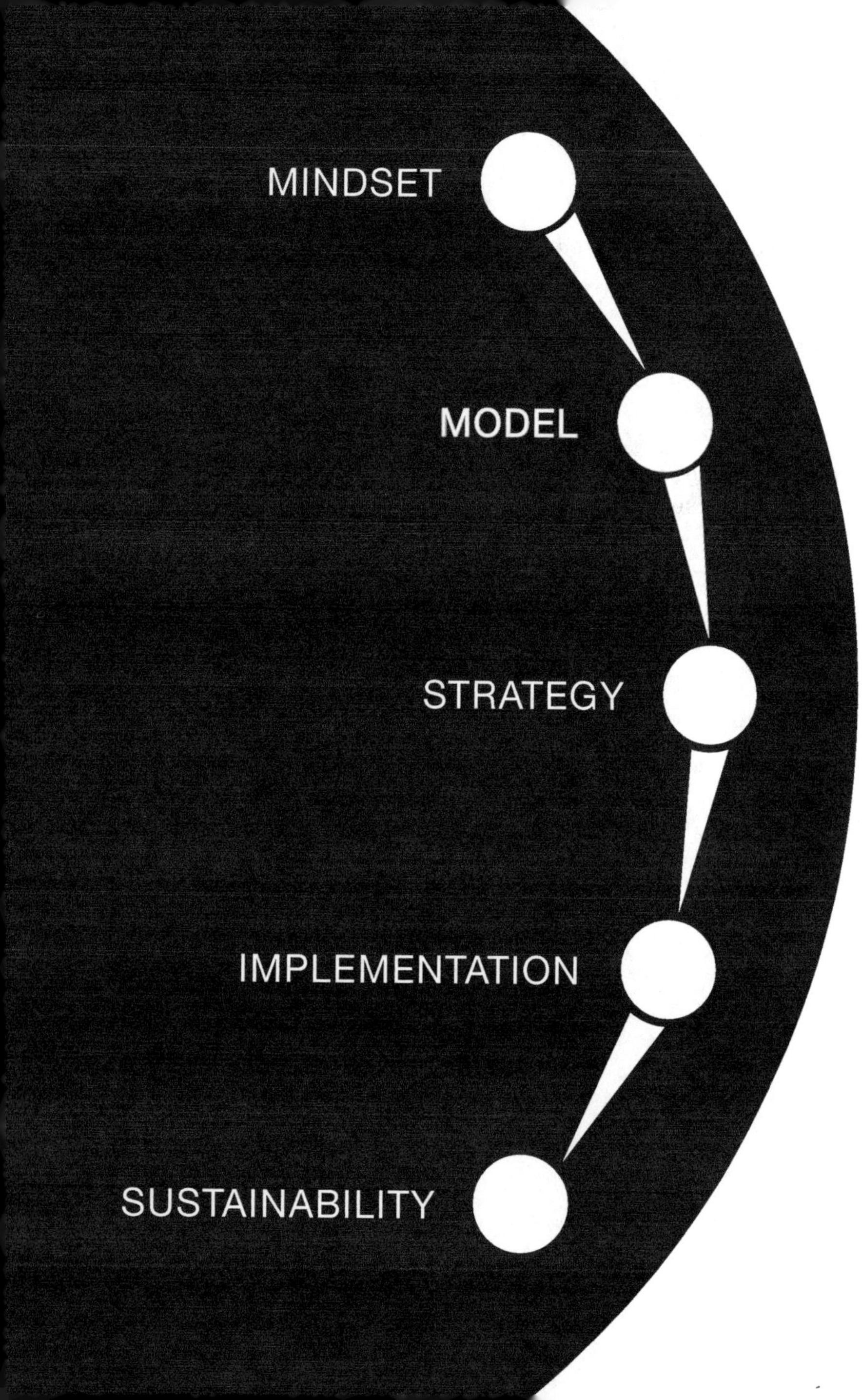

MINDSET

MODEL

STRATEGY

IMPLEMENTATION

SUSTAINABILITY

Chapter 4: Fundamentals of the New Marketing Normal

Chapter 5: Managing the New Marketing Normal

Chapter 6: Integrated Digital Marketing

Now that we have set the context for the *Path to Digital Integration*, we must design a new strategic model that lays the foundation for the *Digitally Integrated Organization*. This model must be adaptive and responsive to the drivers of change, which will continue to transform the marketplace and the organization.

In chapter 4, we outline how the fundamental concepts of marketing have been altered by the drivers of change to create the core components of the *New Marketing Normal*. In chapter 5, we examine how these core components translate into actionable and manageable digital marketing strategies and tactics. Finally, in chapter 6 we introduce a new strategic model, *Integrated Digital Marketing*, which incorporates the best practices of the *New Marketing Normal* to support an organization's effort to achieve sustainable growth through digital integration.

As a reminder, you can access in-depth information, videos, and updates from our *Digital Marketing Resource Center* (www.dmresourcecenter.org) wherever you see this icon.

CHAPTER 4: FUNDAMENTALS OF THE NEW MARKETING NORMAL

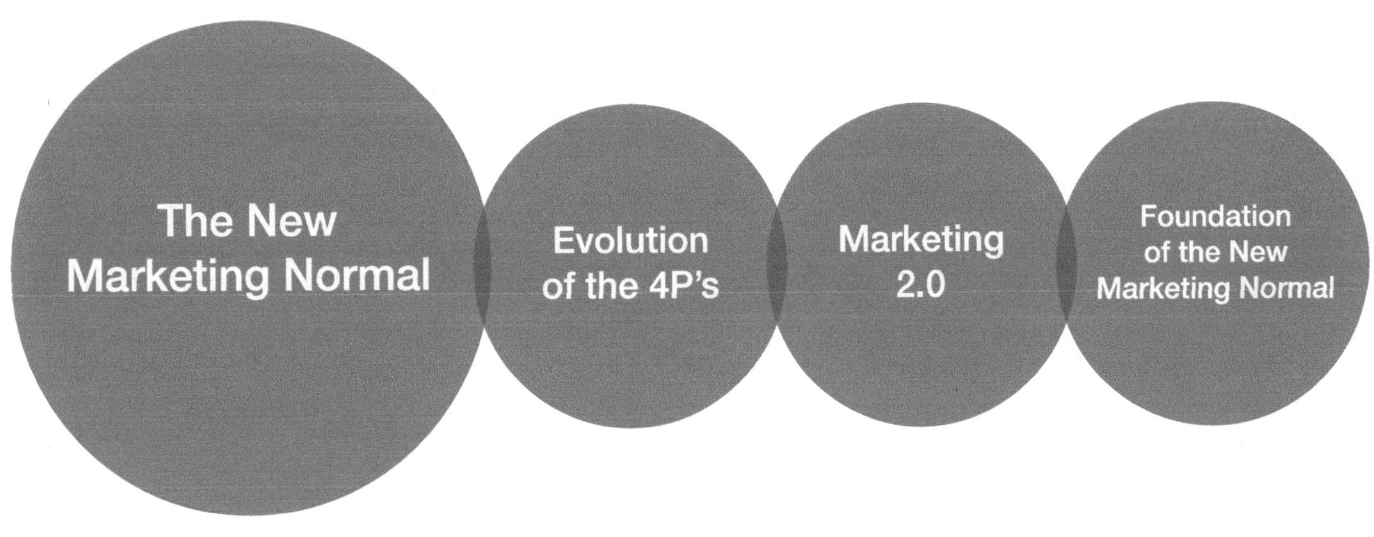

"The Goals Themselves Haven't Changed; the Manner of Accomplishing Them Has."

The American Marketing Association defines marketing as, "the activity, set of institutions, and processes for creating, communicating, delivering, and exchanging offerings that have value for customers, clients, partners, and society at large."[1]

Going back a bit further, the origin of the word "marketing" comes from the Latin, *mercatus*, "to buy, sell, or trade."

The very idea of marketing has its roots in the village marketplaces of old, where one could go to buy or sell a product or service to another in a climate of openness and equivalency. This reflects the essence of marketing. On its most fundamental level, marketing is all about open engagement and exchange between two equal parties. Somewhere along the line we forgot about this notion; however, with the aid of digital technology, we're finally getting back to it.

THE NEW MARKETING NORMAL

The New Marketing – Engaging Customers in the Digital Age

The old marketing involved marketing brands to consumers. Yesterday's companies focused mostly on mass marketing to broad segments of customers at arm's length. By contrast, the new marketing is customer-engagement marketing. Today's companies are using a rich new set of digital and social tools to refine their targeting and engage consumers directly and continuously in shaping brand conversations, brand experiences, and brand community.

Customer-engagement marketing goes beyond just selling brands to consumers. Its goal is to engage customers more deeply and interactively by making brands a meaningful part of their conversations and lives. In this digital age, consumers have more information about brands than ever before, and they have a wealth of digital platforms for airing and sharing their brand views with others. Greater consumer empowerment means that companies can no longer rely on marketing by intrusion. Instead, they must practice marketing by attraction—creating market offerings and sparking brand conversations that engage consumers rather than interrupting them. Successful engagement marketing means making relevant and genuine contributions to consumers' conversations and brand experiences.

Gary Armstrong, Blackwell Distinguished Professor Emeritus, Kenan-Flagler Business School, University of North Carolina at Chapel Hill

Regardless the time or place, marketers have been interested in building awareness, generating demand, converting the sale, and maintaining brand loyalty. However, the rise of digital technologies such as the Internet, social, and mobile has tipped the balance of power in favor of the consumer, who has grown in sophistication with exposure to the digital interface.

Today's consumers, always online, expect to find personalized solutions to their wants and needs on-demand; their tolerance for brands that do not provide desired user experiences wanes with each passing day. The Internet is their playground, an online world that does not recognize traditional boundaries of geography, distance, or data capacity. It is into this *Digital Tsunami* that marketers must wade, learning how to compete on a global scale by tapping into a seemingly limitless pool of information in order to navigate the unceasing tumult of consumer expectation.

Welcome to the *New Marketing Normal*.

When asked what precipitated this shift to the *New Marketing Normal* from the consumer perspective, John Battelle, digital thought leader and Founder and CEO of Federated Media Publishing, had this to say:

"It started about a decade ago with search…what search offered the consumer at scale was the ability to declare an intent and have the world organize around that intent in a fraction of a second. That changed the expectations of all of us in terms of how responsive we expect a brand to be…the new marketing is all about figuring out how to be in conversation with a customer at scale."[2]

Sounds like the traditional rules of marketing engagement, only at greater speed and scale.

The Breakup

Figure 4.1: The Breakup – Video[3]

Video Credit:

Client: Microsoft Digital
Contact Client/Trade Marketeer: Geert Desager
Agency: Dallas Antwerp (www.dallas.be)
Creatives: Stef Selfslagh, Stijn Gansemans

Account Manager: Mathias Delmote
Production: Caviar Films LA
Director: Ben Zlotucha

What does the breakup between the Advertiser and Consumer reflect?

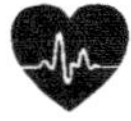

- List some attributes of the Advertiser and the Consumer cultures.
- How can the Advertiser transform himself to be more effective?
- Does this dynamic reflect practices in your organization?

EVOLUTION OF THE 4P's

In the 1960s, the prevailing worldview was that marketing was king; product had longevity and audiences were reached by mass media. Jerome McCarthy established the 4P's (Product, Price, Promotion, and Place) as the four core variables that comprise the marketing mix. The 4P's served as the guiding force in marketing for 40-plus years.

Recently, a new worldview has emerged, driven by digital technologies. In this emerging techonomy, the consumer and his or her digital interface are the central focus; product is morphing daily, its target audience a patchwork connection of social conversations and online communities. Thus the 4P's, as they were originally conceived, have become an anachronism in the digital age.

One of the best ways to understand the *New Marketing Normal* is to trace the evolution of the 4P's. In its traditional sense, the 4P's model can be considered to have three major components: the Value Creator who initiates the marketing message, the functions or variables that serve to transfer or communicate the message, and the end recipient for whom the message is intended.

In this model (Figure 4.2), the Value Creator is the marketer, his functions or variables the 4P's, and the end recipient the Customer, who is expected to share the marketing message through word of mouth and other limited formats. In the traditional view of marketing, the 4P's are controlled by the Value Creator.

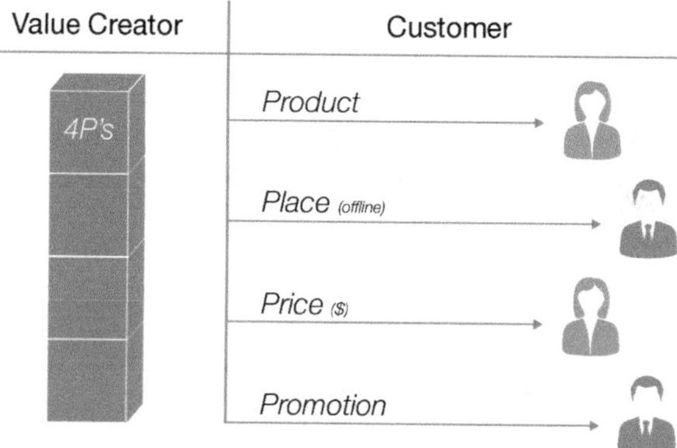

Figure 4.2: The 4P's

MARKETING 2.0

The next iteration on the 4P's, known as Marketing 2.0 (Figure 4.3), reflected the changes brought about by the widespread use of the Internet and social media. Marketing 2.0 can be defined as a marketing model that integrated traditional print media with online marketing in ways that were more effective and efficient. As a result, the concept of integrated marketing communications was developed.[4]

In this model, the Value Creator evolved into the Value Builder, and now included the Company, its Employees and Partners, and the Customer, all interacting to create added value. Additionally, the notion of the Customer expanded into that of the User, as people began to interact through numerous social media contexts (user-generated reviews, online forums, videos, Tweets, etc.) to add to or detract from brand value.

In Marketing 2.0, the 4P's expanded to reflect the new interactive social environment, where Product was now User-driven and the brand was social; Place was both online and offline; Price expanded beyond mere monetary value to include time, ease of acquisition, and corporate social responsibility; and Promotion reflected an integrated approach to marketing communications, adding social and mobile to traditional efforts. Moreover, the Marketing 2.0 model added a fifth P into the mix: Participation, where communication was two-way and open engagement drove the marketplace.

In this model, the conception of the end User was no longer monolithic; messages were communicated to different Users, including consumers, job seekers, publishers, and thought leaders. The interaction moved beyond one-way to become truly interactive, with all parties influencing the Value Builder, as well as one another. The Value Builder had some control of the 5P's, but each of these variables was also affected by the Users.

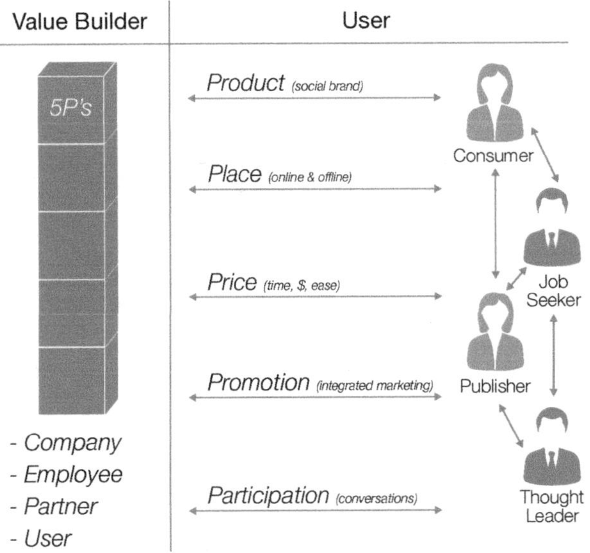

Figure 4.3: Marketing 2.0

Our continued immersion in the digital culture has brought forth a third iteration of the 4P's, which we refer to as the *New Marketing Normal*.

THE NEW MARKETING NORMAL

In the *New Marketing Normal* (Figure 4.4), the Value Builder, with unfettered access to big and broad data, evolves into the Value Generator, as companies large and small begin to align core values with consumer-driven actions. The Value Generator, which includes the Company, its Employees and Partners, Users, and now Data, all interact dynamically and symbiotically to create value for all parties.

Product is now defined by consumer experiences and touch points, or all the interactions a User has with the Value Generator; **Promotion** represents the seamless integration of various marketing media reinforcing one another, as Users simultaneously augment the brand message by driving it to their social communities; **Place** becomes truly ubiquitous, as product is available everywhere, thanks to the widespread adoption of digital

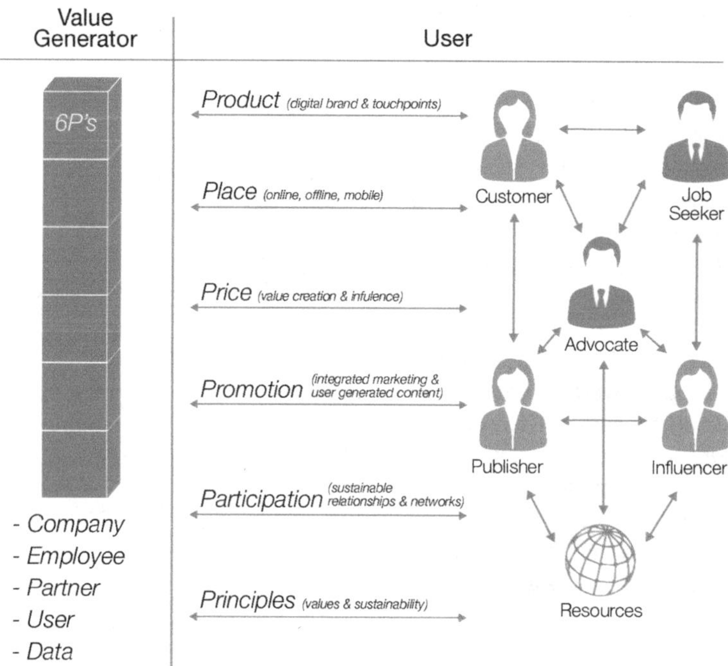

Figure 4.4: The New Marketing Normal

technologies such as smartphones, tablets, wearables, and the cloud; augmented reality applications transform online and offline ads into immediate calls-to-action (CTAs); **Price** is about overall value creation. Online reviews build consumer trust and influence, while perceived value and cultural transparency create a level playing field for competitive pricing. Brands now have social value.

In the *New Marketing Normal*, **Participation** is expanded beyond mere engagement to building sustainable relationships. Finally, a 6th P is added into the mix: **Principles**. Adapted from Professor Philip Kotler's Values-Driven Marketing, Principles includes the infusion of individual and organizational core values and how they translate into actions that not only benefit the bottom line of the organization but the health and well-being of its employees and partners and the greater community as a whole.[5]

In the *New Marketing Normal*, the concept of the User now expands to include advocates and super fans who generate social and online content favorable to the brand, and engage with and introduce new Users locally and globally to the brand through their social networks.

The evolution to the *New Marketing Normal* is summarized in Figure 4.5.

	Traditional Marketing – 4P's	*Marketing 2.0 – 5P's*	*New Marketing Normal – 6P's*
Variables	Product, place, price, promotion	Product, place, price, promotion, participation	Product, place, price, promotion, participation, principles
Core Principles	Product-centric marketing	Customer-oriented marketing	Values-driven marketing
Objectives	Sell products; Increase consumer spending	Satisfy and retain customers with better quality and service	Grow customer loyalty and advocacy; sustainable growth
Driver of Change	Industrial Revolution	Social Media Revolution	The Digital Cultural Evolution
Initiator	Marketer, push driven	User, pull driven	User, data driven
Key Marketing Concept	Product development	Differentiation	User value and experience
Interaction	One-to-many	One-to-one	Many-to-many
Data	Ad hoc, collected by marketing research	Inconsistent, semi-automated data collection	Systematic, fully-automated data collection
Goals	Profit	Profit, people	Profit, people, planet, community
Relationships	One way	Interactive conversations	Sustainable; based on shared values

Figure 4.5: From the 4P's to the New Marketing Normal[6]

FOUNDATION OF THE NEW MARKETING NORMAL

With all the changes in marketing during the last decade, we searched for an overarching concept that would serve to redefine marketing in the digital age. The *New Marketing Normal* was selected because, though the core components of marketing (e.g. market segmentation, branding, consumer behavior, sales process) which have defined it as a timeless practice remain, the ways in which these components have manifested themselves in recent years have fundamentally changed.

The following are five core marketing components which, though understood in a certain light for nearly forty years, by necessity have been redefined in the context of the digital marketplace. Each reflects the rapidly shifting standards of consumer behavior in the digital age (e.g. reading online reviews before a new car purchase, or asking Facebook friends their recommendation for a new car and local a dealer they can trust). Collectively, they serve as the foundation of the *New Marketing Normal*:

1. Market Segmentation – From Target Consumers to Consumer Networks
2. Branding – From Strategic Branding to The Social Brand
3. Product Features – From Product Experience to Customer Experience
4. Sales Process – From Short-Term Engagement (Sales) to Long-Term Value
5. Customer Decision Process – From Consumer Behavior to Influence Marketing

1. Market Segmentation: **From Target Consumers to Consumer Networks**

The emerging standards of the *New Marketing Normal* require marketers to rethink how to reach out to, or target, their intended audiences.

What is Market Segmentation?

Market segmentation is a marketing strategy which involves dividing a broad target audience into one or more subgroups of people with common wants and needs, and then designing and implementing strategies around various media channels and other touch points considered most likely to reach each subgroup. Market segmentation enables businesses to better target their products and services to the right consumers at the right time by aggregating prospective buyers into groups (segments) that have common needs and, as such, will presumably respond similarly to specific marketing initiatives.

Lifetime Value of a Mobile User

"There is a realization that brands need to get much smarter about segmentation and thinking about how to identify and value, and recruit and retain, loyal users of those [mobile] applications."

Jeremy Lockhorn, Vice President of Emerging Media, Razorfish[7]

Digital marketing expands on this practice, challenging marketers to redefine their understanding of market segments and encouraging them to stop targeting consumers and start building networks of advocates. Greater access to data is hastening this change, as sophisticated behavioral information collected from websites, search engines, mobile devices, and social media networks allows marketers to delve far deeper than basic demographic and geographic segmentation.

Indeed, today's digital marketers can tap into a plethora of locational information, including interaction and behavioral metrics from social, local, mobile (*SoLoMo*) initiatives like geofencing, social check-ins, locally-targeted mobile advertising, mobile apps, mobile search and browsing data, SMS text, user-generated reviews and comments on social local sites like Yelp, web and social content, micro-segmented email campaigns, ad retargeting, online behavioral profiling, and anticipatory recommendations; the list goes on, and is added toevery day.

With the aid of these digital tools, marketers can segment based on new sets of data-driven criteria that are timely and actionable:

- Current interests, lifestyle changes, keyword searches (*e.g. organic diet, new car purchase, Florida family vacation, etc.*).
- Brand loyal vs brand agnostic.
- Shopping preferences (*e.g. in-store, online research, mobile interactive, sales and coupons, shopping list or spontaneous, experimental or fixed choice*).
- Profiled interests and values (*e.g. using data from Facebook, Google, etc.*).
- Digital personas (*e.g. profiles of online behavior, up and downstream click data, device preferences*).[8]

Traditionally, marketing was focused on targeting a small number of segments with a high potential for conversion, but broad data has changed this practice. It allows marketers to target many micro-segments, each of which can be reached one impression at a time through web, search, social, and mobile interfaces and with real-time interactions.

Digital media and the data they produce are giving rise to a new kind of market segmentation based on networks of consumers or other groups with common interests and values. Whereas geographic, cultural, and generational divisions once kept these people apart, digital technology is bringing them together. These affinity-based market segments communicate, share, and identify with each other through an ever-expanding host of interlocking and intersecting consumer networks made possible by continually advancing digital technologies.

Thus, the prevailing market segmentation strategy in the *New Marketing Normal* is to engage, inspire, and activate influencers in each targeted consumer network so they will carry your mutually advocated message to their social communities.

Has your organization's approach to market segmentation changed in the last 3 years? 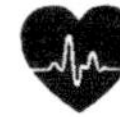

- Do you really understand the people within each of your target segments (their language, where they hang out), or is your understanding based on outdated misconceptions?
- Are you targeting consumers or their social communities?
- Are you segmenting based on shopping preferences?
- Are you actively monitoring changes in your target segments?

2. Branding: From Strategic Branding to the Social Brand

A generation ago, brands were tightly controlled assets that were nurtured and protected. Through strategic branding, marketers controlled the brand by defining, designing, and communicating brand value in a one-way conversation to consumers. As one marketer put it, brands have been conditioned to provide Pavlovian stimuli in the hopes of a positive consumer response.[9]

The digital evolution has changed all that, turning brands into platforms for collaboration rather than assets to be leveraged. The social brand (Figure 4.6) interacts with fans and followers to co-produce the compelling experiences that keep consumers engaged. In this way, the social brand is an interactive platform or open ecosystem where the consumer plays an active role in its continuous evolution. Through the real-time feedback mechanism of social collaboration with its target audience, the social brand is able to market more organically and effectively.

The Tale of the Social Brand

Figure 4.6: The Tale of the Social Brand – Video[10]

In 2011, UK-based social brand agency Headstream began issuing its Social Brands 100 rankings to provide a benchmark of social performance for brands spanning all industry sectors.[11] The Headstream initiative defines a social brand as one that adopts the following three underlying principles:

- *Win-win relationships* – focus on equitable and fair value exchanges with all stakeholders.
- *Active listening* – monitor conversations on the social web and then act on what is found in a timely manner.
- *Appropriate social behavior* – provide a consistent brand presence that is compelling, honest, authentic, and transparent, and that acknowledges the particular etiquette of each social community.

The top social brands featured in the agency's 2013 rankings span numerous industries; among the top ten highest ranked are a number of well-known organizations, such as American Airlines and Tesco, as well as innovative firms like innocent fruit juice. Much can be learned from the Social Brands 100 initiative that can help support organizations along the *Path to Digital Integration*.

For marketers and business owners, the emergence of the social brand underscores the notion that brand loyalty requires affinity, and affinity requires relevance. If the social brand does not provide relevance to the end consumer, he or she is unlikely to develop affinity for the brand. Likewise, any organization operating in alignment with its core values and business goals will have little interest in developing affinity with consumers who do not find relevance in their brand.

3. Product Features: *From Product Experience to Customer Experience*

Traditional marketing focused on the product experience through the lens of product features – characteristics such as quality, usability, convenience, and price. In today's consumer-centric digital age, the customer experience (CX) has expanded to include the sum of all touch points a customer has with a supplier of a product or service during their entire relationship, from the initial purchase through ownership and servicing; this includes recommendations to others.

For organizations, the principle focus of CX strategy is to deliver consistent value to the customer. Here are seven hallmark attributes that contribute to a positive CX with a product or service:

- *Goal* – Does the product or service help the consumer resolve a want or need or achieve a desired objective?
- *Functionality* – Do its features, price, and quality meet or exceed expectations?
- *Usability* – How easily can the customer use and service it?
- *Emotion* – How personally meaningful are the customer's experiences with it?
- *Expectations* – Does it meet the customer's expectations relative to the initial brand promise and experiences with competitors?
- *Consistency* – Does it provide consistent and reliable value?
- *Employee Interactions* – Does post-purchase customer service meet or exceed expectations?

With feedback from one or more of these seven attributes, CX reflects the overall impression a customer has of a given product or service.

Data from a 2010 TARP analysis found a significant portion (40% to 60%) of customer dissatisfaction is not caused by employee error or attitude, but instead by products and services that do not meet expectations, marketing miscommunication, and poorly designed processes. Further, employees are often not equipped with effective responses to help resolve such problems.[12]

Taking proactive measures to identify and resolve issues before they occur, CX strategy plays a critical role in the *New Marketing Normal* by:

- *establishing trust and building brand loyalty.*
- *serving customer needs by problem solving and improving design and function.*
- *providing feedback on the seven attributes of CX, allowing brands to make continual adjustments.*
- *leveraging relationships to retain current customers and attract new ones.*

How can CX Impact Brands in the Digital Age?

Social media offers the perfect conduit to disseminate both positive and negative customer experiences at lightning speed. An example of the latter is the *United Breaks Guitars* (Figure 4.7) video that went viral with some 4 million views shortly after it was uploaded to YouTube in the summer of 2009.

United
Breaks Guitars

Figure 4.7: United Breaks Guitars – Video[13]

The video features United Airlines passenger Dave Carroll strumming a song he wrote after enduring a terrible customer service experience with United in which his Taylor guitar was destroyed by the airline's baggage handlers during a flight. Afterward, the company repeatedly declined to reimburse him for the damage.[14] The negative PR still lingers for United five years later, with the video now reaching over 14 million views at the time of writing.

The United Breaks Guitars video teaches us that in the digital age, every customer experience has the potential to deeply impact a brand, regardless of its size or market position. Just ask United Airlines. The United Breaks Guitars debacle forced the airline to become more transparent, eventually using the video as a training tool for customer service.

Oracle reported the following in a global survey of 1300 senior executives:

- 93% of senior executives said improving CX is among their top three priorities during the next two years; 81% believe delivering a great customer experience today requires leveraging social media effectively.[15]

- What makes customers fall in love with brands? 73% said friendly customer service representatives; 55% said easy access to support.[16]

- 89% of customers surveyed switched brands after poor customer service; 25% posted complaints on Facebook and Twitter - 79% of these complaints were not addressed.[17]

As CX has grown in importance, so have the standards for its evaluation. Here are three popular measurements:

- *American Customer Satisfaction Index (ASCI)* is an annual survey of US companies by industry relating customer complaints and loyalty with product expectations, quality, and value.[18]

- *Net Promoter Score* is a rating system that benchmarks how a company scores after asking its customers the question, "How likely is it that you would recommend us [your company] to a friend or colleagure?"[19]

- *Customer Effort Score (CES)* is a survey related to the question. "How much effort was needed to do business with X brand?"[20]

4. Sales Process: *From Sales Funnel to Digital Involvement Cycle*

The move to the *New Marketing Normal* ultimately impacts the entire sales process, as organizations move away from coaxing prospects down the sales funnel, opting instead to foster deeper customer relationships through ongoing digital involvement.

Traditional Sales Funnel

The sales funnel was created in 1898 to reflect the AIDA model (Awareness, Interest, Desire, Action). It assumes that the consumer will consider many brands upon entering the Awareness stage. Through a series of inputs and interactions with the consumer, these brands are winnowed down until the dominant brand prevails at the Action stage where the sale is made. All inputs are one-way and occur in a downward direction.

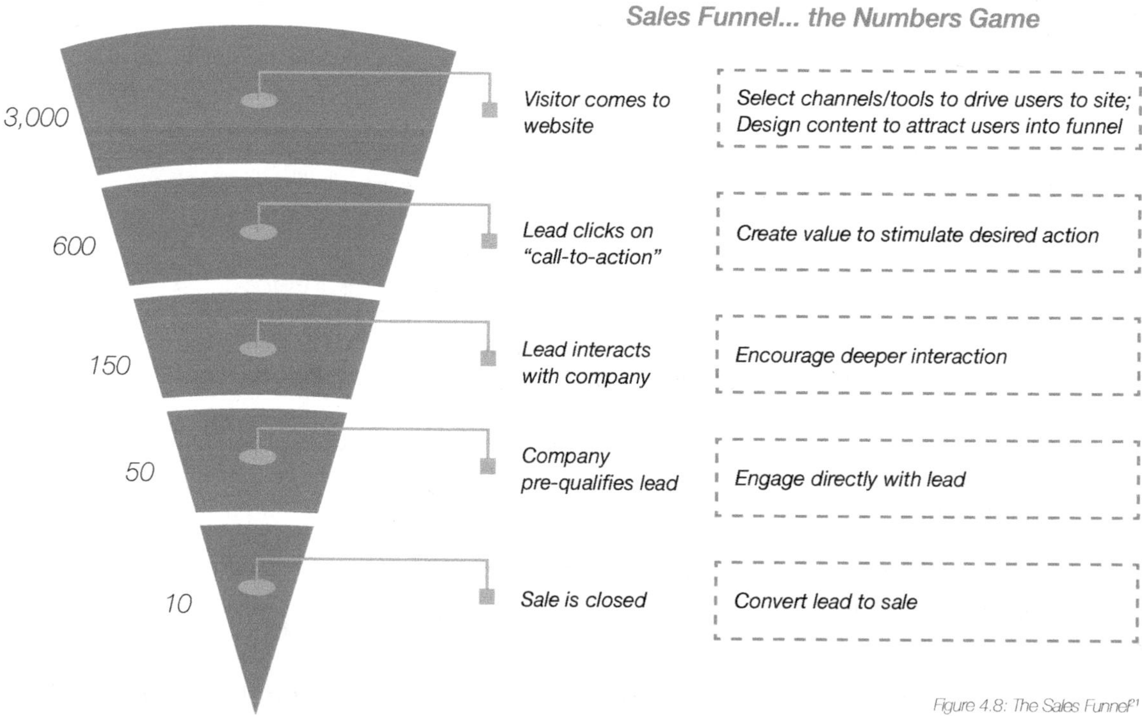

Figure 4.8: The Sales Funnel[21]

In essence, the sales funnel is a numbers game (Figure 4. 8).The brand leverages various channels and tools (e.g., sales staff, email, call centers, website) to shepherd prospects down the funnel to the Action stage. This model is heavily focused on short-term, if-then engagement metrics: *"if I engage X number of contacts, then I should be able to generate Y leads and Z sales."*

Digital Involvement Cycle

The *Digital Involvement Cycle* (Figure 4.9) more accurately reflects the existing customer decision process; the customer moves through the pre-decision process to Commitment and from Commitment through the post-decision process to Champion. In the digital marketplace, the customer is interacting with numerous networks of touch points as they move through each stage of the *Cycle*, searching, differentiating alternatives, selecting, and then evaluating their choice. In this way, the customer decision process is not linear but iterative, building incrementally upon all inputs and moving through repeated cycles until he or she takes a defined action (e.g. purchase a product or service, subscribe to an offer, attend an event, etc.). At this point, a second *Cycle* begins as the new customer grows into a loyal customer, sharing their CX on social media, advocating for and ultimately championing the brand.

Contrary to the sales funnel, the ***Digital Involvement Cycle*** is designed to produce long-term assets and "social capital" in the marketplace. The focus shifts from achieving short-term gain to developing sustainable relationships based on reciprocal value.

What distinguishes the Digital Involvement Cycle from the Sales Funnel?

- Movement was one directional (down), linear, and contracting; now, it's an interactive, swirling *Cycle* with expanding touch points at each stage before and after the Commitment (Action) stage.
- Movement ended at Commitment; now, it expands to Loyalty, Advocacy, and Champion.
- Potential customers used to enter at Awareness; now, they can enter at any stage.
- Customers were targeted at Awareness; now, they are targeted at each stage along the *Cycle*.
- Media tactics were focused on selling; now, various content strategies and tactics are employed to inform and entertain prospects, providing value and building loyalty.
- Goals were short-term and engagement-driven; now, they are long-term and value-driven.

For additional information about the *Digital Involvement Cycle* ->

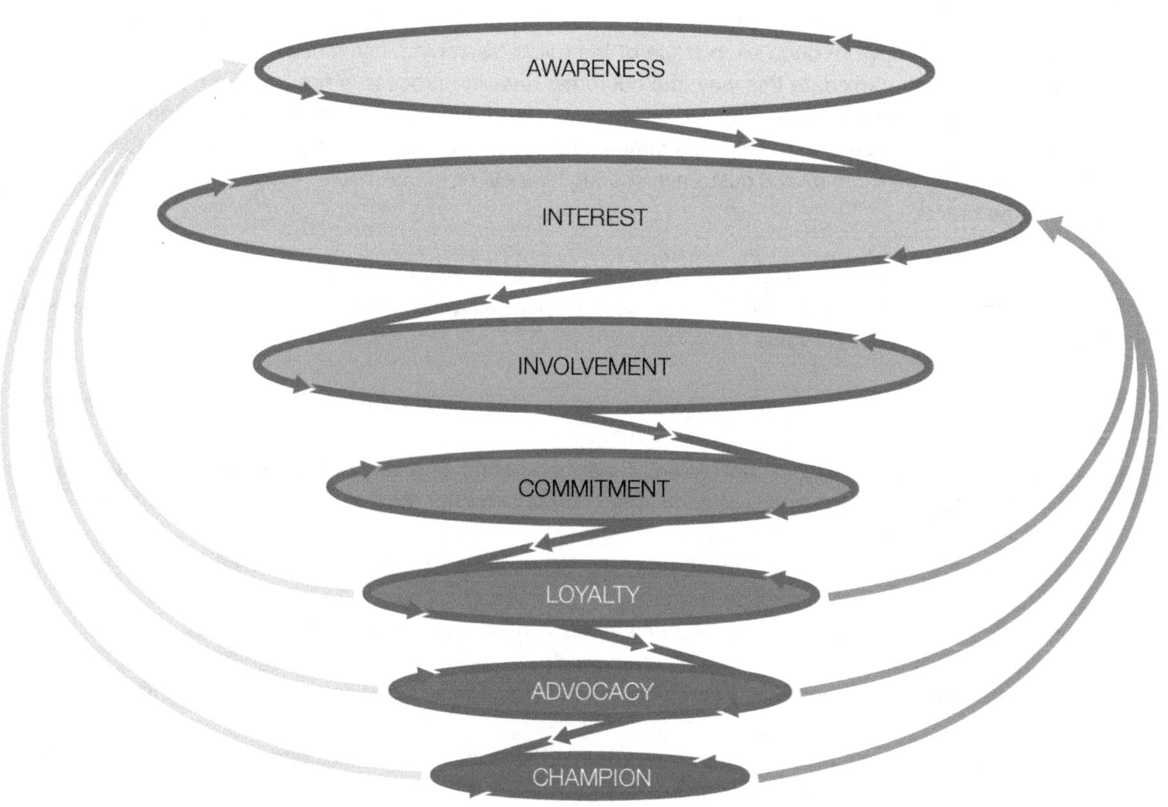

Figure 4.9: The Digital Involvement Cycle

Is your brand measuring users' movement through the customer decision process? 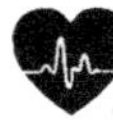

- Do you use different tactics at different stages of the process?
- Have you placed significant resources on post purchase/customer service and loyalty?

5. Customer Decision Process: *From Consumer Behavior to Influence Marketing*

This transition from short-to long-term marketing is also reflected in the shift from consumer behavior to influence marketing. In the past, consumer behavior analysis was utilized to better understand the customer decision process by researching the internal characteristics and external influences of consumers.

In recent years, relationship marketing has attempted to reaffirm the importance of the consumer in the marketing process, recognizing the long-term value of customer relationships over the short-term payout of advertising and promotion. Fueled by the power of the social consumer, influence marketing, or the practice of building relationships with individuals who have influence over a target audience of buyers, can be viewed as a logical extension, and in a sense an affirmation, of relationship marketing for the digital age.[22]

Social Influence

In the digital age, the traditional concept of influence based on classical models of power is being turned upside down. Social media expert Mark Schaefer notes how social platforms such as Twitter, Facebook, LinkedIn, and Google Plus are upending traditional patterns of influence. According to Schaefer, ROI no longer means return on investment, but rather, return on influence.[23]

Online influence graders such as Klout and PeerIndex are using complex algorithms to tap into the social data streams to score millions of people based on their level of social influence. This, in turn, gives brands (e.g., Disney, Nike, Microsoft) an opportunity to use social scoring to identify, quantify, and nurture valuable word-of-mouth influencers who can uniquely drive demand for their products.[24] Influence marketing is becoming an integral aspect of the *New Marketing Normal*.

Social scoring attempts to quantify social influence; social influence relies on social sharing and on the exponential nature of digital media to achieve its greatest impact.

This raises two important questions: How does social sharing equate to social influence? Moreover, does social influence really impact the customer decision process?

Jonah Berger, an Assistant Marketing Professor at the Wharton School of the University of Pennsylvania, has been conducting extensive research on why people share for years. His data suggest that word of mouth is the primary factor behind 20-50% of all purchase decisions.[25] This becomes especially interesting when you factor in that McKinsey Quarterly predicts word-of-mouth (WOM) marketing will be a $5.6 billion industry by 2015.[26]

Mass consumer adoption of digital media is the primary driver behind this emerging sharing economy, where organizations must leverage digital media to activate prospects and customers and turn them into brand advocates and super fans.

Another approach to developing an organization's social influence is to target those likely to be influencers by collecting the right information from the right person in the right place at the right time. G-Male (Figure 4.10), a satirical video, highlights some of the pros and cons of this strategy.

- Many Fortune 500 companies now require a Klout score on a candidate's resume for marketing positions.

- Consumer products firms are beginning to offer special discounts based on Klout scores.

Is G-Male an aberration or a reflection of the *New Marketing Normal*?

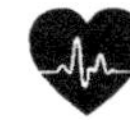

- Is your organization using any of the data points accessed by G-Male to become more informed?
- How can information such as that shared by G-Male impact your organization's marketing strategy?

G-Male

Figure 4.10: G-Male – Video[27]

In the past, marketing practitioners controlled the 4P's; now customers have major input on the marketing mix. The 6P's, along with the foundational components of marketing as they have been redefined, come together to form the *New Marketing Normal*. Marketing practitioners need to understand these changes in order to successfully operate in today's fast-moving digital culture. The next step is learning how to manage it all!

TAKEAWAYS

- Our continued immersion into the digital culture has brought forth a third iteration of the 4P's – the 6P's – which we refer to as the *New Marketing Normal*.
- Market segmentation begins with targeting social influencers and then building networks of loyal customers and advocates.
- The digital evolution has changed the control of the brand, turning brands into platforms for collaboration rather than assets to be leveraged.
- CX (customer experience) is designed to deliver value to the user.
- The sales funnel, developed more than 100 years ago, is still used by most companies to understand the customer decision process, which is more accurately reflected in the *Digital Involvement Cycle*.
- ROI no longer means return on investment, but rather, return on influence.

CHAPTER 5: MANAGING THE NEW MARKETING NORMAL

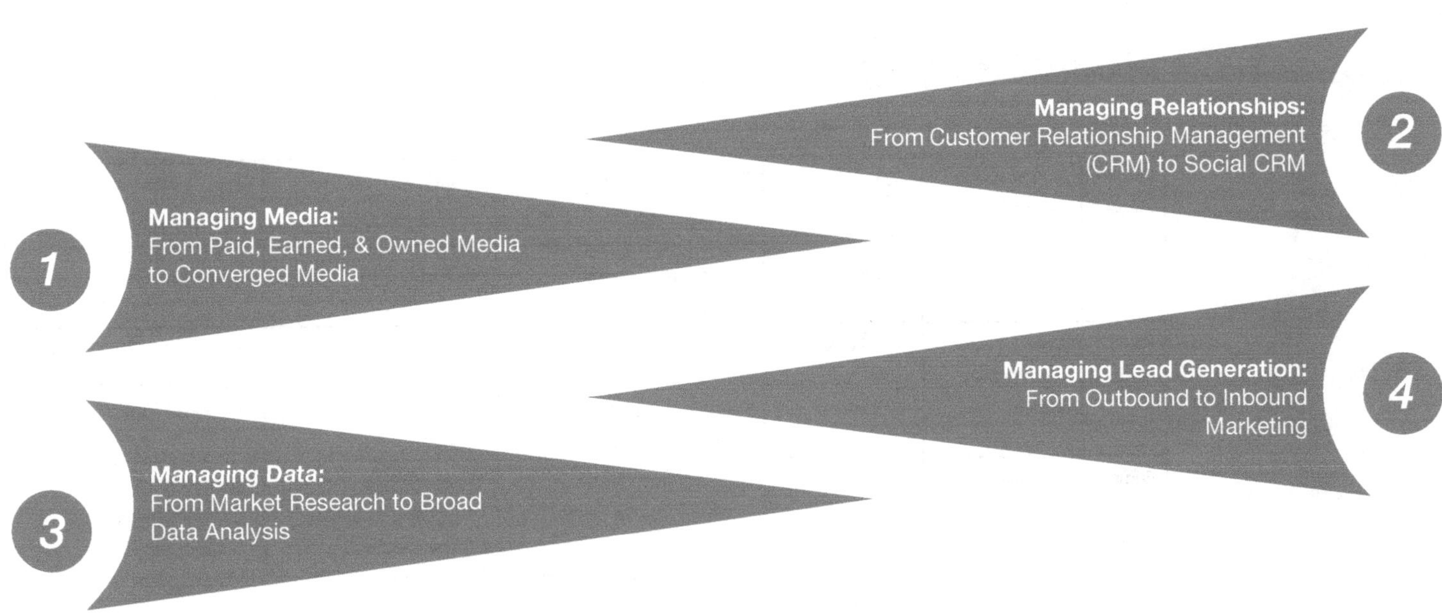

In chapter 4, we introduced the foundational components of the *New Marketing Normal* that have so drastically altered the traditional marketing mix, which include customer networks, the social brand, CX, long-term sales process, and influence marketing. This next chapter demonstrates how these foundational components can be translated into actionable and manageable digital marketing strategies. For example, a foundational component of the *New Marketing Normal*, the social brand, requires a unique platform to facilitate collaboration and win-to-win relationships. The traditional customer relationship management (CRM) system is focused on collecting, storing, and managing customer data. To leverage the interactive environment characteristic of the social brand, the social CRM (SCRM) system is focused on actuating and managing customer engagement.

In this chapter, we examine four actionable digital marketing strategies based on the foundational components of the *New Marketing Normal*.

MANAGING MEDIA:
FROM PAID, EARNED, & OWNED MEDIA TO CONVERGED MEDIA

In response to the changing marketplace, marketing practitioners recently have begun categorizing media into three silos: paid, earned, and owned. Nokia was an early pioneer in using this model to sort out its media options and then prioritize them.[1] Each approach has different benefits, applications, and challenges (Figure 5.1).

Media	Definition	Examples	The Role	Benefits	Challenges
Owned Media	Brand controls the channel	• Website • Mobile Site • Blog • Facebook	Build for longer-term relationships with potential and existing customers and earned media assets	• Control • Cost efficiency • Longevity • Versatility • Niche audiences	• No guarantee of results • Company communication not always trusted • Takes time to scale
Paid Media	Brand pays to leverage the channel	• Display ads • Paid search • Sponsorships	Shift from foundational element to a catalyst that feeds owned media and creates earned media	• On demand • Immediacy • Scale • Control	• Clutters the user experience • Declining response rates • Poor credibility
Earned Media	Customers become the channel	• WOM • Buzz • "Viral"	Listen and respond – earned media is often the result of well-executed and well-coordinated owned and paid media initiatives	• Most credible • Key role in most sales • Transparent and sustaining	• No control • Can be negative • Unpredictable scale • Hard to measure

Figure 5.1: Paid, Earned, & Owned Media[2]

Paid media is any form of media in which the brand pays the media owner to insert the brand's message. Central to this exchange is the idea that the media owner has gathered an audience the brand wants to connect with, and as such the brand is willing to pay to reach. Examples of paid media include broadcast advertising, billboards, display ads, and paid search. It is scalable and immediate but has low credibility.

Earned media represents any form of positive brand messaging that is produced and diffused by unpaid influencers. It is often user-generated content that is shared by others. Examples of earned media include social media posts, reviews, and social mentions. It is organic, trusted, long term, and sustainable.

Owned media is any kind of content or media outlets created and owned by the brand. Examples of owned media include a brand website, ebooks, blogs, or a company's Facebook or Google Plus page. Owned media is targeted and cost effective, extending the brand's reach in an organic manner.

What's the status of the Paid, Earned, & Owned Model?

- *Categorization vs Actionablity* – The model provides a convenient way of organizing media that is not evident to targeted audiences, but it does not serve as a strategic framework for implementing actions.
- *Control vs Reach* – Underpinning the model is the control of the media. The digital world focuses on two-way engagement and dialogue, which translates into reach.
- *Siloed vs Converged Media* – Each of these media outlets cannot stand as independent entities, but must necessarily integrate to properly function.

A study comparing paid and earned media for car purchasing concluded, "the combination of brand (i.e. owned), earned and paid media lead to significantly greater brand awareness compared with using just one media type."[3] Siloed marketing does not work in the digital age. In recognition of this *New Marketing Normal*, marketers are beginning to take a holistic, converged approach to paid, earned, and owned media that is greater than the sum of its parts.[4]

Converged Media

The advent of converged media breaks down marketing silos, providing an opportunity to create a content strategy that combines and optimizes the power of all media channels.

Marketing research and advisory firm Altimeter Group defines converged media in the following way: *"Converged media utilizes two or more channels of paid, earned, and owned media. It is characterized by a consistent storyline, look, and feel. All channels work in concert, enabling brands to reach customers exactly where, how, and when they want, regardless of channel, medium, or device, online or offline."*[6]

Converged media integrates paid, earned, and owned media to support an organization's goals. It reflects the customer's seamless journeys between devices, channels, and media; given this, it requires careful implementation and adjustment.

Nancy Bhagat, Vice President of Sales and Marketing at Intel, recently took the plunge into converged media: *"I merged my Social Media team and Global Media team together, driving cross media opportunities with our partners and thinking about a new world where the idea of "paid" or transactional media dissolves. I found we were having similar conversations across teams.... The role of communities is not exclusive to the social space. Our paid media partners are looking for ways to drive engagement and conversation in ways previously unheard of. Our social partners are open in an exciting way to new product ideas and testing. The idea of 'test and learn' has never been so real."*[7]

Examples of converged media are beginning to surface, as organizations seek to seamlessly integrate two or more media types. News and sports broadcasts are incorporating live tweets into their TV shows, directing the content of the TV discussions. Bloggers and PR professionals are telling stories through earned media while driving users to various owned and paid media channels via integrated marketing campaigns.

New York Giants – Live Tweeting

New York Giants were the first team in professional sports to integrate live Tweets in game broadcasts, both in their television broadcast and in stadium. The results exceeded expectations. The Giant's Twitter followers grew by 122% in less than two months. With more than 306,000 Twitter followers, the Giants quickly ranked 3rd for most Twitter followers in the NFL. The "Extra Effort Player of the Game" initiative, which encouraged fans to vote by Tweeting the hashtag of a specific player, increased online sales for the winning player's jersey.[8]

To learn how brands are integrating converged media into their marketing strategies ->

The Convergence of Paid, Earned, & Owned Media

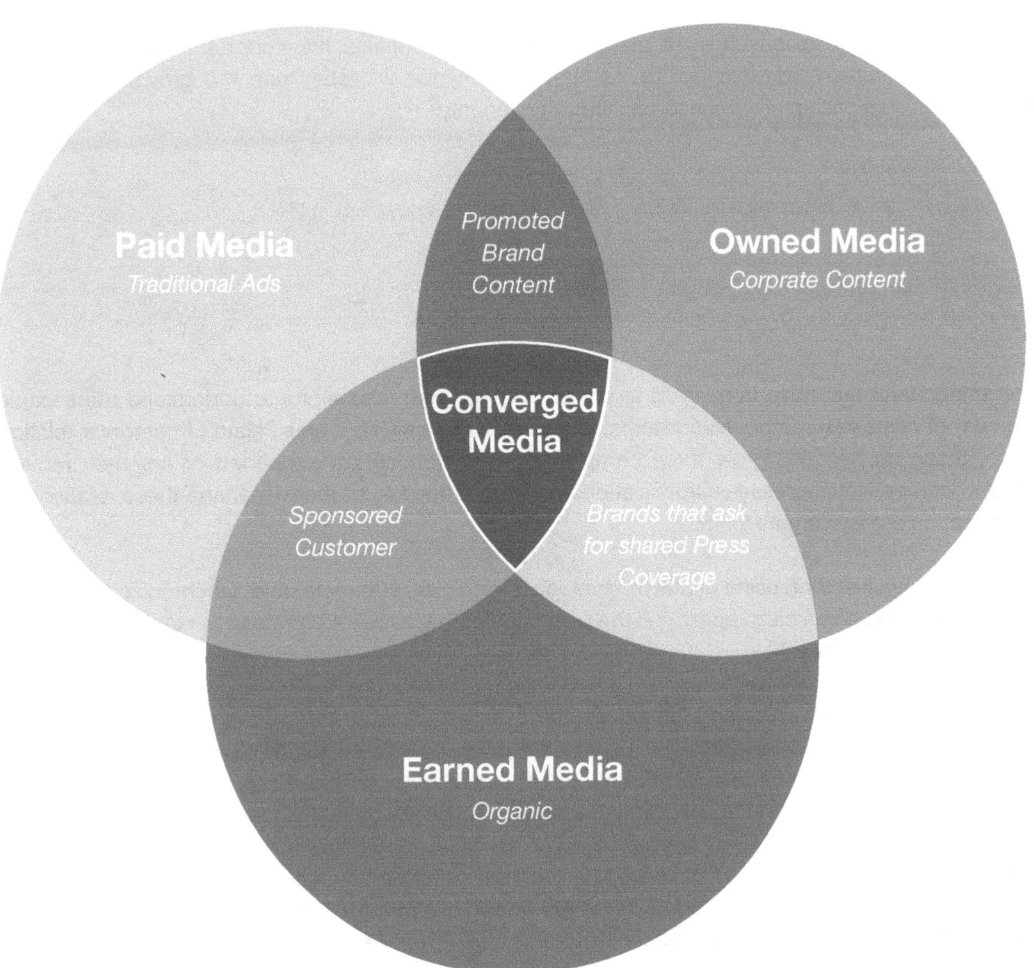

Figure 5.2: Converged Media[5]

MANAGING RELATIONSHIPS:

FROM CUSTOMER RELATIONSHIP MANAGEMENT (CRM) TO SOCIAL CRM

"The Customer is King" is an oft-used marketing tag which reflects the important idea that the direction of a business is ultimately determined by its customers. Once a cliché, with the growth of digital media, customer-centric relationships have become a strategic priority.

> *"Traditional CRM strategies are not equipped to address this new social medium."*[9]
>
> IBM Study: *From social media to Social CRM*

To better understand the move from CRM to social CRM (SCRM), it's helpful to understand the evolution and management of customer-centric relationships. A business begins with a clean slate of customer relationships. Over time, these connections grow more complex as expectations are exceeded or not met, requirements change, and competition increases. Organizations develop a need to properly manage these relationships and share information across various teams.

A CRM system does just that, using digital technology to organize, automate, and synchronize sales, marketing, customer service, and technical support. It is the nerve center that allows a company to manage interactions with current and future customers.

CRM developed in the late 1980s and has grown to become a core element of the marketing mix. It helps the organization manage its business relationships and the data and information associated with them. CRM uses sales, marketing, and customer service to move the customer through the lifecycle of engagement and sales conversion. It is a "one-way" effort to collect and store data from customers and prospects in one central location.

By contrast, SCRM is in its infancy. Figure 5.3 highlights some of the differences between CRM and SCRM. As noted CRM guru Paul Greenberg shared in ***CRM at the Speed of Light***, *"The underlying principle for Social CRM's success is very different from its predecessor.... traditional CRM is based on an internal operational approach to manage customer relationships effectively. But Social CRM is based on the ability of a company to meet the personal agendas of [its] customers while, at the same time, meeting the objectives of [its] own business plan. It is aimed at customer engagement rather than customer management."*[10]

Evolution of CRM to SCRM

CRM		SCRM
assigned departments	WHO	everyone
company-defined process (1,2,3)	WHAT	customer-defined process
business hours (9-5)	WHEN	customer sets the hours
company-defined channels	WHERE	customer driven, dynamic channels
transaction ($)	WHY	interaction
inside out	HOW	outside in

Figure 5.3: Evolution of CRM to SCRM

The growth and impact of social media creates a strategic imperative for marketers to update and upgrade their CRM strategy to a SCRM program. Further, they must constantly re-invent their SCRM programs to be aligned with the demands and expectations of the digital consumer. Given its ability to enhance the customer experience, SCRM is a vital component of the *New Marketing Normal*.

SCRM respects and engages today's consumer. Customer service was a department in a traditional organization, focused on addressing customer's issues. SCRM prioritizes the customer service function, giving rise to the notion of customer service excellence. SCRM is focused on "doing the right things" and planning to "do things right." It's about anticipating, listening, and quickly responding to customer needs. In this way, SCRM helps the organization enhance the customer experience.

SCRM is the Top Priority for CMOs

"Long-term, brands are focusing on developing deeper relationships with their customers. Social media is becoming more ingrained in the business. The natural next step is to integrate social data to CRM systems."[11]

John Whitehurst, Global Head, iStrategy

- 89% of consumers have stopped doing business with a company after experiencing poor customer service.[12] (RightNow Customer Experience Impact Report)
- A customer is 4 times more likely to buy from a competitor if the problem is service related vs price or product related.[13] (Bain & Co.)
- 55% of consumers would pay more for a better customer experience.[14] (Defaqto Research)
- A 10% increase in customer retention levels results in a 30% increase in the value of the company.[15] (Bain & Co)

To learn how organizations are using SCRM to enhance the customer experience ->

How can SCRM be achieved? How do you make it a reality?

1. *Management Buy-in* – The executive suite must make SCRM a strategic priority.
2. *Strategy* – The marketing team must develop a holistic strategy to integrate CRM and SCRM, including standards, staff, budget, and technology.
3. *Consistency* – The marketing team must live the guidelines and procedures to "walk the walk," and consistently deliver customer service excellence to all touch points.
4. *Integration* – They must also integrate existing channels to make the customer experience (CX) more seamless and less interrupted.
5. *Flexibility* – SCRM technology and processes must be flexible, caring, and responsive to the customer base to facilitate open dialogue.
6. *Social Participation* – Current and potential customers need to be engaged on social platforms – neutral turf – to gain trust and establish thought leadership with the organization's target audience.
7. *ROI* – Marketers need to be active in measuring and evaluating SCRM strategies to determine their effectiveness and contribution to achieving organizational goals.
8. *Value* – SCRM strategies must create value for consumers and the organization.

What value does SCRM bring to your organization?

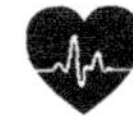

- Is SCRM a priority in your organization?
- If customer service has such a high ROI, why is it not a priority for organizations?

MANAGING DATA:

FROM MARKET RESEARCH TO BROAD DATA ANALYSIS

Until recently, marketing departments and advertising agencies were all about market research and web analytics. They ran focus groups to help clarify their brand message, conducted surveys and interviews to gain insight into the customer experience, designed ratings and "short" questionnaires to gauge brand awareness and recognition, and tracked website metrics and ad click-through rates to better understand consumer intent.

This patchwork of market research was then put together to calculate the ROI of a particular campaign, or to determine which marketing interventions were most effective and needed adjustment. This type of "old think marketing" was based on a lot of guesswork and intuition derived from years of experience.

However, as consumers became more accustomed to digital media use and buying habits, many of these relatively slow-moving market research techniques began to lag behind the actual customer experience. With the proliferation of data and improvements in computer processing and storage capacity, many marketing opportunities have been missed or gone unrealized altogether.

Enter the *New Marketing Normal*, which is greatly dependent on the collection and analysis of real-time or near-real-time customer experience data to inform marketing strategies and tactics. In the *New Marketing Normal*, marketing analytics and broad data analysis transform marketing campaigns from reactionary to predictive. They help organizations realize their goals by minimizing the guesswork.

The Digital Consumer

Digital technologies have forever altered the consumer discovery process, changing how we seek and consume information. When checking out a new product, we might "Google it," post a question to our social network, read online customer reviews, download an app, or initiate a voice-activated search on our smartphone or tablet. There are so many ways for us to access feedback and reviews and quickly digest inputs from various places before we buy a product online or offline. Regardless of whether our buying experience or the product we receive was exceptional or not quite up to our expectations, we can easily share the "customer experience" with our vast networks. Every online exchange is a data touch point; every post contains keyword data; nearly every action is somehow connected to a social network. All of this feedback, action, and reaction – all of this data – can be collected and processed instantly to make timely adjustments; it can be monitored and sent as real-time information alerts to customer service departments.

This kind of data, which is collected from diverse sources in aggregated fragments of small and (sometimes) contextually related data points, is generally known as "big data." However, a more precise term may be "broad data," which reflects the shift from a small number of organizationally controlled data sources (e.g. bricks-and-mortar stores, websites, and customer data warehouses) to myriad data sources of varying nature and size. Both are relevant, depending on the size of the organization and its expected goals from data analysis.[16]

What is the Role of Traditional Market Research in a Broad Data Environment?

The future of traditional market research tactics such as surveys and focus groups is undecided. One can see how they will have a diminished role as broad data analysis allows marketers to aggregate consumers' real-time actions and comments about a product or brand rather than their retrospective feelings about the same. Marketing teams may decide that such new, quantitative data analysis techniques will displace any need for qualitative market research. After all, traditional marketing research is based on the controlled experiment with research participants, a stimulus and a measured response. Today's insights are based on transparent, open data collection, where the consumer is free to co-create the brand, product, etc.[17]

Consider the soft drink brand Mountain Dew's *DEWmocracy* social campaign, in which Mountain Dew fans were asked to whittle the initial field of potential new products from seven to three, and finally chose *White Out*. *DEWmocracy* had consumers openly picking flavors, names, packaging, and advertising.[18] The digital initiative created a lot of buzz, significantly increasing Mountain Dew's social media presence.

Viewed from another perspective, traditional market research can provide qualitative context to quantitative measurement, infusing the "Why?" into the picture, thereby making the "What?" that big/broad data can offer more valuable.[19]

For example, data analysis can spot a trend among seniors showing interest in traveling to the Canadian Rockies by monitoring online metrics such as keyword use on social networks, inquires on websites, and YouTube downloads. But the data doesn't necessarily reveal *why* seniors are interested in that location versus another tourist destination such as New England or the Blue Ridge Mountains in Virginia. Market research may be able to provide the answer, delivering qualitative insight into the underlying motivational force behind certain consumer preferences. Combining broad data and market research to complement and augment each other can be a powerful force for competitive advantage.

By in large, digital technologies have sped up the process of consumer purchase decision. Organizations must respond by increasing the speed by which they research trends, design strategies, market products, and evaluate impact. Today's digital consumers devour and expend vast amounts of information. Organizations must nimbly leverage market research, broad data, and marketing analytics, tapping into the infinite channels and data trails left by digital consumers to deliver what they want, when, how, and where they want it.

MANAGING LEAD GENERATION:

FROM OUTBOUND TO INBOUND MARKETING

Traditional marketing orthodoxy has had an outbound focus, with marketers trying to reach their target audience through a variety of means, including print & television advertising, junk mail, spam, trade shows, seminar series, email blasts to purchased lists, internal cold calling, and outsourced telemarketing, to name a few. These efforts could be rightly characterized as taking a "shotgun approach" to marketing.

Outbound marketing is proving less effective over time for two reasons. First, your average consumer is inundated with thousands of marketing interruptions each day and is finding new ways to block them out, including caller ID, spam filtering, DVR, and satellite radio. It's still possible to use these channels to convey an effective message, but it is becoming more expensive.

Widespread consumer adoption of the Internet, social, and mobile has given rise to a tectonic shift in marketing communications. Empowered consumers no longer have to rely on outbound marketing to be told about new products and services. They now have an alternative method of discovering and researching brands, of learning about and buying products and services. This new method, inbound marketing, has become a two-way dialogue, much of which is facilitated by social media.[20]

Inbound marketing is a holistic, data-driven strategy that helps organizations attract and convert visitors into customers by providing personalized, relevant information and content instead of interruptive messages. By following them through the sales experience with ongoing engagement, inbound pulls consumers toward an organization's products and services by aligning published content with consumer interests.[21] To return to our gun analogy, if outbound marketing represents a "shotgun approach" to marketing, inbound marketing is wielding a sharpshooter's rifle.

Inbound reflects a shift from campaign-based, interruption marketing to consistently measureable, closed-loop marketing initiatives that attract interested prospects and customers with a view to creating lasting relationships. Given the ubiquity and reach of digital technologies like social media, organizations can no longer afford to pass off shoddy products and customer service. In today's consumer-driven era, organizations need to operate transparently and communicate openly. Inbound marketing realigns the organization's internal focus on sales, marketing, and product, toward strategic decision-making based on the wants and needs of the customer.[22] Inbound marketing focuses on earning, not buying, a person's attention, which is done through social media and engaging content, such as blogs, ebooks, videos, webinars, and podcasts. This content is interesting, informative, and relevant, creating a positive connection with the consumer, thus making him or her more likely to engage with a brand and buy its products.[22]

- 44% of direct mail is never opened; 86% of people skip through television commercials.[23]
- 84% of 25 to 34 year olds have clicked out of a website because of an "irrelevant or intrusive ad."[24]
- Inbound-marketing-dominated organizations experience a 62% lower cost-per-lead than outbound-marketing-dominated organizations.[25]
- In 2013, 60% of companies adopted some element of the inbound methodology into their overall strategy; 41% of marketers confirm inbound produces measurable ROI.[27]

Thanks to improvements in online search engines such as Google, along with the proliferation of sophisticated mobile devices and social media platforms, researching and shopping over the Internet is now more efficient and convenient than ever. The Internet is fast becoming the method of engagement preferred by the majority of consumers. These factors have conspired to usher in an age of rapid Internet growth. In recent years, businesses have begun shifting money out of previous forms of outbound marketing into content creation, search engine optimization (SEO), and social media – all elements of the inbound marketing mix.

Lead Generation Tactics of Inbound Marketing

Most successful inbound marketing initiatives combine these three core lead generation techniques into one integrated approach.

Content creation is the primary tool that attracts potential customers to an organization's website and social media platforms. The name of the game is relevance. Brands must produce quality content that is informative, entertaining, educational, or otherwise exceptional; this content should effectively engage its intended audience with information they find relevant and useful. Quality content establishes a brand as an industry thought leader, buildingtrust with those who matter most: prospects and customers who are looking for an organization's product or service offerings.

Search engine optimization makes it easier for prospects to find an organization's website and collateral online content by maximizing its ranking in search engines, where most customers initiate the buying cycle. Optimizing web content for search engines essentially "magnetizes" a website, drawing in prospects already interested in a brand's products or services. Inbound marketing takes SEO a step further, utilizing web and social based calls-to-action (CTAs) that link to landing pages designed to convert visitors into prospects and prospects into sales.

Social Media is the megaphone that amplifies a brand's content and messaging, efficiently disseminating both throughout its social networks. From web-based forums and industry-specific blogs to sites such as Facebook, Twitter, and LinkedIn, social media is an effective way to spread content organically, providing breadth and legitimacy.

Inbound marketing gives brands an efficient way to scale their marketing message. Organizations with attractive products and services can now compete with companies who have traditionally enjoyed a much greater reach thanks to larger marketing budgets. Inbound marketing acts as the great leveler, allowing smaller organizations to compete with their larger industry rivals on a more even playing field.

This is especially true for non-profits, which can use inbound marketing best practices to spread their mission and accomplish their work.

Transitioning to Inbound Marketing

Here are four best practices to follow when making the transition to inbound, taken from leading inbound marketing software platform HubSpot's 2013 State of Inbound Marketing report:[28]

Become an Early Adoptor – The early adopters of new business paradigm shifts always see the best results. With the decline of traditional marketing's effectiveness, marketers cannot afford to wait for their leads to dry up before refocusing their marketing practices.

2. *Fully Commit to the Inbound Marketing Model* – Inbound is a theory, but it only works if you actually do it. For an inbound strategy to work, it needs both resources and company-wide allegiance. Companies must educate cross-functional teams on inbound marketing's goals and framework. Ultimately, inbound results will reflect how much, or how little, the organization changes its everyday business practices.

3. *Allocate the Budget and Resources to Properly Implement* – Organizations must ensure their marketing team is armed with sufficient staff to execute their inbound goals. Similarly, cross-functional teams must have the tools they need to implement, optimize, and test inbound initiatives.

4. *Tie Results to Hard Data* – Inbound marketing must integrate with the larger business goals of the organization. Without connecting marketers' lead generation and sales efforts, marketers are doomed to be seen as a cost center, which is counter-productive to the goals of inbound marketing. Inbound provides a wealth of data analysis. "Softer data," such as brand awareness and even traffic is fine to be aware of, but reporting to the executive team means knowing which numbers clearly impact the bottom line. Organizations must be able to accurately measure how their inbound marketing efforts are contributing to overall revenue.

Now that we have an understanding of the foundational components and actionable strategies of the *New Marketing Normal,* we need a comprehensive strategic model that encompasses the best practices of the *New Marketing Normal* and ensures their effective implementation. For this, we turn to *Integrated Digital Marketing*.

How have your marketing practices changed in the last 5 years?

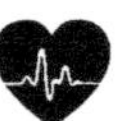

- In what ways have they impacted your organization?

- What changes have you resisted?

TAKEAWAYS

- Paid, earned, and owned media is a convenient way to organize media types but does not serve as a strategic framework for implementing actions.
- Converged media breaks down marketing silos and provides an opportunity to create a content strategy that combines and optimizes the power of all media channels.
- SCRM is focused on "doing the right things" and planning to "do things right." It's about anticipating, listening, and quickly responding to customer needs.
- Traditional marketing research is based on the controlled experiment, with research participants, a stimulus, and a measured response. The new social insights are based on transparent, open data collection where the consumer is free to co-create the brand, product etc.
- Combining broad data and market research to complement and augment each other can be a powerful force for competitive advantage.
- Organizations have begun shifting money out of previous forms of outbound marketing into content creation, search engine optimization, and social media – all elements of the inbound marketing mix.

CHAPTER 6: INTEGRATED DIGITAL MARKETING

In chapter 3, we noted how the drivers of change are fueling the rapid pace of digital transformation, posing a number of unique challenges for organizations of all sizes and necessitating a fundamental paradigm shift in the existing marketing function. Taken as a whole, we call this paradigm shift the ***New Marketing Normal***. In chapter 5, we noted how the foundational components of the *New Marketing Normal* require a comprehensive strategic model that incorporates their best practices and ensures their effective implementation, all while supporting an organization's effort to achieve sustainable growth through digital integration.

We call this strategic model *Integrated Digital Marketing*.

This chapter will address the following questions:

- What is digital marketing?
- Is all marketing now digital?
- Why must digital marketing be integrated?
- What is *Integrated Digital Marketing (IDM)*?
- How does the *IDM Strategic Model* relate to the *Digitally Integrated Organization (DIO)*?

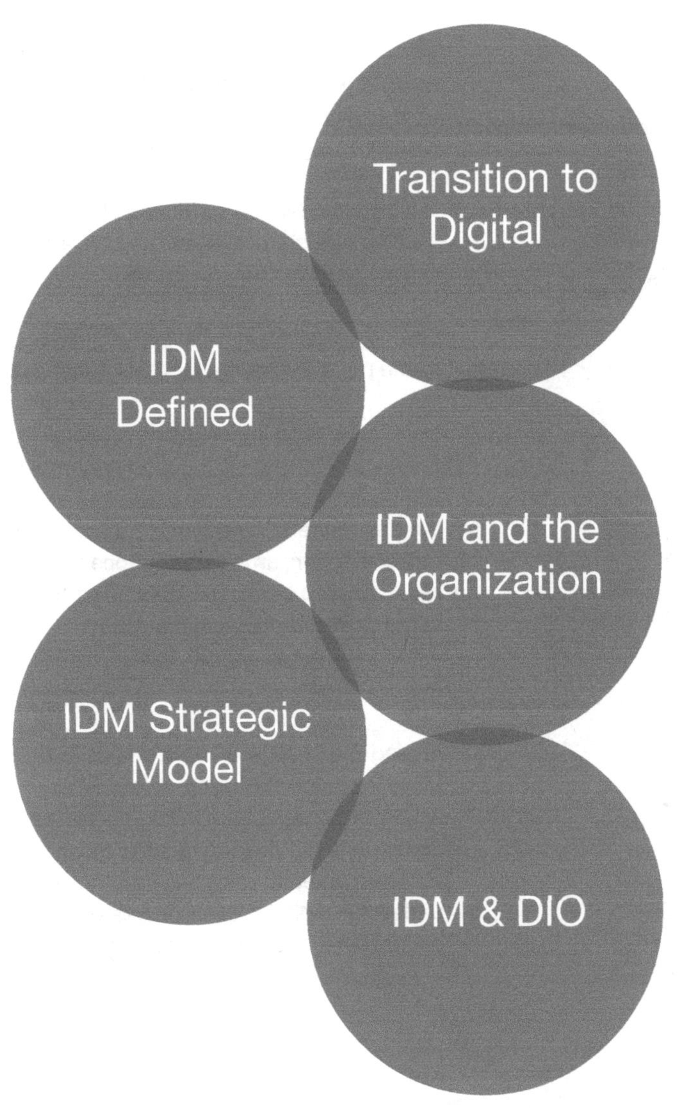

THE TRANSITION TO DIGITAL MARKETING

As we wrote in the introduction to this book, one hears the term "digital" expressed all the time, often paired with nearly every conceivable device and action of daily life. So much so that by now, the term may seem a bit buzzy or even annoying to many. However, in our treatment, we have deliberately chosen to refer to digital in its most fundamental sense:

"...in contrast to the continuous and variable analog world of human experience, digital is finite and non-variable. It utilizes discrete data points that are either on or off, ones or zeros. As such, digital is the language of the computer in its many forms."

Given this definition, what is the difference between digital marketing and "offline" or traditional marketing? More to the point, what specifically is it that makes a marketing action digital?

Here is our working definition of digital marketing: *A marketing action is digital if it is reliant on a digital medium to execute its specific function or complete its intended action.*

We use the term "medium" in the sense of *channel, instrument, manner, or device*. In this way, the Internet is a digital medium, as are smartphones and tablets, along with the innumerable apps that run on them; television and radio are also digital media, at least to the extent that they are broadcast utilizing a digital signal, as is the case in the United States and many other countries. In fact, by this definition the whole print media ecosystem, along with nearly every conceivable piece of "online or offline" marketing content, also falls under the aegis of digital, at least insofar as they rely on some kind of digital media for their design or production.

Indeed the final *"...or complete its intended action"* clause of our definition serves to underscore how virtually every relevant marketing action is now, in one sense or another, digital. For example, a trade show banner displaying a website URL and social share buttons would be understood as a piece of digital marketing content, as the action it intends to initiate is in whole, or in part, a digital one (e.g. visiting a website or social site). This places marketing channels long considered traditional, such as print media and TV and radio spots, squarely under the digital banner (increasingly, these channels are leveraging some kind of digital-dependent call-to-action, whether to visit a website, engage on social media, download a mobile app, etc.).

On a practical level much of this may seem like semantics, but it is important to recognize, especially for the many business and marketing executives who have been dismissive of digital but are starting to get squeezed because of it.

Digital Marketing Must Be Integrated

If we are prepared to acknowledge that virtually all marketing is now digital marketing, we must also understand that, to function properly, digital marketing must be integrated. The growing size and complexity of the digital marketing landscape necessitates an integrated approach. Marketing silos must be torn down; communications processes must be re-worked; long-held paradigms must be shattered; marketing orthodoxy must evolve. To respond to the greater sophistication and heightened expectations of the hyper-connected consumer, to meet the formidable challenges of the digital marketplace, organizations need *Integrated Digital Marketing*.

"Companies have no choice if they want to stay competitive"

INTEGRATED DIGITAL MARKETING (IDM) DEFINED

Integrated Digital Marketing is a comprehensive marketing strategy that merges multiple digital channels, platforms, and media to help organizations achieve their goals by providing value for and building sustainable relationships with their target audience.

In many ways, *IDM* is the logical progression of its precursor, integrated marketing communications (IMC), a term that emerged in the late 20th century regarding the application of consistent brand messaging across myriad marketing channels. The term has varying definitions, and the differences can impact how IMC is viewed and used:

- The initial definition for IMC came from the American Association of Advertising Agencies in 1989, where it was explained as, *"an approach to achieving the objectives of a marketing campaign through a well-coordinated use of different promotional methods that are intended to reinforce each other."*[1]
- In the 1990s, Northwestern University's Journal of Integrated Marketing defined IMC as, *"a strategic marketing process specifically designed to ensure that all messaging and communication strategies are unified across all channels and are centered around the customer."*[2]
- As recent as 2013, IMC has been defined as, *"the development of marketing strategies and creative campaigns that weave together multiple marketing disciplines (paid advertising, public relations, promotion, owned assets, and social media) that are selected and then executed to suit the particular goals of the brand."*[3]

Characteristics of IDM

- Integrates principles (core values) into all marketing decisions.
- Integrates the customer experience (CX) across all stages of *Digital Involvement Cycle*.
- Integrates a consistent brand message across all channels.

- Integrates silos; end goals are unified and not conflicted. By integrating all marketing and communications efforts into one overarching strategy (incorporating content, social media, mobile, search [paid and organic], email, sales, advertising, etc.), not only does every department have a better understanding of what other departments are doing, but end goals are unified and not conflicted.
- Integrates various digital channels, platforms, and media to optimize and augment each other.

In its essence, the idea behind *Integrated Digital Marketing* is simple: by establishing a seamless online presence over web, social, and mobile, your organization can more efficiently convey and promote its brand message, attracting and converting new prospects and staying connected with existing customers, all the while measuring results to refine your efforts.

Today's digitally enabled consumers expect highly personalized and relevant online experiences. They're looking for content that informs, entertains, or otherwise adds value to their daily lives. To stay competitive, your organization must form meaningful connections with the people who matter most: those who find value in your brand.

You can do this by producing original content that is exceptional, personalized, and relevant, optimizing for any platform or device on which it could potentially be viewed or consumed. You must then engage with your audience in real time over multiple channels. Finally, relying on user feedback and data analytics, you need to constantly tweak your brand's message to fit the ever-changing demands of each segment of your target audience.

IDM AND THE ORGANIZATION

Unfortunately, this is easier said than done. According to a global survey of more than 1,000 business respondents carried out by Econsultancy and Adobe in November of 2013, only 12% of businesses take an integrated approach to all marketing activities. For many organizations, the principle culprit is a growing inability to leverage relevant technologies. For example, only 19% of respondents are currently using multichannel campaign management technology; only 22% are utilizing marketing automation software to manage campaigns and measure ROI; less than half (47%) are employing a social media management platform.[4]

According to a 2013 survey of marketers conducted by Ignition One, only 24% said their teams are set up to support an *Integrated Digital Marketing* strategy. Here are the top five perceived challenges to doing so:[5]

- Technology is too complex
- Teams are not set up for it
- Data is not centralized
- Too expensive
- Too time consuming

The real-world complexities of executing a successful *Integrated Digital Marketing* strategy are aptly reflected in the following video case study of an *IDM* campaign conducted for Lexus South Africa:

IDM – Lexus of South Africa

Figure 6.1: Fully Integrated Digital Marketing Campaign Case Study with Lexus – Video[6]

Effective implementation of *Integrated Digital Marketing* is not easy; it takes a cross-organizational effort to align resources, goals, technology, data, and measurement.[7] Specifically, it requires a set of coordinated strategic components supported by a subset of actionable, goal-oriented tactics and tools. In other words, it requires a new framework or model.

IDM STRATEGIC MODEL

The following four strategic components, which we will expand on in the following unit, come together to form the *IDM Strategic Model*:

- *Define and Establish* – The first step is to Define your organization's values, goals, and message, and use them to Establish a seamless online presence across all relevant digital channels.
- *Convey and Promote* – The second step is to employ various digital content media to effectively Convey your organization's brand message, and leverage organic and paid search, social, and mobile initiatives to Promote this message throughout your organization's website, social, and mobile channels.
- *Connect and Convert* – The third step is to engage and Connect with your target audience anywhere, anytime, over any device; the goal is to form personal connections that will Convert short-term leads into sales and foster long-term relationships.
- *Measure and Refine* – The fourth and final step is to evaluate and Measure actual outcomes against expected performance, and then use these insights to further Refine future *IDM* initiatives.

Figure 6.2 on the following page outlines the four components of the *IDM Strategic Model*, providing strategic analysis and enumerating related tactics for each component.

Integrated Digital Marketing Strategic Model

Define & Establish	Convey & Promote	Connect & Convert	Measure & Refine
Strategic Analysis	**Strategic Analysis**	**Strategic Analysis**	**Strategic Analysis**
Are your organization's values and goals in alignment? Are all elements of the Brand Blueprint Analysis (see Figure 6.3) consistent, and integrated with organizational values and goals? Have you taken time to perform an *IDM Strategic Analysis* (see below)?	Is your content engaging and effective? Does it reflect your organization's values and goals? Are you reaching your intended audience? Are you interacting with them?	Is your online presence optimized for mobile? Does each of the seven stages of the *Digital Involvement Cycle* correlate to the goals, targets, and tactics designated for each stage?	For each stage of the *Digital Involvement Cycle*, are analytics monitored and measured and KPIs evaluated against goals?
Tactics	**Tactics**	**Tactics**	**Tactics**
Clarify Values Define Goals Shape Brand Message Establish an Online Presence	Content Marketing Social Media Marketing Paid Social Promotion Search Engine Optimization (SEO) Paid Search	*SoLoMo* Lead Nurturing Lead Conversion	Website Performance Management Social Performance Management Integrated Performance Management

Figure 6.2: Outline of the IDM Strategic Model

For a detailed analysis of the *IDM Strategic Model* ->

Integrated Digital Marketing (IDM) Strategic Analysis

In the next section, we will review six analytical approaches, known collectively as the *IDM Strategic Analysis*, that your organization can use when designing its own *IDM* strategy. Taken together or in part, these tools will help you to fully operationalize the *IDM Strategic Model*.

As you begin to develop an *IDM* strategy for your organization, its critical that you take the time to reflect on a number of key factors. Specifically, you may want to assess your brand's overall position in the marketplace; examine its strengths, weaknesses, opportunities, and threats; evaluate the competition; align your brand message with your organization's values and goals; review the extent to which your current or proposed marketing efforts embody a well conceived and executed *IDM* strategy; and finally, evaluate which stage(s) of the *Digital Involvement Cycle* particular *IDM* initiatives should focus on. Here are six analytical approaches.

Reputational Analysis

- Gather marketing insights from consumers and employees:
    - Collect data though surveys.
    - Analyze online reviews and customer feedback.
    - Determine impressions through focus groups.
- Determine digital footprint:
    - Monitor online/social presences (alerts, search).
    - Assess sentiment and tone of mentions (see Monitoring Tools in chapter 7).

SWOT Analysis

- Generate a SWOT analysis: a framework to analyze your organization's Strengths and Weaknesses, and to examine Opportunities and Threats.
- Have your managers review each SWOT element and suggest ways to: build on their Strengths, correct their Weaknesses, grow Opportunities and protect against internal vulnerabilities and external Threats.

Competitive Analysis

- How are your competitors positioned in the marketplace?
  - Brand
  - Reputation
  - Market share
- What are your competitors' media strategies?
  - Website
  - Promotions
  - Social media
  - Mobile
- Given your competitors' positioning, what opportunities are available for your organization to seize?

For further insight on competitive analysis and *IDM* ->

Brand Blueprint Analysis

- Brand blueprint analysis helps your organization shape various aspects of its brand message to ensure each aspect aligns with its values and goals. Brand blueprint provides the marketing team a snapshot of the organization's current brand positioning and how it reflects the organization's values, allowing the team to resolve discrepancies and target areas that need work. Figure 6.3 outlines the key elements of brand blueprint analysis (for more detail on certain key elements of brand blueprint, see chapter 7, page 128).

Element	*Definition*	*Alignment with Values and Goals*
Competitive Context		
Target Markets		
Brand Image (External)		
Desired Behavior/Action		
Challenges to Overcome		
Customer Insights		
Brand Properties		
Brand Essence		
Brand Promise		
Universal Selling Points		
Value Proposition		
Brand Recommendations		

Figure 6.3 Key Elements of Brand Blueprint[8]

SERVAS Digital Analysis

SERVAS Digital Analysis uses six benchmarks to evaluate your organization's digital marketing initiatives in the context of the *IDM Strategic Model*. This analysis can be applied to various phases of a campaign:

- Strategic Phase – to position the product/organization.
- Design Phase – to anticipate results.
- Market Testing Phase (via team discussion or focus group) – to refine the product or presentation.
- Final Evaluation Phase – as a campaign post mortem to understand the adjustments needed.

Here are the Six Benchmarks:

Sustainable Goals

Engagement

Relationships

By probing and asking related questions for each benchmark, you can gain insight into the likelihood of specific marketing efforts achieving desired results.

Sustainable Goals – What are the goals of each content piece, social initiative, or digital marketing campaign? Who is your target audience? Are these goals achievable and sustainable?

Engagement – How effective is your brand messaging in attracting or engaging with your target audience?

Relationships – Does the marketing effort foster interactivity or shared dialogue with its intended audience?

Value – Does it communicate added benefit for the individual or organization for which it is intended?

Action – Does it move them to act?

Synergy – Is it a one-off or add-on to an existing marketing initiative, or is it integrated into a broader digital marketing strategy?

For additional information on the *SERVAS* tool ->

Digital Involvement Cycle Analysis

Digital Involvement Cycle Analysis gives the management team a way to define on which stages of the *Cycle* they should focus their *IDM* strategy for any given marketing initiative. For each of the seven stages of the *Digital Involvement Cycle* (see Figure 6.5), the management team needs to define specific goals, targets, and tactics.

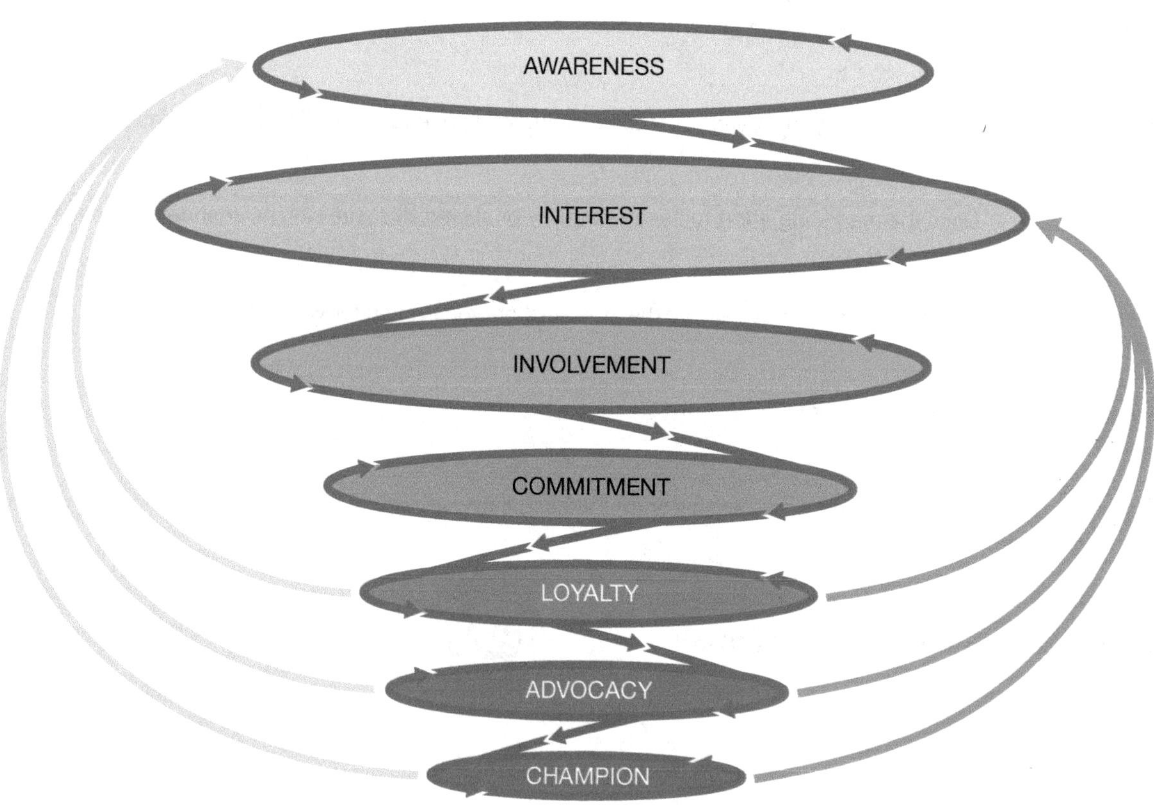

Figure 6.4: The Digital Involvement Cycle

For each of the seven stages of the *Digital Involvement Cycle* (see Figure 6.4), the management team also needs to monitor and measure analytics against expected outcomes and evaluate KPIs to ensure goals are achieved.

	Strategy		Tactics	Measurement	
Stage	**Goals**	**Targets**	**Tools**	**Actions**	**Metrics/KPIs**
AWARENESS	Gain Exposure	Target Demographic	Email, Banner Ads, AR Icons, Swarm (Foursquare)	Open Email, Engage with Banner, Snap AR Icon, Check-in on Swarm (Foursquare)	Open Rate, Click Through Rate, Views, Brand Equity
INTEREST	Foster Interactivity	Potential User/ Customer	Facebook, Twitter, Pinterest, Social Contests	User Likes, Shares, or Comments on a Post, Submits/Engages with Contest	Follows, Likes, Retweets, Engagement
INVOLVMENT	Encourage Inquiry	Prospect	YouTube, Blogs, Newsletter, Loyalty Programs	Watch Video, Subscribe to Blog/Newsletter, Sign Up for Program	Number of Subscribers
COMMITMENT	Generate Conversion	Customer/ Client	Coupons, Social Buzz, Opt-ins, Calls-to-Action	Redeem Coupon, Buy Product or Service, Attend Event, Register/ Subscribe	Conversion Rate, Customer Aquisition
LOYALTY	Serve Customers	Loyal Customer	Social Customer Relationship Management (SCRM)	Service Interactions (Phone, Online, Chat, Store), Service Reviews	Mentions, Reviews
ADVOCACY	Reward Loyalty	Advocate	Social Share Buttons, Surveys, Comments & Reviews, Referral Links	User Shares Blog Content, Fills Out Survey, Leaves Comment or Review, Shares Links	Number of Times Shared, Revenue Generated from Referral Links
CHAMPION	Engage Passion	Super Fan	User-Generated Content, Case Studies/ Testimonials, Access Social Community	Initiates Digital Campaign for Brand; Mobilizes Network around Brand	Number of Connections, Downloads, and Participants

Figure 6.5: The Digital Involvement Cycle with Related Strategies

For added insight into the application of the *Digital Involvment Cycle* to *IDM* strategy ->

The Importance of Creating an Integrated Digital Marketing Strategy

Pay no attention to the man behind the curtain, Dorothy, it's not about the technology. *We're well beyond the stage in which digital media is a fad – it's quickly becoming the dominant means by which consumers communicate with their friends and family (especially among younger consumers). Many companies don't fully appreciate just how rapidly the mobile device category is changing the ways in which we communicate with each other. Businesses who don't appreciate this are missing a big opportunity to re-think how they want to engage with their target audience.*

Companies who are waiting until others have become successful in digital marketing are in for a rude awakening. *That's because there is a first mover advantage in making a shift to an integrated digital marketing strategy. A company that is willing to engage with consumers in ways that were impossible to imagine a few years ago can now create and build deep relationships with its target audience on a regular basis. Companies who wait until their competitors have figured out how to do this are going to be at a double disadvantage when they finally decide to commit to a digital mindset and strategy. They will need to learn the lessons their competition has already turned into best practices and convince consumers to shift their loyalties to their company (which is a tough sell!).*

You don't have to radically change what your company is currently doing to create an integrated digital marketing advantage. *One of the biggest advantages of digital marketing is that, unlike traditional marketing, you can "make a little, sell a little, learn a lot."*

Reduce your marketing cost and improve your consumer insights while offering your customers more value. *There is a lot of waste in many companies' marketing budgets. It is amazing that social media gets such an intensive budget review on relatively small funding while massive TV budgets are approved simply because "that's what we've always done."*[8]

Kip Knight, President, International and US Franchise Operations, H&R Block

For a detailed outline of a sample *Integrated Digital Marketing* plan ->

IDM AND THE DIO

As with many other tools in this book, we have designed the *IDM Strategic Model* to help organizations like yours merge *IDM* strategy with values and goals to facilitate organization-wide digital transformation.

In practice, you may find *IDM* implementation to be a difficult proposition, full of complexities and challenges. The best place to start is at the beginning, asking a number of simple but important questions. What problems are your target audience trying to resolve? How are they going about doing so? What exactly are you doing to help? Are you communicating the right message to the right people at the right time? What is your organization doing to make sure you are found by prospects and customers wrestling with a problem to which you can provide a solution? How are you measuring the success or failure of your efforts?

Once you've reviewed these questions, you can begin to implement the *IDM Strategic Model*, which will help your organization leverage digital media, channels, and platforms to maximize operational efficiency. Just remember, *IDM* is not a silver bullet. However, when properly implemented, it is a responsive strategy that provides your organization an opportunity to listen to and address the wants and needs of your target audience, thereby enhancing the customer experience.

To optimally function, *IDM* requires holistic thinking. What are the fundamental values and principal business goals of your organization? How can you realign organizational processes to realize these? Asking these questions will help you prioritize *IDM* strategic implementation. Recognize that you may not be able to accomplish all of your objectives, at least not right away. Think about how you can incorporate digital into your current and future plans. Prioritize based on immediate relevance, but also take the long view. How do specific digital strategies, tactics, and tools fit into your future vision? Are some more relevant than others? Why? Recognize that the only constant is change. In today's hyper-paced digital culture, paradigms are made and broken all the time. To compete, you must stay mentally flexible and agile.

Above all, your organization must stay committed to its core values, using them as guiding principles when implementing the *IDM Strategic Model*, a critical step along the *Path of Digital Integration*. The final destination in the journey is the *DIO*, which combines digital technology and *IDM* with core values to create abundance for its stakeholders.

In the four chapters of the next unit, we will examine in greater detail the tactics and tools necessary to effectively implement the *IDM Strategic Model*.

TAKEAWAYS

- A marketing action is digital if it is reliant on a digital medium to execute its specific function or complete its intended action.

- If we are prepared to recognize that virtually all marketing is now digital marketing, we must understand that, to function properly, digital marketing must be integrated.

- *Integrated Digital Marketing (IDM)* is simple: by establishing a seamless online presence over web, social, and mobile, your organization can more efficiently convey and promote its brand message, attracting and converting new prospects and staying connected with existing customers, all the while measuring results to refine your efforts.

- Effective implementation of *IDM* is not easy; it takes a cross-organization effort to align resources, goals, technology, data, and measurement.

- *SERVAS Digital Analysis* uses six benchmarks to evaluate your organization's digital marketing initiatives in the context of the *IDM Strategic Model*.

- Above all, your organization must stay committed to its core values, using them as guiding principles when implementing the *IDM Strategic Model*.

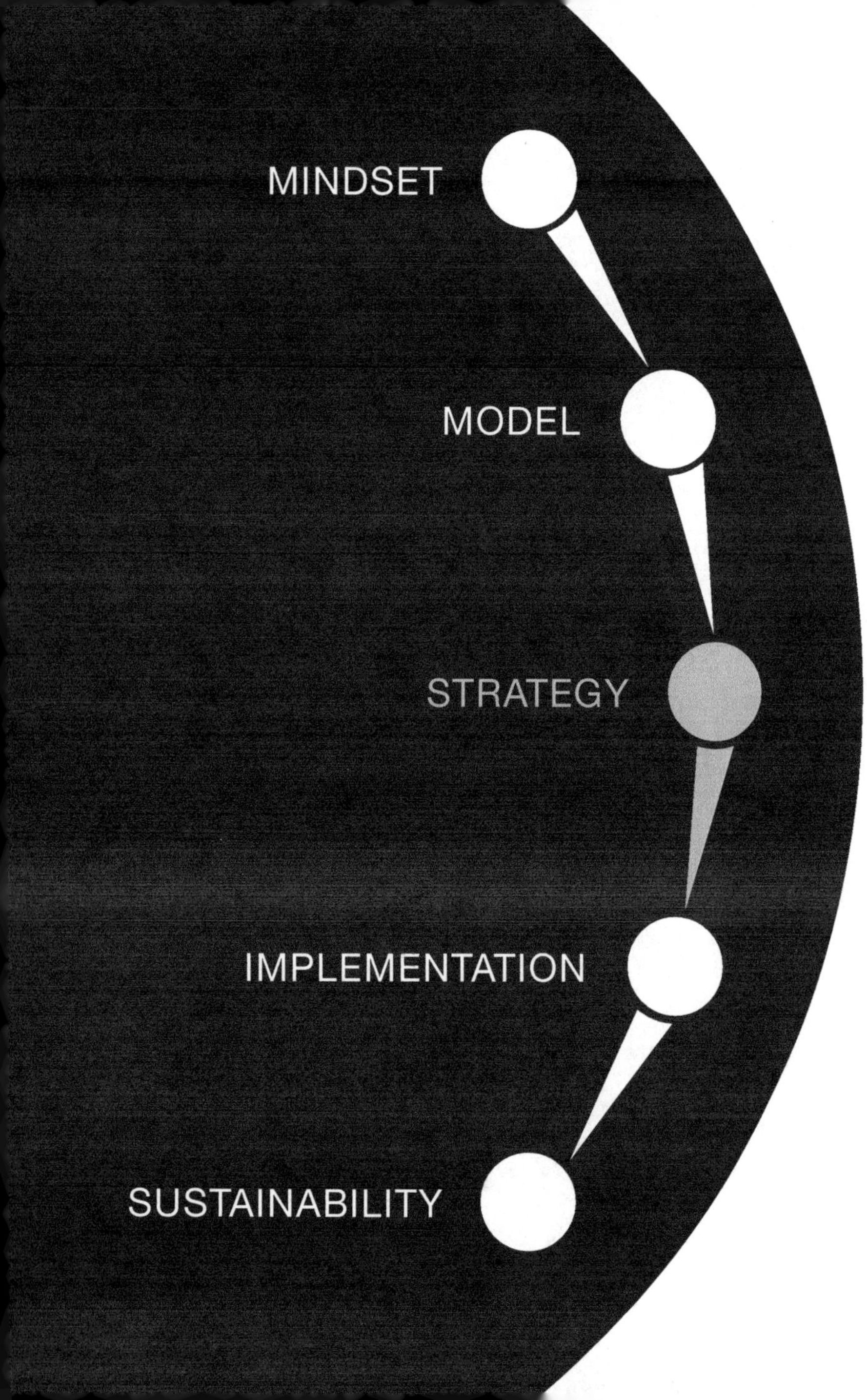

MINDSET

MODEL

STRATEGY

IMPLEMENTATION

SUSTAINABILITY

Chapter 7: Define and Establish

Chapter 8: Convey and Promote

Chapter 9: Connect and Convert

Chapter 10: Measure and Refine

Integrated Digital Marketing (IDM) is an over-arching strategy to help organizations build meaningful relationships with those who find value in their brand (i.e. their target audience) across all digital platforms. Digital marketing is a complex, ever-changing field with many moving parts; new trends come and go each day. As it is impossible to catch lightning in a bottle, so too is it impossible to offer a comprehensive and exhaustive set of *IDM* tactics and tools in an introductory guidebook. Recognizing this, in the following four chapters which comprise the "Strategy" unit, we endeavor to provide a foundational subset of actionable tactics and tools necessary for your organization to execute an effective *IDM* strategy.

As a reminder, you can access in-depth information, videos, and updates from our *Digital Marketing Resource Center* (www.dmresourcecenter.org) wherever you see this icon.

CHAPTER 7: DEFINE AND ESTABLISH

The first step in implementing the *IDM Strategic Model* is to Define and Establish your brand for the digital age. We use the term "Define" in the sense, to identify, specify, or discern; we use the term "Establish" in the sense, to lay the foundation, launch, or initiate. To find success with *IDM*, your organization must first Define its values, goals, and message and use these to Establish a robust online presence. This may be a confusing exercise for organizations that regard their brands as already Defined and Established, however, it is a necessary one.

The transparency and authenticity of the digital culture necessitate that brands live their values or face the consequences (e.g. accusations of hypocrisy, bad reviews). Clarifying values allows you to clearly Define your business goals and shape your brand message – all preconditions for your organization to Establish a seamless online presence across relevant digital channels.

By investing the time and effort upfront, you can lay a solid foundation for an effective *IDM* strategy. This chapter provides the tactics and tools you need to accomplish this worthy goal.

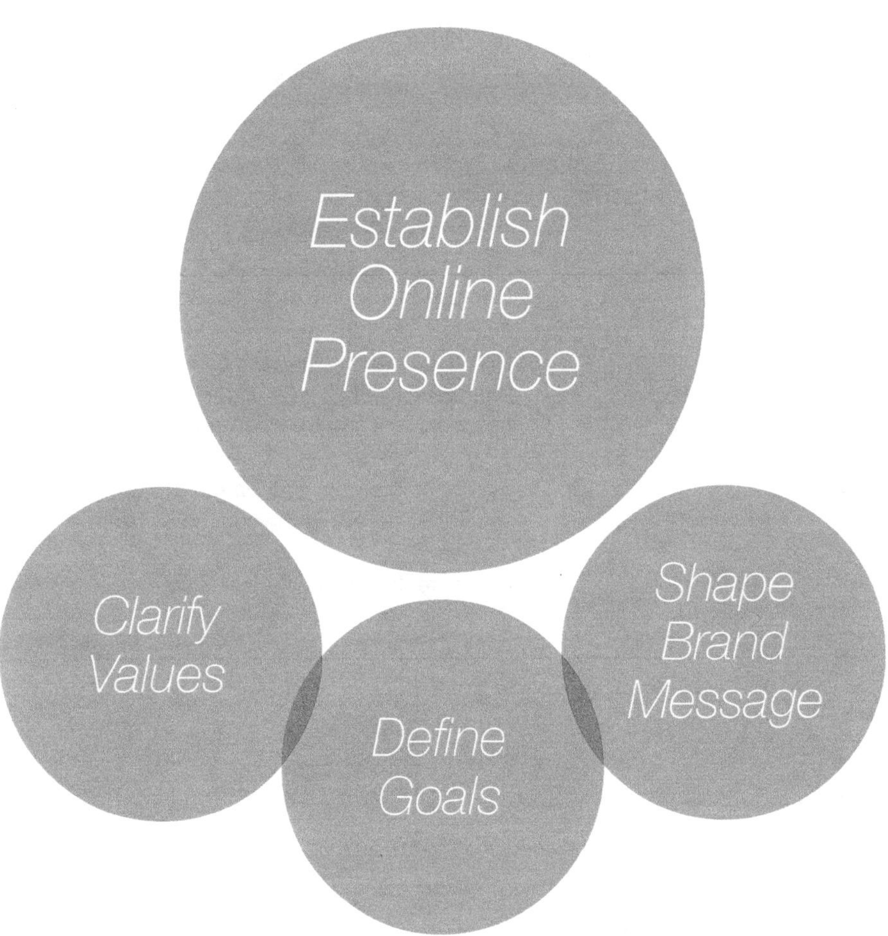

TACTIC: CLARIFY VALUES

In chapter 3, we introduced "Principles" as the 6th P of the *New Marketing Normal*, which necessitates that businesses integrate individual and organizational values to achieve success. Organizational values are those things or beliefs your organization finds important and meaningful. Clarifying and defining these core values is necessary to building an authentic and transparent brand.

Suggested Action – Determine the core values of your organization:

- Survey the executive team and selected managers and employees for their input.
- Compile the results, and then discuss with your senior leadership.
- Come to agreement on the core values that you want to represent the organization as touchstones for all work, both internal (e.g. communications, performance, customer service, collaboration) and external (e.g. website, brand, content, social messaging) to the organization.
- Survey or interview your partners, suppliers, customers, prospects, and social communities to see if they acknowledge your core values.
- Compare the results. If there is no consensus, you have some work to do!

TACTIC: DEFINE GOALS

Now consider your organization's goals, as they are the standard by which you measure organizational performance. Are you a healthcare company that wants to be one of the top five regional providers in the next three years? Are you a software manufacturer that wants to launch a new project management tools and capture 5% of the market? Are you a local craft beer brewery that would like to achieve regional reach within the next five years while still keeping with your commitment to donate 25% of all profits to charity?

While most business goals tend to reflect standard, "bottom line" metrics such as brand position or ROI, they can also encompass holistic, "sustainable values" metrics (e.g. 100% organic certified foods, 10% increase in local job creation). Defining specific business goals that are well thought out and reflect the future direction of the organization is a critical component of *IDM* strategy.

Prepare a short survey for your organization's board and management team to gain agreement on goals. Each partcipant will allocate 100 points among a list of goals broken out by stakeholder. The results will be shared and discussed among both groups until consensus is reached.

Stakeholder	Goal in Year X	Rating
Shareholders/Owners	Increase Revenue by 10%	20 pts.
Prospects	Increase Brand Recognition	10 pts.
Current Customers	Improve Customer Service	30 pts.
Suppliers	Cut Costs by 12%	5 pts.
Employees	Encourage Innovation	15 pts.
Local Community	Provide 20 New Jobs	20 pts.

Figure 7.1: Organizational Goals Ranking Sheet

Suggested Action – align values and goals:

- Review organization's stated values (mission) and goals.
- Compare and resolve the differences, if any, between the organization's stated values and goals and its actual or operational ones.
- Mesh the organization's values tightly into achievable/measurable short- and long-term goals.

TACTIC: SHAPE BRAND MESSAGE

It is clear that both organizational values and goals influence the message your brand conveys to the greater world. The following tools will help further shape this message.

Build Buyer Personas

To effectively define your brand's message, you must first clarify with whom it is trying to build relationships. The *New Marketing Normal* encourages brands to stop targeting consumers and start building networks of advocates. To do so, your organization should create nuanced buyer personas for all relevant market segments or buyer groups that demonstrate affinity to your brand. These buyer personas should include standard demographic information as well as insights into buyer behavior.

Below are some basic questions to consider when developing your buyer personas:

1. ***Demographic Profile*** – Age, gender, income level, education level, marital status, children, etc.
2. **Employment Information** – What industry do they work in? What is their role in the company? What is their seniority level?
3. **Pain Points** – It's hard to provide a solution if you don't understand your buyer's problems and challenges. Go into detail. How do they feel about their pain points? How they are trying to resolve them?
4. ***Values/Goals*** – What does your buyer value? What will get them excited to work with you? What are they trying to accomplish with this relationship? Consider values as the flip side of pain points.
5. ***Information Consumption*** – Where does the buyer turn to for information? Friends, family, online search, social networks, books, newspapers? What keywords or phrases are they using when searching online?
6. ***Anticipated Experience*** – What features and benefits is the buyer looking for? What type of experience is he/she expecting when buying your product or service?

7. ***Objections*** – Know what you're up against. Why would the potential buyer not purchase your product? To the extent that you can expose buyer objections, you can tailor your *IDM* strategy to resolve them early on in the buying cycle.

This is simply the beginning of a process; buyer personas are not meant to be static, but rather always evolving. The most helpful buyer personas reflect how consumers grow in relation to your brand and how different situations (e.g. marriage, layoffs, etc.) may affect their relationship with your brand.

Understand Brand Properties

The next step is to understand your brand's properties. Think of brand properties as having three components:

Essence

Your brand essence is an encapsulation of its fundamental qualities and characteristics; a pithy articulation of your brand's unique Identity; the few words that serve as the consistent touchstone for all of your marketing efforts. Is your brand essence chic and sophisticated, or is it efficient and smart? For example, *Nestlé's* brand essence may be defined as nurturing and holistic. The *NFL*, who in the past may have been "aggressive and competitive," is now becoming "community-orientated" (partly in response to increasingly challenging questions concerning the danger of the sport). Your brand essence is not to be flaunted in the media, but rather serves as the "quite foundation" of all external touch points and internal actions.

Voice

Given your brand's essence, how might your brand speak? You must not only define your brand voice but also embody and execute it at every consumer touch point, from website copy to tweets to email campaigns. Remember from chapter 4 that "Product" is now defined by all the interactions a User (i.e. your target audience) has with the Value Generator (i.e. your brand). Authenticity and consistency are key components of brand voice; the right voice will show your personality, elicit an emotional response from your customers, differentiate you from competitors, and help to attract the right audience for your brand.[1]

It's important to note the difference between voice and tone. Think of voice as your brand's consistent identity or the execution of its essence. It doesn't change. Tone, however, changes based on the situation. Your brand's tone will probably sound different in a personalized "Happy Birthday" email to a consumer than it does in a detailed, informative ebook. Remember, though, all tones must come from the same brand voice.

How would you define your brand essence?

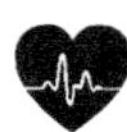

- How do you incorporate brand essence into your marketing efforts?
- Is your brand essence aligned with your organizational goals?

"If your brand could talk, how would they speak? What sorts of things would they say? Would they speak with a folksy vernacular or a refined, erudite clip? Describe the specific aspects of your brands voice, and how it might change in various communication situations. People change their language and tone to fit the situation, and so should the voice of your brand."

Aaron Walter, excerpt from "Designing for Emotion"[2]

MailChimp's Voice

MailChimp has treated the development of its brand's voice as if it was developing a customer persona. The company seems to have asked itself, "If MailChimp was a person, what would that person be like?" MailChimp easily could have made the company sound all-business, but instead went for a persona that is a bit more easy-going. Once the brand decided on a solid persona, the rest of the content was tailored to be reflective of this friendly image. In fact, MailChimp has an entire site dedicated to explaining its tone and voice respective to all the content it produces.

For an in-depth look into MailChimp's brand messaging ->

Promises

Brand promises are the things your brand guarantees to its consumers. What value does it add to their lives? What need does it fulfill? What problem does it solve? Don't set a limit on the number of promises your brand makes, but do be sure that all promises are authentic and truthful. No use in making promises you can't deliver on.

Content Audit

When defining your brand properties, you may find a content audit helpful in understanding how your brand has been portraying itself. Gather all of your organization's digital assets (e.g. website copy, social media profile copy, etc.) and physical content (e.g. brochures, pamphlets, etc.), and ask the following questions:

- How do you feel as you read the content? What emotions and first impressions come up?
- What tone characterizes the copy?
- Given the emotions you feel and the tone you perceive, what brand identity do you conclude?
- How does this perception compare with internal perceptions of your brand identity?

Although you can't rid yourself of all bias, the closer you align yourself with a consumer perspective, the more fruitful, and perhaps revealing this exercise will be.

Value Proposition

Your buyer personas and brand properties will help you create your brand's value proposition. Simply defined, a value proposition is a positioning statement that succinctly explains what problem you solve, for whom you solve it, and how you solve it uniquely well. Establishing your company's value proposition requires thought, care, and time. Don't finalize it too quickly; take time to consider all of the possible directions.

Your value proposition should articulate in one sentence (approximately 20 to 30 words) why people should buy your company's products or services. Ideally, it should answer the following questions:

- What product or service do you provide?
- Who are your customers/targets?
- Why is your offering unique and different?
- What end benefits/expected improvements does your offering provide?

For examples of effective value propositions ->

Once your organization is able to Define its values, goals, and message, it will have laid the foundation for an effective IDM strategy. The next step is to Establish an online presence over web, social, and mobile platforms.

TACTIC: ESTABLISH AN ONLINE PRESENCE

Your values are clarified, your goals are set, and your message and delivery are crafted. Now, you need to establish an online presence to effectively relay your unique brand message.

Establishing Your Brand's Online Presence

Figure 7.2: How-To-Video – Establishing your Brand's Online Presence

Acting as your brand's virtual storefront, your website is the hub of your organization's online presence. It is a powerful tool for conversion on a number of levels. A well-functioning website can effectively communicate your brand message, attract prospects, generate leads and sales, and build long-term advocacy. In fact, it's more than powerful; it's vital. Below are the key components of a website built for C-O-N-V-E-R-S-I-O-N:

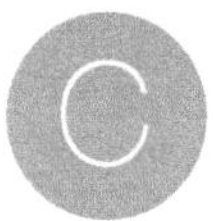

Compelling – Your website should encapsulate the best of your brand, merging crisp visuals with concise, well-written copy that promotes your unique value proposition. Your site must do more than give out information about your products and services – it must successfully make the case why people should consider, or continue, working with you.

Original – Be transparent, and be yourself. Share testimonials, case studies, and/or samples of your work; if you're a start-up, emphasize your vision and values. Humanize your brand with an About Us page that tells your brand story, ideally with pictures and videos. Show your face: familiarity builds trust and fosters brand affinity.

Navigable – The navigation system (site map) is one of the most important elements of your company's website. A clear navigation tells the user where they are on your site at any given time. Give hierarchy to navigation in order to clarify what the site contains and where the user should go next. If the route through the website isn't clear, it's more likely your user will feel confused and leave.

Versatile – Make sure your website messaging and content reflects the multi-dimensional nature of your brand. Don't shy away from audio and visual content. Try new things, and put in some honest effort. Think of your website as your online storefront; put as much thought into the online experience as you would the in-store or in-office experience.

Educational – Many people are coming to your site for information; they're trying to resolve a want or a need, or gain a better understanding of what it is you do or what you have to offer. Don't disappoint. Blogs, ebooks, infographics, and videos are great educational tools. We will discuss these in the next chapter.

Reliable – Stability and reliability breed trust. In the online world, this begins with consistent web-based messaging and formatting. Do what you say, and say what you do. Make sure your website is as reliable for search engines as it is for people. Index your site with the major search engines, and delete redundant copy and duplicate pages. Make sure your brand's message, content, look, and feel are consistent over all media.

Simple – People are coming to your site for a reason. Help them, don't hinder them. Create a clear site structure and layout for an exceptional user experience. If relevant, provide a clear path to the sale with calls-to-action (CTAs) or hyperlinks to online check outs or bottom-of-the-funnel (BOFU) offer landing pages.

Integrated – This is an *Integrated Digital Marketing* strategy, isn't it? Sync your website with other elements of your digital presence, especially social media platforms. Embed social share buttons in relevant site pages and other web-based content assets such as ebooks and infographics. Bolster your email campaigns with links to dynamic web and social content. Above all else, make sure your messaging is integrated over all digital platforms.

Optimized – As we've discussed in previous chapters, the growth of mobile necessitates that your brand is optimized for devices of all shapes and sizes. A responsive web design (RWD) eliminates the need to create a separate mobile site, saving time and money. It also provides users with a seamless experience across devices and access to the same information no matter how they access your site. This helps companies maintain brand integrity by delivering consistent messaging to any web user and creates an experience focused on people rather than on devices.

For additional information on RWD for your organization ->

Nurturing – If your business is like most others, you are probably selling some type of product or service. If so, your website should also function as your top online sales rep. Attractive CTAs that link to actionable landing pages, and sophisticated email lead nurturing campaigns orchestrated by marketing automation software are but two ways to make your website a nurturing one; we'll explain these in greater detail in the following chapters.

As we've noted previously, the lines separating online and offline are blurring. In today's hybrid business environment, your company website must be built for conversion on all levels, turning visitors into leads, leads into customers, and customers into brand advocates. Websites built for conversion encourage "Participation," the 5th P of the *New Marketing Normal*, and foster sustainable relationships with new prospects and existing customers.

Web Optimization: Mobile App Development

In chapter 3, we touched on the exponential growth of mobile. Responsive web design is but one mobile optimization solution. Many brands have found success with mobile apps. As of now, three types of mobile applications have emerged – native, mobile web, and hybrid:

1. *Native Mobile Apps* do not need to be connected to the Internet to be used because they are specific to the mobile device they run on (hence the term "native"). Native apps are distributed within popular marketplaces like Apple's App Store and Google Play.

2. *Mobile Web Apps* are developed using technologies such as HTML5, JavaScript, and CSS3, and run on the mobile device's Internet browser. Mobile web apps are not really apps at all, but rather websites that look and feel like native applications, and can work across multiple devices and be compatible across multiple operating systems. As more websites utilize HTML5 technology, the distinction between mobile web apps and normal web pages is blurring.

3. *Hybrid Mobile Apps* are a mix between the two. They essentially operate as native apps with embedded HTML technology, producing cross-platform apps that access a mobile device's native features. Hybrid apps can be downloaded from app marketplaces and have all the features of a native app, but require updates from the web to function.

For a detailed discussion of the pros and cons of each type of mobile app ->

Tool Website Creation: Content Management System

Thus far, we have considered the functions and priorities of your brand's website. However, you may be asking, what's the best way to build it? Good question.

The key to website design within an *IDM* strategy is, well, integration. You need a system that is part content system and part personalization engine, and that is customizable for you, your team, and each individual visitor.[3]

Enter the content management system (CMS), a computer program that supports content publishing and editing as well as workflow management. WordPress, Joomla, and Drupal are widely considered to be the most popular CMS options on the market. However, the entirety of the CMS landscape, as well as that of other web design options, is too numerous to detail here.

To learn about the current CMS landscape ->

Social Platforms

Acting to complement and augment the reach and impact of your website and brand message, your social platforms serve as the other foundational element of an effective *IDM* strategy.

While some brands still use their social platforms as shameless PR megaphones, shouting obnoxiously at disengaged, annoyed (or absent) consumers, most have begun to understand the true nature of social platforms. They are, in fact, open channels that flow two ways, between the brand and its consumers.

Here are four ways social media can help your organization establish its online presence:

- *Increase Brand Awareness* – Social platforms give your brand exponential reach, empowering you to leverage your content and messaging more efficiently than traditional marketing channels.
- *Build Reputation* – Social platforms help your brand tell its story (both the good and the bad). When what you share on your blog, Facebook, and Twitter truly represents you, people feel safe, and are therefore more likely to move beyond mere interested bystanders to a more meaningful relationship with your brand.
- *Drive Web Traffic* – Social channels can drive relevant visitors to your website – users who have found your site via content on your social channels are users who have already fostered some level of affinity for your brand.
- *Improve Relationships* – Loyalty and trust play vital roles in social media success. Your organization can use social media to build brand influencers and advocates.

- In 2012, half of Internet users ages 18 to 23, and 43% of users ages 24 to 32, used social networks as their go-to Internet-discovery resource, according to a report Forrester Research.[4]
- Social networks are "the preferred means of discovery" for nearly a third of all Americans.[5]
- 20- to 30-year-olds (Gen Y), are twice as likely to seek information or advice from social media as the previous generation (Gen X), and almost four times more likely to than the Baby Boomers.[6]

The following graphic from UMass Dartmouth's 2013 study of social media usage among Inc. 500 companies underscores the importance of social media for business:[7]

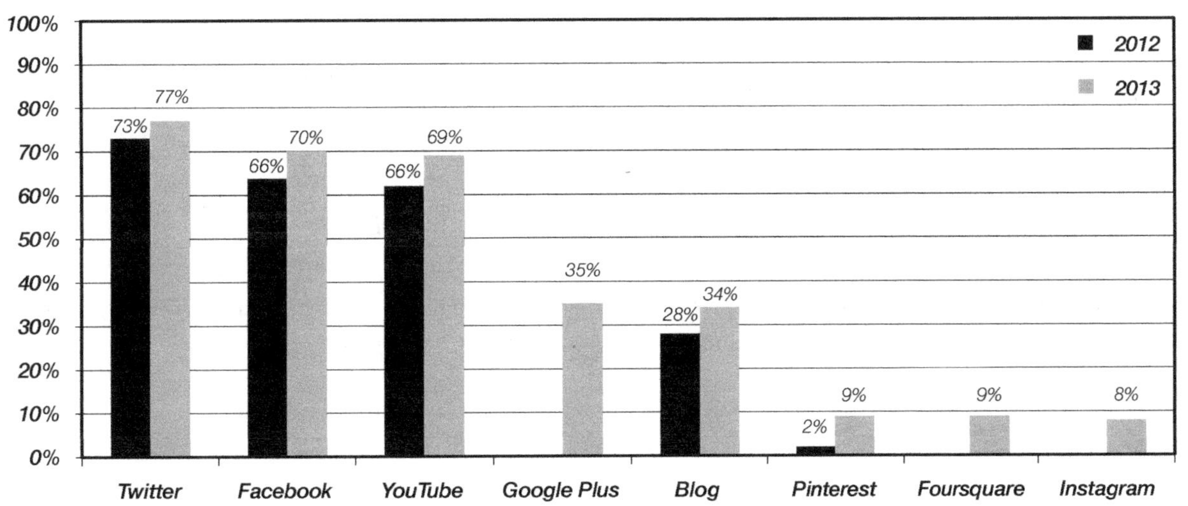

Figure 7.3: Fortune 500 Corporate Social Media Usage (2012-2013)

After having evaluated your brand's values and goals and reviewed the various benefits of social media as outlined above, you need to identify the most profitable and relevant social channels for your organization. Remember: just because EVERYONE is on Facebook doesn't mean your company necessarily should be too. Ask yourself, are your consumers there? With social media, as with many other things in life, quality trumps quantity. Remember to set down your shotgun and grab a rifle.

Questions to ask when determining the right social channels for your organization:

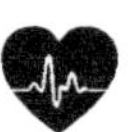

- *Mind the Four W's* – Who, What, When, and Why. Who is using the channel (do they match my target audience); What are they doing on it; When are they most active; Why have they chosen the social channel?

- *What Types of Content Do People Share*? Are the products and services your business provides relevant to the content people are sharing?

- *How Much Time and How Many Resources* does this channel require of my brand to stay current?

The "Big Seven" Social Channels:

Facebook, Twitter, Google Plus, LinkedIn, Instagram, Pinterest, YouTube

It seems that each month a new social media channel emerges. While the field is always in flux, the *"Big Seven"* social channels are established mainstays that you can count on surviving the year.

- 73% of online adults now use a social networking site.[8]
- Some 42% of online adults now use multiple social networking sites.[9]
- Facebook is the dominant social networking platform in terms of number of users.[10]

Below is a brief explanation of how each channel could be relevant to establishing your brand's online presence, as well as a few facts about each.

Facebook

As the largest global social networking site, Facebook has come a long way since Mark Zuckerberg first built it in his Harvard dorm room. With its "Timeline" profile format and scrolling Newsfeed, Facebook for individuals as well as brands is focused on storytelling, especially through photos and videos.

- *Over 1.3 billion monthly active users.*[11]
- *23% of users check their account more than five times a day.*[12]
- *The demographic of 45- to 54-year-old users has grown 46% since the end of 2012.*[13]

Twitter

Twitter favors short, pithy snippets of information limited to 140 characters. It's an excellent place to post quick updates or links to more in-depth content. It's an easy platform for brief conversations with other users, including consumers or other brands.

- *235 million monthly active users.*[14]
- *55- to 64-year-olds is the fastest growing user demographic.*[15]
- *500 million Tweets are sent each day.*[16]

Google Plus

While slow in gaining popularity, Google Plus (G+) is a growing platform. Similar to Facebook, G+ favors highly visual content. It also features "communities" which foster more intimate discussions and sharing. It's worth considering that G+ is the proprietary social platform of Google, the biggest search engine on the market. Given this relationship, many marketers and SEO experts view Google Plus as the "back door" to higher Google search rankings.

- *Over 500 million users.*[17]
- *The "+1" button is used over 5 billion times a day.*[18]
- *70% of brands now have a presence on Google Plus, up from 4% in the last quarter of 2012.*[19]

LinkedIn

The self-proclaimed "largest professional network," LinkedIn is much less focused on visual content than Facebook and G+. Rather, this social channel is an excellent place for brands to provide relevant organizational and educational information. Companies can create LinkedIn brand pages that other users can "follow" instead of "connect" with.

- *Over 300 million members globally.*[20]
- *More than 3 million companies have LinkedIn Company Pages.*[21]
- *Over 2.1 million LinkedIn groups.*[22]

Instagram

Instagram is a photo-sharing platform that rewards beautiful and compelling shots. An excellent way to showcase your brand's personality, Instagram allows you to post photos directly onto its platform as well as push photos to your other social channels such as Twitter and Facebook. Brands can attract followers using popular hashtags.

- *Over 200 million monthly active users.*[23]
- *Instagram receives 1,000 comments every second.*[24]
- *Average of 60 million photos uploaded every day.*[25]

Pinterest

Pinterest is more than just a DIY-er's dream; the social platform allows brands to pin and re-pin posts of both their own products as well as other items and scenes they (and their consumers) find inspiring or otherwise valuable. Pins, which are the equivalent to posts on Facebook and tweets on Twitter, can be linked to any other web page or URL (i.e. an order form or e-commerce check-out page), making the site very sales-actionable.

- *Over 70 million active users.*[26]
- *57% of posts discuss food-related content, making food the network's top category.*[27]
- *More than 69% of users are female.*[28]

YouTube

YouTube is the king of video and, therefore, a necessary platform for any brand considering adding video to their content repertoire. YouTube recently added homepages that allow users to upload photos and an introductory video, making it more of a social channel in itself rather than simply a video hosting site.

- *Over 1 billion unique monthly visitors.*[29]
- *The second-largest search engine behind Google.*[30]
- *Over 6 billion hours of videos are watched each month.*[31]

Niche/Industry-Specific Social Channels

Beyond the *"Big Seven"* social channels, countless social platforms have cropped up over the of years tailored to specific industry segments and niche social markets. For example, Houzz is similar to Pinterest but specific to the home remodeling and construction industry; Reddit is the highest supplier of news among social sites; Vine is a mobile video sharing app with a maximum clip length of six seconds; StumbleUpon is a discovery engine that finds and recommends web content to its users; SnapChat is a photo messaging app that is now one of the fastest growing social platforms among youth.

For additional information on these unique social channels ->

Now that we've reviewed how your organization can Define its values, goals, and message to Establish a seamless online presence, you must learn how to properly Convey and Promote this information throughout your digital channels. For this, we turn to chapter 8.

- The *New Marketing Normal* necessitates that organizations align their values and their business goals in order to achieve success.
- Taken together, your organizational values and goals will shape your brand message.
- Building detailed buyer personas and defining specific brand properties are vital to a solid, foundational value proposition.
- Your brand's website is the cornerstone of your digital presence and, therefore, must be built for converting leads into valued consumers and brand advocates.
- Although the *"Big Seven"* are popular social channels, not all will be right for your brand. Careful consideration of each channel's demographic profile and use will help determine which channels are right for your organization's *IDM* strategy.

CHAPTER 8: CONVEY AND PROMOTE

In the previous chapter, we explained that the first step in implementing the *IDM Strategic Model* is to Define and Establish your brand presence. In this chapter, we will examine the second step, how to Convey and Promote your brand message.

We use the term "Convey" in the sense, to make known or communicate. A carefully implemented *IDM* strategy leverages digital content media to efficiently Convey your organization's brand message, product and service information, expertise, and creativity throughout your website, social, and mobile channels.

We use the term "Promote" in the sense, to advance, advocate, elevate, or augment. A well-crafted *IDM* strategy utilizes organic and paid search and social channels to effectively Promote your organization's brand message and content. As you will see, a successful *IDM* strategy relies on both for its proper execution.

TACTIC: CONTENT MARKETING

Content is an integral element of *IDM* strategy. But what exactly is "content," anyway? Used in a digital marketing context, content can be virtually any form of written, auditory, or visual media (e.g. blogs, ebooks, whitepapers, social posts, webcasts, webinars, podcasts, videos, emails and more). Effective content marketing often reflects an organization's goals while still speaking to the wants and needs of its target audience.

With the widespread adoption of the Internet, social, and mobile, consumer demand for digital content is increasing geometrically. Each day, more than 92,000 pieces of content are posted to the Internet.[1] As more brands shift budgets to digital, this number is bound to go up exponentially in coming years.

What is the Essence of Content Marketing

"Instead of trying to get attention of prospects and customers while they are engaging in someone else's content, brands are becoming the content. Becoming the media. Brands are creating content so useful and interesting that prospects and customers are drawn to them. It's marketing that doesn't specifically sell, but opens the door to conversations. In essence, content marketing is about taking your marketing and sales hat off and putting on your publishing hat."[2]

Joe Pulizzi, Founder, Content Marketing Institute (CMI)

The very notion of content marketing poses some challenging questions for organizations of all sizes: how can we produce the amount and type of quality content needed to get found in a rapidly expanding Internet ecosystem? In such a crowded online environment, what is it going to take for our brand's content to deliver the right message to the right people at the right time? How can we build meaningful and sustainable relationships with our intended audience?

Organizations with limited resources often find it extremely difficult to compete with the sheer volume of online content produced by their better-funded peers. If your brand falls into this category, the name of the game is quality, not quantity. A good place to start is to create a well-defined content strategy that is laser-focused on resolving the wants and needs of your target audience. Value and relevance are two key factors. To survive and thrive in an increasingly competitive online marketing environment, your brand needs to produce useful content that solves problems and adds value to the daily lives of its prospects and customers.

Content Marketing is Survival

The essential benefit of content marketing is simply this: survival.

Currently, content marketing is a choice. Brands can stick to old-school outbound marketing tactics, hedge their bets by moving some of their advertising budget into content initiatives or make the full leap into content marketing. But companies that don't make the transition soon will suffer and, eventually, die.

Because customers are not only demanding content from brands, they are creating content of their own. They're writing reviews and blogs and blasting them through social media. Brands that fail to develop their own content marketing strategies will find themselves at the mercy of their customers (and former customers.) If people can't get the information they want from one brand, they will find it from another.

Many companies will not make the transition – or they will make it too late. Content marketing is a long-term, holistic approach to converting customers that doesn't fit comfortably in the "results NOW" mentality of traditional marketers. But customers can no longer be pushed into funnels against their will. They will go where they wish to be led.

Content marketing works because it is like courtship from a candid suitor: it woos customers, not just with candy-coated, flowery prose, but with an honest appraisal about the value of committing to your products or services.

Customers liked to be wooed, but not misled.

Katherine Kotaw, CEO, KOTAW Content Marketing

Blogging

A blog is essential to your *IDM* strategy and a simple way to house content right on your website. Given that each blog page creates its own unique URL, blogging also provides SEO benefit. To successfully build connections with your consumers, your organization's blog should have a clear focus that is relevant to both your brand and its target audience. Your business goals, content strategy and, ultimately, resources will determine how often you post on your blog, but as a general rule once a day is best. A 2013 survey by HubSpot found that 82% of marketers who blog on a daily basis acquire a customer using their blog, as opposed to 57% of marketers who blog monthly.[3]

Other factors, such as blog length and layout, can significantly impact your blog's effectiveness. Blog length depends on your industry as well as your topic, but as a general rule 400-800 words is sufficient. Blogs that contain visuals, especially statistics, tend to resonate with readers, especially on mobile devices, so much so that many brands are now adding video blogging (Vlogging) into the content mix.

To increase your blog's reach, consider submitting your blog for syndication on other sites. Many industries now have online communities that welcome submissions from readers and brand representatives. These online communities usually have a larger readership than your blog will initially have, so they're excellent places to begin building your own following.

As with most content marketing, success in blogging often comes down to following this simple approach: clearly define and listen to your target audience, provide solutions that address their pain points, needs, and wants, and keep your message simple, concise, and relevant.

For additional insight into effective business blogging ->

Tool *Premium Content*

As a complement to blogging (which usually requires comparatively little investment of time and resources), premium content serves as the anchor of your content strategy. Premium content pieces offer more expansive or in-depth information than a single blog post may contain. Examples include webinars, SlideShare presentations, ebooks, and whitepapers, which you can host on your site and offer to consumers as a free download. While the line between ebooks and whitepapers is blurred, ebooks are generally more graphics heavy, whereas whitepapers are more text heavy. For an integrated content strategy, consider accenting the content of a comprehensive ebook with several blog posts that delve into the specific topics covered in the ebook more thoroughly.

Tool Multimedia Content

Content marketing is not limited to words; in fact, today's mobile-device-toting consumers often prefer multimedia content. To meet this demand, consider adding infographics, videos, audiocasts, or webcasts to your content production. Exercise the same care, however, as you did when establishing your brand on various social channels. Just as not all social channels will be relevant and useful to your brand, not all forms of content will either.

To learn about infographics and other multimedia used in content marketing ->

Why is Content Marketing so Critical for the Enterprise?

In the past, enterprise brands had to have a robust paid strategy (advertising, sponsorship, traditional PR) to have any kind of success. Today, brands can attract and retain customers through consistent, valuable storytelling. More brands, like Coca-Cola, Red Bull, Cisco, IBM and thousands of smaller companies, are focusing on owning their audiences instead of renting them through advertising like they did in the past. Today, brands are working to have a long-term relationship with customers through value-driven content.

That said, smart companies need to use a balanced approach of paid and owned (hopefully working in concert) to make the most impact. The biggest difference today is that there are literally no barriers to entry for brands to get into the publishing business. Fifteen years ago, publishers spent hundreds of thousands of dollars just to get into the publishing game. Today, a brand can get a blog up and running in five minutes with minimal cost. Since consumers are in complete control, and the majority of the buying process is over before the company is contacted, content needs to carry that new weight in the enterprise. So, it's of critical importance.

Joe Pulizzi, Founder, Content Marketing Institute (CMI)

Editorial Calendar

An editorial calendar is a monthly (or weekly – whatever structure works best for your brand and team) schedule of all content to be published for that time period. It usually contains all of the information needed to produce each content piece, such as the topic, author, keywords, links to resources, and draft and publication due dates. Most editorial calendars are organized by author, content type, or campaign. Editorial calendars are critical project management tools to keep your team organized and help them produce quality content in an efficient manner.

For further information on editorial calendars and their uses, including examples ->

- 93% of B2B organizations are marketing to customers and prospects with a range of content-based tactics; 73% are producing more content than they did one year ago.[4]
- Nearly three-quarters (73%) of digital marketers agree that "brands are becoming publishers."[5]
- 53% of marketers say they're failing to create enough content to resonate with readers.[6]

Newsjacking

Newsjacking is a relatively new term, but it has quickly become a mainstay in any content marketing strategy. Newsjacking is simply "hijacking" a popular news story and using it as content for your brand. This is another tool for brands to form relevant connections with consumers.

The key to successful newsjacking is quick, creative action. News stories come and go, and when they fade a day or two later, so too will your content's relevance. So be spontaneous, but also be ethical; consider the nature of the content of a news story before "jacking" it. If it involves a natural disaster or other tragedy, think twice before using it to promote your brand's message.

Newsjacking in Action: Royal Baby Craze

The birth of Prince George to Kate Middleton and Prince William in July 2013 provided ample newsjacking fodder for brands. Global news outlets extensively covered the event, and upon the actual news of Prince George's birth, brands from Pampers to Volkswagen sent their congratulations and best wishes to the Royal Family.[7]

Smart Content

As digital technologies advance, consumers are increasingly expecting a personalized experience. To meet the demands of this new expectation, "smart" content is emerging. Smart content is content that adapts, or personalizes, based on who's consuming it. This is made possible by sophisticated content management system (CMS) software, which is baked into many marketing automation software platforms. When planning your content strategy, consider leveraging these "smart" technologies to continue forming relevant and meaningful connections with your consumers.

Branded Content

Also known as "native advertising" or "advertorials," branded content is a novel approach to content marketing in which the brand attempts to connect with the end user by providing customized content designed to naturally and contextually "fit in" with the content that it appears alongside. Branded content can take on virtually any form, such as videos, news articles, social media posts, even television shows. Examples of branded content in social media include Facebook's Sponsored Stories, Twitter's Promoted Tweets, and YouTube's TrueView Ads.

The idea behind branded content is to make paid media feel less intrusive and thus increase the likelihood users will engage with it. There is some controversy surrounding the practice, especially its use by leading news organizations, with many business leaders and consumer groups beginning to voice concern over the ability of end users to tell the difference between "actual" content that is meant to be objective and "branded" content that is presumed to be pushing a commercial agenda.

- 74% of online consumers become frustrated with websites when the content they see has little or nothing to do with their interests.[8]
- 28% of consumers would be willing to give up social networks for a week in order to receive appropriate content based on their personal interests.[9]
- 57% of consumers are OK with providing personal information on a website as long as doing so benefits them and is used responsibly.[10]
- 62% of adults under 34 are willing to share their location to receive more relevant content.[11]

TACTIC: SOCIAL MEDIA MARKETING

When using social media, it's important to remember what social channels actually are. They are not platforms for spamming sales-focused messages. They are, instead, platforms for sharing your brand's content: content that entertains, informs, or is otherwise useful to your consumer. In fact, a 2013 CMI/Marketing Profs study found that 93% of B2B marketers now use social media for content marketing.[12]

Social Media: The Rules of Engagement

Figure 8.1: How-To-Video – Social Media: The Rules of Engagement

Social channels are also channels that flow two ways, and as such are ideal places for sharing and fostering conversation. For many brands in today's digital marketplace, their social channels may be the only places where they will ever get the opportunity to directly interact with prospects and customers. One of the keys to effective social media marketing, then, is to be sure to listen and engage with others more often than you post.

The "Big Seven" Social Channels

When considering the *"Big Seven"* social channels, we will be focusing on how you can use each to complement your overall *IDM* strategy, first through organic and then through paid means. Standard tips and suggestions follow, but remember that social channels have few practical boundaries, so get creative and inspired when it comes to posting and interacting.

Trying to engage with consumers on social media with even the best of intentions doesn't guarantee that those consumers will be awaiting you with open arms. In an article for the *Huffington Post*, Chris Abraham offers these words of warning:[13]

"Communities are so used to being abused that you'll be surprised and insulted by the level of caution, dread, and mistrust you'll wander into, even if your intentions are pure and you're just looking for ways to discover, engage, and help folks online.

So, approach the attempt to expand your online presence as you would a dinner party you weren't invited to. Meet the host, be honest and, of course, bring booze. Be upfront yet gracious. Listen 80% of the time, and promote your content the other 20% of the time."

Chris Abraham, founder, Gerris digital

Facebook

Facebook is generally more of a private platform, with users expecting to see pictures of family and friends or announcements of babies and weddings. Therefore, keep your posts friendly and personal – Facebook is a great place to humanize your brand. Posting photos of your team around the office or out-and-about creates familiarity and breeds brand affinity.

When first engaging on Facebook, fill your Newsfeed with information that is relevant to your brand, such as industry news or stories about other people and companies you find inspiring. Doing so will alert you of posts that you can engage with through comments and likes, and will serve to authentically project your brand's vision and values.

Quick tips:

- *One to two posts a day is appropriate; more than that and you might be considered overbearing.*
- *When posting your own content, such as a blog post or premium content offer, post a photo with the link.*
- *Be vigilant with monitoring comments and messages, as you want to be sure to respond in a timely fashion.*

Twitter

Twitter is fast-paced like a newsroom, and given the 140-character limit of tweets, consistently posting shortened URL links with your tweets is appropriate and welcomed. Pushing your brand content more heavily on this channel is considered acceptable, but counter this practice by sharing relevant content from other sources as well. As a rule of thumb, for every 10 Twitter posts, four can be brand specific, and one can promote a content offer.

Quick tips:

- *When posting content that features an organization or person, tag them in your tweet.*
- *Use relevant hashtags (#) to engage your brand in conversations with other users.*
- *When another user mentions your brand in a tweet, follow-up with either a simple "thank you" or a comment to start a conversation.*
- *If you have enough relevant and meaningful content, multiple tweets an hour is appropriate. But do not post simply to post.*

Google Plus

Google Plus (G+) is similar to Facebook. The highly visual platform welcomes engaging photos and allows you to tag other users in posts. Perhaps the biggest benefit of G+ for brands is the SEO boost content shared on the platform receives, given G+'s deep integration with Google's search engine.

Quick tips:

- *Join relevant communities, and respond more often than you post your own content. Google does not circumscribe post length; comments such as "great post" are not as useful as more detailed, thoughtful comments that offer follow-up content.*
- *One to two posts a day on your own profile is acceptable; however, more frequent engagement in communities is recommended.*
- *G+ Hangouts (instant messaging and video chat platform) provides an excellent way to collaborate and network with industry thought leaders and colleagues.*

LinkedIn

Owing to its role as the "professional" social network, LinkedIn tends to be more buttoned down; photos aren't as prevalent. However, posting blog articles or links to other web-based premium content on your LinkedIn Company Page is common practice.

Quick tips:

- *Utilize the Group function to both join and start other groups relevant to your industry.*
- *Given the nature of this channel, both your posts and engagement within your Groups can be more thought provoking and inquisitive.*
- *One to two posts a day on your company page is appropriate.*
- *Connect with LinkedIn influencers to build your following and expose your content to a wider audience.*

YouTube

YouTube has less strict etiquette rules than other social channels. When posting videos, however, be sure to include a title and description. It's also a good idea to embed YouTube videos in your blog or elsewhere on your website to generate more cross-platform traffic.

Quick tips:

- *Generally, keep videos short, at about two to four minutes. These short-form videos must still provide useful information or entertainment to keep users engaged.*
- *On YouTube, more is better. Because most people don't use YouTube like a social network they check often, frequent posting won't seem overbearing, and will build up your profile on the planet's second largest search engine.*
- *Just do it! Video production intimidates many brands, but consistent video filming and posting will help refine your tactics.*

Instagram

Instagram is not a social channel to vigorously post your content, such as blogs and ebooks, for two reasons: 1) links don't work within the channel and 2) people want to see beautiful pictures. Therefore, keep your content focused on people and projects around the office as well as images that inspire you.

Quick tips:

- *As long as your photos are aesthetically pleasing and relevant, post as many as you want.*
- *Research popular hashtags and use them to gain more visibility for your photos. You can do so on sites such as "TagsForLikes.com" and "HashtagIG.com." Also, instead of posting a maximum of 30 hashtags in your photo description, add them in a comment below the photo.*
- *Try out different apps to complement your Instagram use, such as VSCO Cam, Whitagram, and PicFrame. New ones come out regularly, so don't be afraid to experiment.*

Pinterest

Pinterest allows you to create several "boards," which gives you plenty of freedom when "pinning." Like Instagram, Pinterest is a completely visual platform, but unlike Instagram, it allows you to post a mix of original content and other images.

Quick tips:

- *Create boards showcasing your products and services. You can also embed links with your pins to drive users to specific web-based landing pages or check-out pages.*
- *Pinterest is an excellent platform to host user-driven contests. However, be sure to follow the network's "Acceptable Use Policy" to review specific rules for hosting contests.*
- *"Re-pin" is to Pinterest as "Retweet" is to Twitter.*

For additional tips and suggestions on using the "Big Seven" for business ->

TACTIC: PAID SOCIAL PROMOTION

Paid social ads are appealing because you can use them to target the right audience, drive traffic to your website, and generate new prospects and customers for your business. Marketers are increasingly viewing paid social promotion as an integrated, cross-platform tactic to be used in conjunction with other digital media.

The "Big Seven" Social Channels

Facebook

Facebook offers several options for advertising. Though the company's Facebook for Business website lays out a step-by-step process for doing so, here are some quick features of advertising on Facebook:

- *Ad Create Tool walks you through the creation process. It tailors your ad to accomplish specific business goals, whether that's to get more Page likes, highlight specific Page posts, promote a new app, or increase event attendance.*
- *Comprehensive targeting options allow you to target your ad based on location, gender, interests, etc.*
- *Page Promotion allows you to simply advertise your company's Facebook Page to increase awareness.*

Twitter

Like Facebook, Twitter dedicates an entire site to walking you through its advertising options. Here are a few key features of advertising on Twitter:

- *Promoted Accounts allows your brand to feature its account under Twitter's "Who to follow" section, providing an opportunity to increase your brand following.*
- *Promoted Tweets are an option if you'd like to promote a specific tweet to Twitter users. This can be a smart tool when pushing newsjacked content or special offers.*
- *Promoted Trends pushes your featured hashtag to the top of the trends list. This option can help a special engagement promotion gain traction.*

Google Plus

Google Plus does not offer specific advertising options, but you can link your G+ page with your Google AdWords account. We will discuss AdWords later in this chapter, but for now, note that if you link your G+ page with your AdWords account, your ads will show endorsements from your G+ followers. These endorsements are called "social annotations."

LinkedIn

LinkedIn offers comprehensive direction for creating ads within its network. Here are a few of the more notable features of advertising on LinkedIn:

- *You can set your ad budget to reflect how much you're willing to pay for clicks or impressions.*
- *You are given a wide array of options to define your target audience, including by job title, industry, location, age, seniority, etc.*
- *Your ads can be shown on the following LinkedIn pages: user Profile Pages, Home Pages, User Inbox, Search Results Page, and Groups.*

YouTube

Most YouTube ad options are powered by Google AdWords. YouTube offers the service in "three simple steps," which include 1) uploading your video to YouTube, 2) creating an AdWords, account and 3) launching your video ad. Here are some features to advertising on YouTube:

- *You only pay when people actually watch your ad. If they choose "skip," you don't pay.*
- *Like the other social channels, YouTube offers detailed ad targeting options.*
- *When you pay for ads on YouTube, your ads show up on all devices.*

Instagram

At the time of publication, Instagram is very slowly and carefully introducing ads to its community in the form of "sponsored posts." Right now, the option is only available to brands with a large and dedicated Instagram following, but if you're a visually focused brand, look to this channel in the future for advertising opportunities.

Pinterest

Like its visual counterpart Instagram, Pinterest is also slowly rolling out advertising in the form of "Promoted Pins." Concerned about the user experience, Pinterest has been testing the feature with a select number larger US-based brands and soliciting user feedback. However, in June of 2014, Pinterest is scheduled to begin offering self-service ads to small- and medium-sized businesses. Using an online auction system, Pinterest will allow brands to bid to have their ads placed in specific categories on the platform, which they will pay for on a cost-per-click basis.

TACTIC: SEARCH ENGINE OPTIMIZATION (SEO)

In recent years, the practice of SEO (sometimes referred to as "organic SEO") has evolved to closely align with the consumer-centric focus of *IDM*. SEO is no longer all about ranking #1 in the search engine results pages (SERPS) of Google and others. Instead, it is primarily concerned with creating fresh and original content that addresses the problems, needs, and wants of your target audience. As a brand, only after you've created such content should you focus on "optimizing" it for search engines.

"For every company that is creating useful, sharable content, growing their social networks, and optimizing the performance of their online marketing, there are probably 10 or even 100 more that are solely focused on tweaking keywords and getting links in the hopes of that first page or top 3 listing. 'If only we could reach #1, we'd be in the money.'

Beyond the singular SEO focus is the growing realization that consumers use more than search to find information and make purchases. And to be successful with online marketing, companies need to be where their customers are. They need to be there in a meaningful way. How? By understanding and answering your customers' questions on their journey from awareness to purchase to advocacy."[14]

Lee Odden, CEO, Top Rank

Before we break down the common tools used in SEO, it's important to briefly outline the factors that make up an optimized webpage. When a webpage is "optimized," we mean that the page will

- Have the best opportunity to rank highly in search engines like Google and Bing/Yahoo!.
- Earn traffic from the major social networks like Twitter, Facebook, LinkedIn, and Google Plus (via social share buttons embedded in webpages, blogs, and premium content pieces that help drive traffic to your social media platforms).
- Be worthy of links and shares from across the web.
- Build trust with your target audience, increasing its potential to convert visitors into leads, customers, and advocates.

The following organic SEO tools will help you re-tool your webpages and content to provide a seamless, "optimized" user experience.

Keyword Optimization

When considering keyword optimization, it is important to note that you are not just trying to "rank with Google." Rather, the keywords you use to construct your content should be relevant to your users' needs or desires. In other words, your keywords should be the words your consumers use when performing a Google search or when posting to their social networks. As a best practice, it's a good idea to try and pull a few keywords or keyword phrases that might fit this description from each piece of content after it has been written. Ideally, those chosen keywords would then be placed in your title and section headers. When in doubt, though, always err on the side of writing content for people, not search engines.

What words or phrases is your target audience using when performing an Internet search to resolve a problem or fulfill a want or a need?

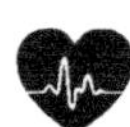

- What words or phrases do existing customers use when talking about your product or service both on your website and on their social networks?
- What words or phrases do existing customers use when speaking with sales and customer relations team members?

In addition to keyword optimization, there are a number of other useful "on-page SEO" techniques (most notably HTML schema markup) that can positively impact page performance.

To learn about on-page SEO techniques ->

Tool *Link Building*

An important search engine ranking factor, link building is concerned with increasing both the number and, more importantly, the quality of inbound links to a webpage. Inbound links are all incoming links to your website or specific webpage, and are also called backlinks, incoming links, inlinks, and inward links. Inbound links are relevant for two reasons: they create additional traffic to your website, and they indicate where that traffic is coming from. Link building or link marketing is a vital aspect of organic SEO. Popular link building tactics include content marketing (especially blogging), guest blogging, contests and promotions, and content sharing on social media, to name a few.

Rel="Author"

Like most humans, Google's search engine tends to place greater trust in content written by authors who consistently prove their authority on the subject they're writing about, and who are willing to connect their name to their work. Google's Authorship program allows you to attach your name to your content for all the world – and Google's web crawlers – to see. Many experts believe doing so can improve your "Author Rank," and thereby increase the likelihood of your content placing higher on Google's search engine results pages. Applying to the program involves linking your content to your Google Plus profile. Details about this process can be found on Google's Support Page.[15]

TACTIC: PAID SEARCH

As with paid social promotion, paid search offers brands numerous ways to micro target prospects and consumers. Here is a brief outline of the most standard tools in the field today.

Google AdWords

Google AdWords is the only way to advertise on the world's largest search engine. Google has greatly streamlined its process over the years, honing it down to just two simple steps:

1. Sign up for account, and design a campaign that includes a timeline and keywords.

2. Your ad will appear on the SERPs when users search for the keyword(s) you selected.

Google AdWords allows you to create text, image and video ads, and even provides a Keyword Planner tool that has a "wizard type interface." The new tool makes selected keywords more efficient and effective for your brand. Google also offers an Enhanced Campaigns function that integrates campaign management no matter the user device or location.

Yahoo!/Bing Network

As the name suggests, this is an ad network by the two other major search engines, which together account for nearly 30% of all online searches in the US. Apart from Yahoo! and Bing, the network features syndicated partner sites such as Facebook and Amazon, as well as networks like The Wall Street Journal Digital Network. For some, the main advantage of Bing Ads over Google AdWords is the customer support, which consists of real people providing actionable tips to solve your problems. Bing Ads generally have lower prices compared to AdWords, which is not surprising given that traffic levels on the Yahoo!/Bing network are lower than that of AdWords.[16]

Ad Retargeting

Thanks to the amazing growth of data aggregation, it is now relatively easy and inexpensive to place your message in front of the right people at the right time with retargeted ads. According to ad retargeting vendor AdRoll, only 2% of shoppers convert on the first visit to an online store.[17] Retargeting tracks the users who visit your site and displays your retargeted ads to them when they visit other sites online. Put another way, ad retargeting connects users with your message multiple times, not just once, increasing conversion rates. In addition to AdRoll, several vendors exist to help you set up and execute an ad retargeting strategy, including Retargeter, Fetchback and Chango.

Demand-Side Platforms (DSPs)

Demand-side platforms are similar to Google AdWords in that they are both buying platforms on which to purchase advertising and create ad campaigns. However, DSPs go beyond AdWords; while AdWords has been constructed primarily around search, keywords, and text ads within the Google network, DSPs have been designed around building display ad campaigns within a vendor-neutral real-time-bidding (RTB) environment.[16] There are many differences between the AdWords platform and DSPs, including the extent of reach, targeting options, data delivery, and pricing.

For an in-depth examination of paid search ->

In this chapter, we have outlined how you can utilize *IDM* best practices to Convey and Promote your organization's brand message throughout its digital ecosystem. Next, we will review how you can leverage *IDM* to Connect with and Convert new prospects and existing customers. For this, we turn to chapter 9.

- In order to break through the overwhelming amount of content on the Internet, your brand needs a clearly defined content strategy to connect the right message to the right people at the right time.

- A successful content strategy for any brand includes a varied mix of personalized content relevant to the consumer, including blogging and premium content.

- Each of the *"Big Seven"* social channels has unique posting and engagement strategies and paid advertising options; your brand's social media marketing efforts will serve to augment its *IDM* strategy.

- While the field of search is changing, organic SEO techniques such as keywords and link building, along with paid search tools such as AdWords and ad retargeting, are still pertinent to your brand's *IDM* strategy.

CHAPTER 9: CONNECT AND CONVERT

In chapter, 8, we explained that the second step in implementing the *IDM Strategic Model* is to Convey your brand message and other brand properties with content marketing, and then Promote the same using organic and paid search and social channels. In chapter 9, we will examine the third step, how to Connect with and Convert your target audience.

We use the term "Connect" in the sense, to establish a relationship or have a rapport. A well-executed *IDM* strategy conveys your brand message across all digital platforms in order to form personalized connections with your target audience, no matter the device or location they receive or access your brand.

We use the term "Convert" in the sense, to bring over or persuade. An *IDM* strategy is ultimately judged by its ability to Convert interested users or content consumers into product or service consumers and, eventually, brand advocates.

TACTIC: *SoLoMo*

Social and mobile technologies are two critical drivers of change fueling digital transformation. The seemingly limitless functionality of smartphones and tablets is opening up a new world of possibilities for consumers; increasingly sophisticated mobile users expect brands to provide contextually relevant online resources and personalized experiences that not only add value to their daily lives but can be conveniently accessed anywhere, anytime, on any device.

The widespread consumer adoption of social and mobile necessitates *SoLoMo* be an integral part of your *IDM* strategy. As you may recall from chapter 3, the term "*SoLoMo*" is an elision of three marketing elements:

1. *Social* – The platform you use to Convey and Promote your message and Connect with your target audience.
2. *Local* – Your area of concentration or relevant proximity; can be geographic or online.
3. *Mobile* – The medium of connection between your brand and its prospects and consumers.

SoLoMo best practices mandate that your brand ***Get Social, Think Local, and Integrate Mobile***.

1 *Get Social* – Actively engage on social media to Convey and Promote your brand message and Connect with your target audience. Content shared on social media channels amplifies your brand's online presence, while transparent social exchanges project its authenticity, fostering longstanding connections with new prospects and existing customers.

Social Data

People share personal information on their social channels. Therefore, think of your organization's social channels as "windows" into the thoughts, desires, wants, and needs of your prospects and customers. Your organization can use the data gleaned from social interactions to gain a better understanding of its audience. This kind of information allows for greater personalization of your brand message and marketing content, which in turn helps your organization form relationships (i.e. Connect) with those who have affinity for your brand.

A number of different software platforms are available to help you collect and manage social data, which we will discuss later in this chapter.

Social Advertising

In chapter 8, we touched on a number of paid social media promotion options (i.e. social advertising). Social advertising offers more than just a way to enhance the reach of your brand message; social advertising helps influence prospects at the Involvement stage of the *Digital Involvement Cycle*. At this stage, your prospects understand what they want or need and are actively searching for a solution provider. Social advertising during the Involvement stage should, therefore, clearly explain how your organization will resolve this want or need and concisely express why prospective buyers should work with you to do so. Product webinars, case studies, data sheets, FAQs, and free demos are some examples of Involvement-stage offers that can be included in social advertisements in order to Connect with your target consumers.

To learn how to incorporate social advertising into your *SoLoMo* strategy ->

2

Think Local – Social has created an environment where consumers expect brands to be online, transparent, and accessible, oftentimes 24/7. Transparency and accessibility create brand affinity. In addition, proximity makes it easier for consumers to find local* businesses that can best resolve a problem or fulfill a want or a need. Together, affinity and proximity create the kind of contextual relevance (top-of-mind awareness and connection) that ultimately drives sales or other conversion actions.

**Though we use the term "local" to mean businesses that are geographically proximate to the consumer, online proximity also exists, chiefly in relation the consumer's ability to find businesses that can most effectively service their needs.*

Each of the following proximity-based marketing tools is most effective when executed with a *SoLoMo* mindset within your *IDM* strategy.

Local SEO

Local SEO allows your organization to attract prospects and customers from your area – people for whom your products and services are most proximate. Here are a few best practices that will help your organization get found locally:

- *Localized Keywords* – To the extent you can, try to rank for local-focused long-tail keywords (i.e. more detailed or specific search queries). For example, if you are Milwaukee-based widget distributor, try and rank for "widget distributors Milwaukee Wisconsin." Don't be afraid to use these localized long tails in paid advertising as well.

- *Google Places/Local* – Google Places has been switched to Google Plus Local, although you still need to register your business by setting up a Google Places account, which you can then merge with your Google Plus Business Page if you already have one (quite confusing, we know). It is important to follow this registration process to ensure your brand shows up on Google Plus Local, Google searches and Google Maps. Keep in mind that customer reviews and recommendations on your Places/Google Plus Business Page are huge drivers of local SEO ranking on Google.

- *Bing/Yahoo!* – Lest we not forget the other major search engines, the Bing Business Portal allows you to manage your local business listing on Bing; Yahoo! Local also offers listings and reviews of local businesses.

- *AdWords Express* – Think of this as Google's geolocational ad targeting solution. With AdWords Express, when people search your area for the products or services you provide, an ad for your business will appear above or beside their search results. Your business will also be marked with a blue pin on Google Maps, helping it stand out to potential customers. AdWords Express is easy to set up, but there are limited ad targeting options, and businesses can only promote one product or service in any given geographic area; brands looking for more comprehensive solutions should turn to Google AdWords.

Social Check-Ins

Social media users can broadcast where they are, or "check-in," at any given time on their chosen network, sharing their location with followers. Social platforms such as Swarm (Foursquare), Yelp, Google Plus, and Facebook all have social check-in features. Admittedly, social check-ins lack the popularity they had a few years ago. However, anytime your patrons check-in at your location, your organization receives some free advertising. Your brand can experiment with the effectiveness of this tool by offering incentives to consumers to check-in at your establishment and then measuring results.

To learn how your organization can capitalize on social check-ins ->

- Among adult social media users ages 18 and older, 30% say that at least one of their accounts is currently set up to include their location in their posts.[1]
- 12% of adult smartphone owners say they use a geo-social service to "check in" to certain locations or share their location with friends.[2]
- Among these geo-social service users, 39% say they check into Places on Facebook, 18% say they use Foursquare, and 14% say they use Google Plus.[3]

Geofencing

A "geofence" is a virtual perimeter established around any physical space, such as a bar or restaurant, a retail location, an airport, or a stadium, that sends text notifications on an opt-in basis to mobile devices within its sphere. If your organization is a bricks-and-mortar establishment, you can use geofencing to entice customers passing by with coupons, discounts, or other promotions.

If your organization is seriously considering geofencing, you must first decide whether to go with an app-based or network-based solution.

For a detailed comparison of app-based and network-based geofencing ->

3 *Integrate Mobile –* Mobile devices are the driving force behind the SoLoMo paradigm. Three factors, in turn, drive the mobile user experience: convenience, simplicity, and proximity.

Mobile devices make our lives more convenient, allowing us to inform and entertain ourselves and communicate with each other more efficiently than ever. Mobile-optimized websites and mobile apps simplify the path to discovery, allowing us to accomplish more with less effort. Convenience and simplicity, when combined with proximity (whether geographical or online), create contextual relevance and top-of-mind awareness.

Mobile Optimization

For the mobile-optimized business, convenience, simplicity, and proximity come together to connect the organization with its target audience, increasing sales conversion and fostering brand advocacy. Here are three tools to help your organization optimize its mobile presence, the cornerstone of any effective *SoLoMo* strategy:

- *Mobile Apps* – Mobile apps are discrete software applications downloaded and installed on a mobile device rather than rendered on a browser. Mobile apps are built to pull content from the Internet (web app), download content onto a mobile device (native app), or operate with elements of both (hybrid app). In addition to a mobile app for your website, your organization may want to create specific-use mobile apps to simplify the user experience with your brand. As mobile usage proliferates, users are becoming more reliant on mobile apps for search and targeted needs discovery. Eventually many brands will offer some form of mobile app to enhance or simplify the user experience.

- *Mobile Website* – A mobile website is designed for the smaller displays and interfaces of smartphones and tablets. Like any website, a mobile website can show written content, data, images, and video. It can also access mobile-specific features such as click-to-call or location-based mapping. Mobile websites are much easier for users to find because their pages can be displayed in search results. In addition, visitors to your regular website can be sent to your mobile site when they are on a mobile device.

- *Responsive Web Design (RWD)* – As noted in chapter 7, RWD is a process for creating websites that optimize for smartphones and tablets of nearly every size. A well-built RWD uses flexible images, fluid layouts, and media queries to achieve a superior design and user experience no matter how it is sized. RWD can be a vital tool to connect with your consumers no matter where they are or what device they are using.

Mobile Optimization: L'Oreal

When L'Oreal launched a mobile website for hair care brand Redken, the company included a salon locator. Before mobile optimization, only 3% of salon searches were coming from mobile; after optimization, this number rose to 10%. After L'Oreal implemented mobile ads, the percentage of mobile salon searches rose to 23%.[4]

Mobile Advertising

Given the time spent with our smartphones and tablets, mobile is one of the best places to spend your ad dollars. Data suggests that mobile users not only click-through, but act on, the mobile ads they come across each and every day.

- In 2013, worldwide mobile ad spending was up 105.9% to over $18 billion.[5]
- 52% of smartphone users prefer receiving offers on their mobile device.[6]
- In 2013, mobile ads accounted for approximately 3.7% of all ad spend ($6.2 billion).[7]

Mobile-Friendly Ad Copy

As your organization begins to experiment with mobile advertising, make sure to craft mobile-oriented ad copy that is relevant to the on-the-go-consumer. Use mobile URLs when applicable; include business phone numbers, CTAs for content offers, and hyperlinks to directions, coupons, or web/social sites (e.g. Yelp, Google Plus, Yahoo! Local, etc.) that offer user-generated reviews of your brand.

Remember that the goal of your *SoLoMo* strategy is to communicate your brand message and product/ service information as efficiently as possible. Efficiency implies seamlessness and unification. Whoever your target audience, they are looking for simplicity, convenience, and proximity (i.e. efficiency). By providing a seamless customer experience over social, local, and mobile, you are adding value, thereby hastening the path to conversion.

TACTIC: LEAD NURTURING

Lead nurturing is not an end goal but rather an ongoing tactic that allows you to leverage content to more deeply Connect with your target audience, and in so doing, to more efficiently Convert leads into customers and brand advocates.

Building Lead Nurturing Campaigns that Connect and Convert

Figure 9.1: How-To-Video - Building Lead Nurturing Campaigns that Connect and Convert

Lead nurturing, in its most basic form, is defined as *"communicating consistent and meaningful touches with viable prospects regardless of their timing to buy."*[8] These "touches" rely on marketing content to Convey a message. As we discussed in the previous chapter, content helps brands form connections with people. Given this, lead nurturing is a tactic that helps your organization build deeper connections with prospects and customers by leveraging the content in which you Convey your brand message. Following are several tools you can use to create and implement lead nurturing campaigns that Connect and Convert.

Premium Content Offers

Premium content offers include ebooks, whitepapers, webcasts, video series, and many other forms of in-depth digital marketing content.

Unlike your business blog, which can be read without providing personal information, premium content offers give your brand an opportunity to turn site visitors into marketing leads. For example, rather than post your ebook on your website, you can offer it as a free download, where users must enter their name, email, and other basic demographic information in order to receive it. By doing so, your organization has now registered a new contact and formalized a new connection.

CTAs and Landing Pages

Premium content offers themselves are not very useful lead nurturing tools without a means of promotion. For this, we turn to engaging calls-to-action (CTAs) and attractive landing pages.

- Call-to-Action: A banner, button, or some other graphic or text on a web page, social platform, or email message directing the user to take a specific action, such as "click here," "download," "submit," or "purchase."
- Landing Page: A webpage that allows your brand to capture visitor information through a customized lead form.

CTAs and landing pages work in tandem to promote your premium content offers. A CTA directs user attention to the content offer, and the landing page "finishes the job," providing your prospects clear direction and leading them to the exact place they need to be in order to sign up for or download your offer.

The design and placement of CTAs and landing pages is tied to the nature of the content offer and its intended audience. As such, the design and placement of each tool requires careful thought and planning.

For further guidance on designing CTAs and landing pages that Connect and Convert ->

Email Campaigns

Your lead nurturing strategy does not end with the user converting to a lead or contact by navigating your CTA and landing page and downloading your content offer. Next, you must coordinate a well-timed, personalized email marketing campaign as a follow-up to their premium content download. Though the structure of the email campaign will vary depending on the content offer and your lead-nurturing goals, here are three general tips to consider:

1. *Number:* You want to send enough emails to build a lasting connection with your prospect, but you also want to avoid the label of "overbearing." While each campaign will have a distinct number of follow-up emails, as a rule, 3-5 is appropriate.

2. *Timing:* Consider the timing of each email. A "thank you" email may be sent immediately after downloading, while additional emails should be spaced out over the span of two to three weeks.

3. *Content:* Your emails must add value to your lead and not simply serve as a platform for your organization's self-promotion. Therefore, each email should include links to content that will provide additional information not covered in the initial premium content offer. Many email lead nurturing campaigns feature emails with progressive content offers for each stage of the buying cycle (e.g. top-of-the-funnel, middle-of-the-funnel, and bottom-of-the-funnel offers). The goal is to bring prospects, by degrees, from Awareness and Interest to Involvement and Commitment and, ultimately, Advocacy and Champion (see *Digital Involvement Cycle* – chapter 4)

TACTIC: LEAD CONVERSION

None of the above tactics and tools used to Connect with and Convert your target audience can be effectively executed without some way to digitally manage customer relationships. As consumers continue to demand more assistance and personalized marketing from brands, closely managing individual customer relationships has become a strategic imperative. Enter social customer relationship management (SCRM) software.

Social Customer Relationship Management (SCRM) Software

In chapter 5, we introduced the evolution of ***customer relationship management (CRM) to social CRM (SCRM).*** The primary purpose of traditional CRM software is to consolidate customer information into one repository, so it is better organized and relationships are more efficiently managed. Additionally, these software platforms automate routine processes and provide tools for measuring performance and productivity.

In the context of the digital marketplace, the "R" in CRM now represents an "interactive relationship." By integrating social media and customer relationship management, SCRM software enables your brand to truly listen to and monitor your prospects' and customers' conversations, participate in these conversations and other digital interactions, and manage ongoing customer loyalty and advocacy. With SCRM, you can track new leads from a Tweet or Facebook post, ebook download, or demo registration, and then interact with them as they move through the various stages of your *Digital Involvement Cycle*.

While systems vary in their functions and capabilities, the best SCRM software will include the following five core functions:

1. *Customer Data Management* – A searchable database to store customer information (such as contact information) and relevant documents (such as sales proposals and contracts).[9]

2. *Interaction Tracking* – The ability to document controlled conversations held by phone, in person, through email, or other channels. Interactions can be logged manually or automated with phone and email system integrations. In an attempt to provide a complete picture of the customer, SCRM also adds layers for tracking open, uncontrolled social interactions. It can document customer

interactions in public venues such as blogs, wikis, forums, social network sites, photo/video sites, and product review sites. With SCRM, organizations can shift to a customer-centric approach that transforms controlled conversations into open-ended dialogue, monitoring into collaboration. SCRM facilitates customer advocacy, co-creation, and input into brand and product development.[10]

3 *Engaging Relationships* – A simple way to engage with prospects and customers on a real-time basis through social media channels, community platforms, enterprise feedback management, product review sites, and social monitoring tools. SCRM shifts the focus from a one-on-one relationship with the customer to a more collaborative experience involving multiple customers and networks talking to each other and the brand.[11]

4 *Workflow Automation* – A means of standardizing business processes, usually through a combination of task lists, calendars, alerts, and templates. Once a task is checked off as complete, for example, the system might automatically set a task for the next step in the process.[12]

5 *Reporting* – Easily accessible reporting tools which management can use to track performance and productivity based on activities logged in the system, such as new contacts added to the database or amount of revenue generated. These tools can also be used for forecasting, such as for the next-quarter sales pipeline.[13]

The SCRM market is both expansive and varied, including such giants as Salesforce, Zoho, and Microsoft Dynamics

For a detailed look into the leading SCRM software options on the market today ->

In this chapter, we have explained how you can leverage your brand message and content to Connect with and Convert new prospects and existing customers. But how do you Measure and Refine these *IDM* best practices to ensure that your organization is operating efficiently and effectively? For this, we turn to chapter 10.

TAKEAWAYS

- Emerging mobile and social technologies necessitate that your organization *Get Social*, *Think Local*, and *Spend on Mobile*, making a *SoLoMo* strategy an integral part of your overall *IDM* strategy.

- Premium content offers, supported by engaging CTAs, attractive landing pages, and valuable follow-up emails comprise an effective lead nurturing campaign, an essential way to Connect with and Convert your prospects.

- Social customer relationship management (SCRM) software helps your organization cater its marketing efforts to the unique relationship each consumer has with your brand.

CHAPTER 10: MEASURE AND REFINE

In the previous chapter, we explained that the third step in implementing the *IDM Strategic Model* is to Connect with and Convert prospects and existing customers across all established digital channels. In this chapter, we will review the fourth and final step, how to Measure and Refine your *IDM* efforts.

We use the term "Measure" in the sense, to assess or consider carefully. To find success with *IDM*, you must consistently and judiciously evaluate all tactics and tools to measure actual outcomes against expected performance.

We use the term "Refine" in the sense, to fine tune or hone. Practitioners of a successful *IDM* strategy not only measure the performance of all tactics and tools, but use those insights to refine future *IDM* initiatives.

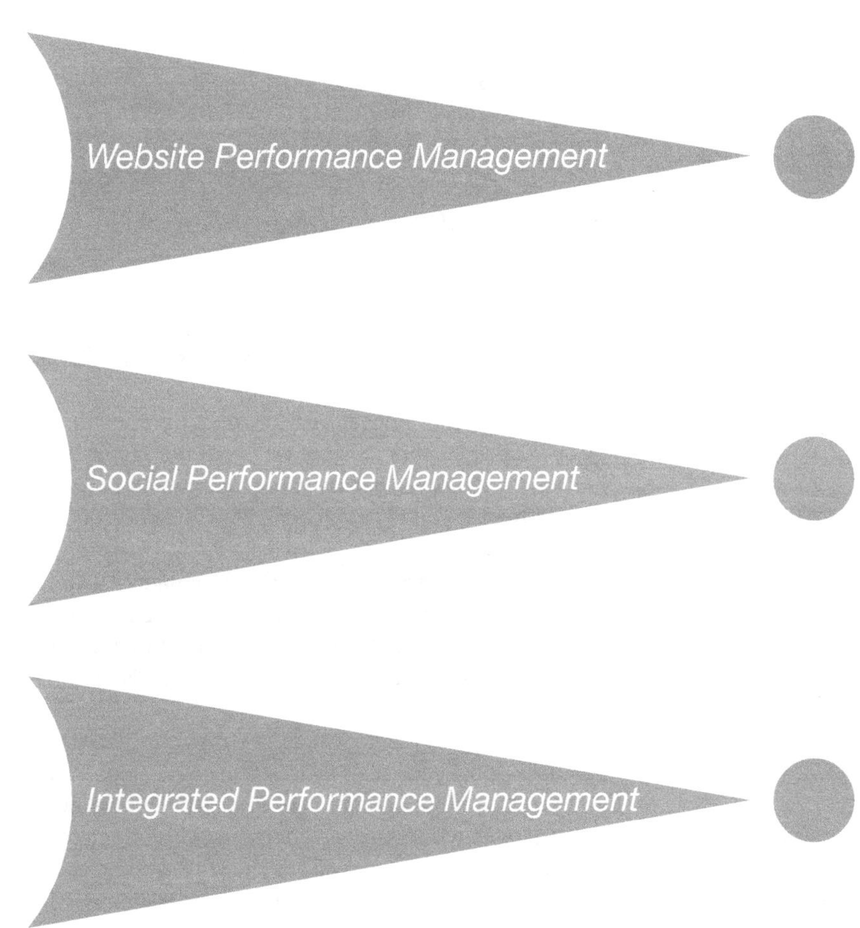

TACTIC: WEBSITE PERFORMANCE MANAGEMENT

As we noted in chapter 7, your website is the cornerstone of your *IDM* strategy. Below are some standard measurements to benchmark website performance. It is important to note that just because your website was effective a year or even six months ago does not mean it is still meeting the needs of your prospects and customers today. Returning to these benchmarks frequently will ensure your website is always optimized to meet their current expectations.

Popular Website Benchmarks

Unique Visitor Traffic – This is a tally of the total number of visitors to your site in a given time period (often measured monthly), not counting multiple visits from the same person or URL. Unique visitor traffic shows whether your web content and campaigns are driving new visitors to your site.

Repeat Visitors – Repeat visitors must be coming back to your site for a reason, presumably because they enjoy your content or connect with your brand message. You want to balance new visitors with repeat ones: too few repeat visitors suggests you're not putting out content that prospects find relevant and useful; too few new visitors means you're not growing your audience enough to generate new business.

Direct Traffic – Direct traffic comes from people who have typed your website's URL directly into their browser, visited your web pages via a bookmark, or clicked on an untagged link from an email or document you produced.[1] It stands to reason that, by creating content that conveys your brand message and then promoting it with social media and lead nurturing campaigns, you'll drive more direct traffic to your site.

Inbound Links – Also known as referral traffic, inbound links originate from a link on another site. Inbound links can help boost your site's search engine rankings. Your list of referring URLs should grow steadily over time as you produce more content that other site owners and bloggers want to share with their audience. Monitoring referral traffic will also give a clue as to which content is most likely to inspire inbound links.

Organic Traffic – This is the traffic generated from "organic" search queries, or search engine queries initiated by people who haven't a preconceived intent to visit your brand's website or engage with its online content. Organic traffic builds up your indexed webpages, i.e. the number of pages on your site that have received at least one visit from organic search. This metric tells you how many of your pages are being indexed by search engines and are getting found by users.[2]

Landing Page Conversion – Landing page conversion tracks site visitors who take a desired action, such as purchasing a product or filling out a lead generation form. By monitoring your conversion rates, you will know how well you have been capitalizing on the traffic coming to your site.[3] Specifically, pay attention to these three metrics:

1. Visitor-to-Lead Conversion Rate – the percentage of visitors who become leads.
2. Lead-to-Customer Conversion Rate – the percentage of leads who become customers.
3. Visitor-to-Customer Conversion Rate – the percentage of visitors who become customers.

Bounce Rate – A bit of a negative metric, bounce rate tracks the percentage of new visitors who leave your site after viewing only one page. Bounce rate tells you if you have the right audience coming to your pages and if you are meeting their expectations. According to Google, the average website bounce rate is 40%. This can be a misleading number, however, as a host of variables factor into website bounce rate:[4]

- industry
- brand credibility
- type of site
- type of page (content)
- where the page is located on the site
- stage of the customer lifecycle
- user intent

Here are Google Analytics' benchmark average bounce rates for various types of webpages:[5]

- 40-60% Content websites
- 30-50% Lead generation sites
- 70-98% Blogs
- 20-40% Retail sites
- 10-30% Service sites
- 70-90% Landing pages

A high bounce rate suggests your web pages are not fulfilling the expectations of your site visitors. Importantly, this may reflect issues with your overall *IDM* marketing strategy, such as having inbound links from irrelevant sources or not correctly optimizing landing pages for specific campaigns. A high bounce rate could also indicate problems with your site itself, such as confusing architecture, weak content, or unclear calls-to-action.[6]

Keyword Performance: Even though HTTPS/SSL encryption is rendering keyword tracking impossible, website keywords themselves are still relevant for SEO. A number of free tools exist to help you analyze keyword performance. For example, Google's AdWords Keyword Planner shares global performance metrics of specific keywords, which can be useful for researching keyword options, while Google Insights shows valuable keyword trends over time.

Organic Search Conversion Rates: One of your most important long-term website goals is conversion; this metric tracks any increases in the percentage of visitors who arrive at your site through organic search and complete a desired conversion action, such as becoming a lead or purchasing a product.[7] To round out the picture, you'll want to track specific landing pages visited throughout the conversion process.

Are visitors to our webpage engaging with your content or quickly pressing the "back" button?

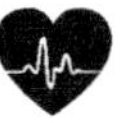

- On which pages of your website do visitors congregate? What's unique about these pages?
- How are visitors finding your site?

Website metrics are critical to your online success: they quantify what people like about your site and what they don't. If tracked and analyzed properly, website metrics can give you valuable insights that will help improve your overall *IDM* strategy and, ultimately, increase your website conversion.

You'll want to factor in all of these metrics when approaching a website redesign. Your organization's website redesign goals should be specific and measurable. Above all, your redesigned website should align with your organizational values and further your business goals.

For further insight into website redesign ->

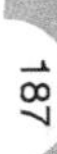

Free Measuring Services

There are several free web analytics software products on the market today, including Google Analytics, Google Webmaster Tools, Bing Webmaster Tools, and Yahoo! Web Analytics. Each of these tools can help you measure website traffic, conversion rates, bounce rates, visitor demographics, and much more.

For a detailed evaluation of the leaders in the free web analytics software space ->

Paid Measuring Services

As you might expect, there are a number of paid measuring services that can offer further insight into your website performance. Two popular ones are Crazy Egg and KISSmetrics. Crazy Egg aggregates your visitor data into heat maps to show you how users are engaging with your site, whereas KISSmetrics provides detailed tracking of your individual customers. Both platforms claim to fill the gaps left by free alternatives such as Google Analytics.

For a detailed evaluation of the leaders in the paid web analytics software space ->

TACTIC: SOCIAL PERFORMANCE MANAGEMENT

You've established your brand's social channels; you are actively conveying and promoting your brand message and connecting with your target audience through these channels. However, such actions mean little unless you know they are working effectively. Several metrics exist to help your organization aggregate and analyze social data, but some reveal more than others.

> *"The trick is to identify specifically what social data is relevant – and to analyze just exactly what that data means. There are a slew of metrics, tools, and services to help you make sense of your business' social data, as with any other data you're managing. As a general rule, seek out rates and more nuanced metrics; avoid overemphasizing simple counts and totals."*[8]
>
> Luke Chitwood, Tech Reporter, The Next Web.

While your organization's specific goals will influence the metrics you use to measure social performance, here is a brief list of common (and important) social metrics:

Channel Reports – Much as you dutifully researched and analyzed various social channels before establishing a brand presence on them, you must continually monitor key performance indicators (KPIs), including how many website visits, leads, and customers each individual social channel is generating.

Customer Response Rates – As more and more consumers take to social channels to engage with organizations, they rightfully expect responses from these brands. Therefore, it is vital to measure both the mentions of your brand on all social channels and your team's response rate to these mentions. Your team should aim for a 100% response rate to consumers, but resources and an overwhelming amount of mentions may inhibit achieving this goal. Nevertheless, monitoring your team's customer response rate is a useful exercise for understanding where you are at currently and for benchmarking future performance.

Customer Service Savings – This metric helps you quantify the actual cost savings generated by your organization's customer service efforts on social media. To calculate, multiply the average time of a customer service transaction on social media by the hourly cost of customer service, and multiply this by the number of customer service inquiries completed via your social channels. In other words:

Average Time x Costs per Hour x Customer Service Inquiries Completed = Savings[9]

Audience Growth Rate – While total number of followers is important, audience growth rate tracks your social media momentum. As your social media efforts progress from their inception, you can track different growth periods: did an event on your social channels two months ago have a similarily high audience growth rate as an event two days ago?

Average Engagement Rate – This metric goes beyond counting the number of "likes," "shares," and "retweets" a post receives. Your average engagement rate compares your posts' engagement with your overall follower base, allowing you to identify those whom are listening among your followers. Increasing your average engagement rate can positively impact your organization's social reach on Internet search engines and within the social platforms themselves. Here are two examples:

1. *Social Search* – Search engines take social cues, such as social shares, into account when they rank your content. For example, if you tweeted your article and have 2,300 followers compared to your competitor's 100 followers, you have a much better chance of generating social shares, and through the process, of ranking higher on SERPs (search engine results pages). In this way, social shares are more important to measure than audience size.[10]

2. *EdgeRank* – Similar to search engines, Facebook determines which posts are prioritized in its News Feed by the favorability of the posts, which is measured by how many people interact with them. Therefore, the more people who interact with your content, the more likely it will generate the activity needed to keep it prevalent in the feed. Make sure your content stays useful – don't waste time and resources employing shallow gimmicks merely to generate social engagement.[11]

- 38% of organizations are only measuring "likes," comments, and interactions on Facebook.[12]

- Only 24% of organizations already measuring their social media efforts are measuring the ROI of their social media campaigns.[13]

Online/Social Monitoring Services

One of the first goals of any organization on the *Path to Digital Integration* is to become customer-centric. Organizations must know what people are saying about their brand at all times; they can accomplish this by monitoring brand mentions on various online and social channels in real time (e.g. social posts, user-generated reviews, blog posts, forum discussions).

Online/social monitoring services can help you discover how and where people are speaking of your brand. The list of such services is varied and extensive in both functionality and cost (free or paid); however, many provide the following three operations:

- Track the keywords and phrases people use to find your website or landing pages.
- Monitor keywords and phrases used by clients, customers, competitors, and influencers in online discussions or social venues.
- Aggregate social data and analyze it based on sentiment, tone, and response required; some even provide the opportunity to respond in real time.

Alerts offer you instant knowledge of any webpage, newsfeed, blog, or discussion containing the keywords you designate for monitoring. Given their ease of set up and use, alerts are one of the simplest tools for online "listening." They are sent as email updates of the latest relevant search results based on your preselected queries. These might include

- Mentions of your brand or other targeted brand names.
- Customer comments or reviews.
- Competitive analysis.
- Industry trends.
- Conversations on developing news stories.

Google Alerts has been the standard for this service for many years. Recently, experts have contended that the service has deteriorated and is not comprehensive.[14] Talkwalker is another free and effective alerts service.

Social Mentions provide an additional layer of online/social monitoring, as they incorporate social media platforms and sentiment analysis to the basic alerts service.

- **SocialMention** is a free, widely used social media search and analysis platform that aggregates user-generated content from across the online universe into a single stream of information. This service monitors more than 100 social media properties, including the *"Big Seven,"* offering daily alerts and an API for embedding its feeds into other applications. In addition to the brand/keyword mentions, you'll be provided with sentiment ratings, top keywords used in conjunction with your brand, top users of your brand name (those mentioning it the most), as well as brand strength, passion, and reach metrics.

- Another popular option is **Mention**, which offers a limited free service with more advanced functionality for paid subscribers.

Multifunctional Dashboards provide a simple way to view from one central location (dashboard) three major social functions: conversation streams and searches, publication of posts, and analytics.

- **Hootsuite** has a robust dashboard which connects with 81 social apps, including the *"Big Seven,"* as well as Foursquare, WordPress blog, Reddit, Evernote, Tumblr, and a number of international platforms (e.g. Mixi {Japan}, Sina Weibo {China}, VK {Russia}). Hootsuite's dashboard allows the user to view multiple streams of conversations and searches, publish and schedule posts on various social tools, and develop reports using 30 different analytics platforms.

- Another option, Buffer, allows you to auto schedule posts throughout the day and week, and even provides performance analytics. In December of 2013, the company rolled out its enterprise-level solution, Buffer for Business.

Social Insights

There are many free services available to help your brand glean information and insight from particular social media platforms. Each of the *"Big Seven"* has their own analytics tools which provide a variety of data points. For example, Facebook has a comprehensive measurement system available on its site; Twitter provides an activity dashboard with detailed information on numerous engagement metrics, including tweet impressions, mentions, retweets, favorites, replies, and follows. YouTube also offers extensive analytics, including historical data on visitor demographics, traffic sources, retention, subscribers, comments, and sharing. See chapter 13 (page 247) for a more comprehensive list of leading social analytics platforms for business.

- **Simply Measured** is a popular tool providing insights from a variety of social platforms. It offers a free social media snapshot report that encompasses key insights from major social platforms like Facebook, Twitter, Google Plus, LinkedIn, Instagram, and Vine, along with a more robust paid subscription option.

Social Media Management

There are a number of paid software tools that allow organizations to manage social media-related activities across the enterprise. Although several of these tools attempt to handle the full range of social-related activity, many have particular strengths in one or more areas, and companies often use more than one product to manage their social media presence.[15] Typical areas of focus include

- Social listening/monitoring.
- Sentiment analysis.
- Social customer support.
- Social publishing/engagement.
- Social campaigns/content.
- Social promotions (sweepstakes/contests).
- Social curation.

Some of the more popular tools include Radian6, Sprinklr, SproutSocial, and Spredfast.

TACTIC: INTEGRATED PERFORMANCE MANAGEMENT

Thus far we have discussed website- and social-specific measuring and monitoring options. Each of these is important; however, in order to effectively Measure and Refine your entire *IDM* strategy, you need an integrated performance management system, also referred to as marketing automation software, which has built-in web, social, customer relationship management (CRM), and content management software (CMS) functions.

Popular marketing automation software options include HubSpot, Marketo, Eloqua, and Lyris. These systems provide in-depth marketing analytics through one unified platform. See chapter 13 (pages 243-5) for a more detailed treatment of marketing automation software.

In this chapter, we have outlined the various metrics you can use to Measure and Refine your organization's website and social performance, thereby completing our review of the tactics and tools needed to properly execute an *IDM* strategy. In the next unit, we will turn our attention to outlining how your organization can efficiently implement such a strategy.

Measuring and Refining Your IDM Strategy

Figure 10.1: How-To-Video – Measuring and Refining Your IDM Strategy

- Routinely measure such metrics as unique visitor traffic, landing page conversion, and keyword performance to ensure your website is continually optimized to meet your consumers' needs and wants.

- Social metrics such as "likes," "shares," and "retweets" are important, however, they don't offer the complete picture of your social performance. For this, look to more nuanced metrics such as average engagement rate and individual social channel reports.

- Although numerous online and social media monitoring services are available, effectively measuring your *IDM* performance necessitates an integrated performance management system.

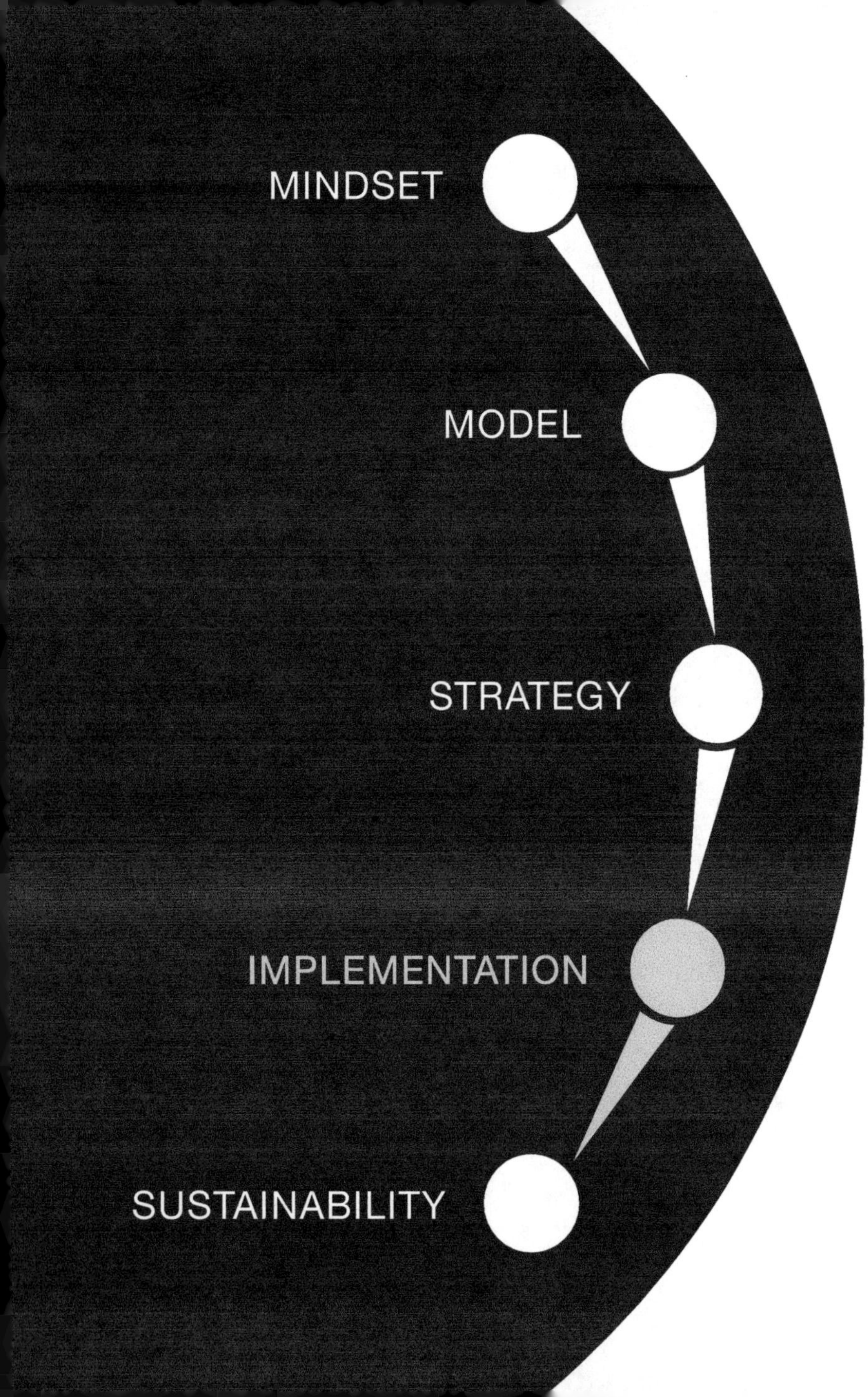

MINDSET

MODEL

STRATEGY

IMPLEMENTATION

SUSTAINABILITY

Chapter 11: Digital Alignment

Chapter 12: Structural Integration

Chapter 13: Evaluation and ROI

Now that you have a better understanding of the tactics and tools used to build an *Integrated Digital Marketing* strategy, you must learn how to properly execute its implementation. Digital implementation is a multi-step process, which will be addressed in detail throughout chapters 11-13. It begins with executive buy-in and the alignment of organizational goals to incorporate digital. It then moves on to digital preparation – understanding how the leaders of an organization must expand their digital mindset, and the staff their digital literacy. For communication to be more open and collaborative, an organization's cultural diversity must be bridged, its structure modified to be less hierarchical and more agile. Finally, a measurement and evaluation strategy needs to be developed to determine the return on investment (ROI) of digital, and to make any adjustments to refine the process.

As a reminder, you can access in-depth information, videos, and updates from our *Digital Marketing Resource Center* (www.dmresourcecenter.org) wherever you see this icon.

CHAPTER 11: DIGITAL ALIGNMENT

Digitally Integrated Organizations are innovators in today's marketplace. Most businesses and non-profits are striving toward that end. This often begins when organizations execute digital media campaigns to grow their brand, and to more efficiently move new prospects and existing customers through the *Digital Involvement Cycle*. If successful, these campaigns often serve as a catalyst for combining traditional and digital media into an integrated marketing strategy, and for introducing digital into other aspects of the enterprise. In fact, many organizations are striving to implement digital at all levels, realizing it is the indispensable ingredient for competitive advantage in the future.

Organizations can accomplish this by following the *Path to Digital Integration*, aligning their core values with their business goals, and then operationalizing these goals with actionable digital strategies, tactics, and tools that can be meaningfully implemented throughout the organization.

 BROAD LEARNING SOLUTION'S APPROACH

To better understand this, let's review **Broad Learning Solution's** approach as the company attempts to implement digital throughout their organizational framework. Here are the actionable components necessary for digital alignment:

- *Align business goals with digital as a strategic imperative; executive and staff buy-in.*
- *Expand executive competencies to guide organization-wide digital transformation.*
- *Adopt a digital mindset and improve technical literacy throughout the organization.*
- *Bridge diverse cultures to facilitate effective communication, collaboration, and innovation.*

To stay competitive, BLS has just purchased a cloud-based language training software application. Bill, BLS' CEO, has set a high priority on launching the app via digital media, and has completely bought in to the necessity of the company developing an online presence. Unfortunately, because of his lack of digital maturity (preparedness and literacy), he will need to delegate this responsibility to Rosa, the new director of digital marketing. As a digital integrator, Rosa has the expertise to design BLS' strategic marketing plan and incorporate it with broad data solutions.

Her first order of business is to audit the level of digital literacy of her staff (which runs the gamut in age and experience with digital technologies).[1] Then she needs to work with CMO Samir to better understand the existing BLS culture, design an *Integrated Digital Marketing* strategy for the new app, and jointly develop their leadership competencies in order to guide this embryonic digital organization. The two will collaborate to provide training for San, Quincy, and other entry-level associates on the strategic priorities for BLS and how to optimize the implementation of the chosen digital tactics and tools. This training will accelerate the junior staff's competencies in marketing strategy and digital media, and teach them effective ways to communicate across the various cultures within BLS.

"Markets today are complex and multidimensional, and leadership isn't about control but about enabling and empowering networks.... The type of leadership we need finds its full expression in the DNA of collaborative technology"[2]

Steve Sargent, President, CEO, GE Australia & New Zealand 

Finally, Rosa will work with Samir and James, the Chief Information Officer (CIO), to select marketing automation software that will enable BLS to monitor customer responses to the company's new app and customer movements through the *Digital Involvement Cycle* (see chapter 4), and gauge the overall effectiveness of its *IDM* strategy.

Now that we've set the scene, let's take a deeper dive into what each of our BLS employees will face as they strive to develop and implement an *IDM* strategy. Bill has invited Rosa into a morning closed-door session to brief him, Samir, and James on the steps required for BLS to do so. The following is a snapshot of their questions and Rosa's answers, the latter of which summarize some best practices of innovative *DIOs*.

Q: What is Digital Alignment?

A: Digital alignment is the harmonizing of the organization's core values and business goals with its digital marketing strategies and tactics, infrastructure, and information systems. Digital alignment is a strategic imperative to enhance performance, ROI, and sustainable growth. As the organization becomes digitally aligned, it develops a new method of doing business, where technology, people, and processes are integrated seamlessly.

Q: How does our CMO align company goals with changing strategies and technologies?

A: Samir must develop an *Integrated Digital Marketing* strategy. Digital alignment requires BLS to be constantly vigilant and agile, to anticipate and make timely changes to any of the *Five Modules of IDM* strategy. (Figure 11.1) All the *Modules* are interdependent: any changes in our core values, marketing tactics, or digital technologies will result in adjustments to both our goals and expected outcomes.

For example, if Apple announced a new iPad designed specifically for K-12 students, BLS would be faced with disruption in both technology and marketing, as we had not previously considered K-12 students and their parents as a primary target market for the company's language learning app. In reality, though, this new Apple initiative might open up significant opportunities.

BLS' adoption of a digital mindset and acceptance of the core values of the digital culture, such as openness to change, will help our staff better prepare for such disruptions, eventually regarding them as strategic opportunities rather than obstacles. By contrast, traditional strategic marketing plans are more linear – goals affect marketing initiatives which, in turn, produce outcomes. Isolated departments compete to leverage opportunities, find solutions, and obtain new company resources.

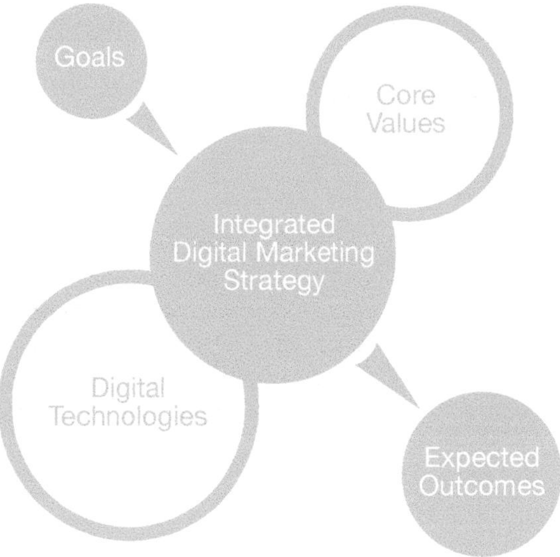

Figure 11.1: The Five Modules of IDM Strategy

In the context of BLS' emerging digital strategy, Samir should recognize the new iPad as a perfect fit for the company's language learning app. He should engage James and the sales director to design a collaborative solution. They should respond quickly, adjusting their goals, *IDM* strategy, expected outcomes, and resources allocated to correspond with the launch date of the new iPad. In this case, BLS' agility in realigning the marketing initiatives and design elements of the new app will give the company a competitive edge.

Q: How do I prepare BLS for the transition to a Digitally Integrated Organization?

A: Bill, given that you have committed BLS to the digital track, we only have one choice – to make the adoption of digital across all departments an organization-wide priority. This translates to training the existing management team and employees as well as hiring new leadership talent.

> *"CEOs are making critical judgments about disruptive technology without firsthand knowledge."*[3]
>
> *Leading Through Connections*, IBM Global CEO Study

The following 11-step process will help BLS prepare for the transition to a *Digitally Integrated Organization*:

Adopt a Digital Mindset – Our executives must understand that the digital evolution is not merely comprised of the next hot social media tool. Rather, it is an all-encompassing paradigm shift that demands a corresponding shift in thinking. The digital mindset is grounded in a foundation of openness, flexibility, collaboration, and shared network thinking. The BLS management team needs to adopt a digital mindset (Figure 11.2) and integrate it into how they communicate and interact with their employees, consumers, and the greater community.

As Mark Begor, Director of GE Capital's real-estate business suggests, *"leaders need to acquire a mind-set of openness and imperfection, and they must have the courage to appear 'raw' and unpolished – traits that may be as challenging for them as developing the creative and technical-production skills."*[4]

2 *Build a Collaborative, Interdisciplinary Team* – In designing and implementing a *DIO*, BLS must first harmonize the company's infrastructure across the traditional silos of sales, information technology (IT), human relations (HR), operations, public relations (PR), advertising, and marketing. Each silo must transition to a collaboration of leaders whose roles (e.g. CMO, CIO) are redefined. Clearly, these departments are not dissolved, but rather are integrated in new ways for more effective decision-making.

3 *Develop an Integrated Digital Marketing Strategy* – Integrated marketing communications (IMC) refers to combining traditional marketing concepts with the Internet and social media to effectively connect with target markets. *Integrated Digital Marketing* builds on IMC by weaving digital, consumer advocacy, and broad data into a more comprehensive and responsive strategy. It recognizes the changing customer touch points and brings together converged media, integrating online, social, and mobile. (See chapter 6)

BLS management needs to design a comprehensive, dynamic *IDM* strategy that leverages the chaos and addresses changes in the marketplace. It can do so by continuously gathering and incorporating target audience data to refine the company's online brand presence and achieve key performance indicators (KPIs).

4 *Understand Consumer Empowerment* – BLS managers need to leverage the new power of the consumer by gaining input on brand, product, and distribution, and by prioritizing customer service. With the explosion of the Internet, social, and mobile, consumers are expanding their influence as product reviewers and sources of trusted information. BLS must build a social community of product advocates and brand champions.

5 *Build a Powerful, Responsive Social Brand* – Social brands need to respond to consumers and generate value to their social communities. They need to combine insights from social engagement and mentions, focus groups, and consumer/employee feedback to develop the brand promise and value proposition. The BLS brand must be aligned with its customers' needs and feedback. By convening an online customer advisory group, BLS can gain valuable input into the design of new products and marketing strategies.

6 *Create Relevant Content* – For BLS, as with other brands, content drives the customer experience (CX). For success in this rapidly changing digital environment, the marketing team must develop content that is easy to access and provides value to its target audience. Content is not about broadcasting ads to sell more language learning software, but about engaging and involving language learning students and creating an unparalleled CX. Regular blog posts on various aspects of language learning would be considered valuable content.

7 *Generate Customers from Social Communities and Global Networks* – The shared network lies at the core of *Integrated Digital Marketing*. Through social network analysis, Samir and James can match common interests and buying patterns with digital consumer behaviors, providing access to new communities of potential consumers. BLS can target emerging markets (e.g. Asia, South America) where digital has been embraced to launch new products.

8 *Leverage Data Appropriately* – Big data is the new digital buzzword for consultants and large corporations. They use it to aggregate and analyze social messages and weave the results into their digital strategy. BLS managers (e.g. small- and mid-size corporate and non-profit managers) need to expand their thinking to encompass broad data, or the collecting and leveraging of appropriate levels of data related to the company's size and goals. There are significant sources of "low hanging data" that can be plucked and readily integrated into marketing strategies. BLS must gather data from language training centers and colleges to anticipate needs and trends in language learning in order to continually adjust their product line.

9 *Monitor Digital Footprint* – Listening to feedback and using social tools to monitor company chatter and social performance are the building blocks of responsive strategies. Alerts, analytics, and social mentions can provide BLS with real-time insight into the organization's digital footprint and guide timely adjustments.

10 *Evaluate Digital ROI* – Digital return on investment (DROI) helps brands analyze the performance of traditional and digital tools in achieving company goals. This expanded ROI (see chapter 13) reflects companywide performance in the digital environment. It considers the impact of digital technologies on brand engagement, customer relationships, and advocacy, in addition to traditional action metrics of exposure, sales, and profit.

Demonstrate the Value of the Social Enterprise – BLS teams need to integrate digital technologies to generate innovation and collaboration throughout the organization to ensure market position and growth. They need to create a social business environment that inspires change and innovative solutions. Doing so will create long-term sustainability.

Developing a Digital Mindset

Figure 11.2: Developing a Digital Mindset – Video[5]

What conditions are critical to the successful organization-wide adoption of a digital mindset?

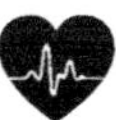

- How the management team personally adjusts.
- How situational leadership is implemented.
- How the organization manages the paradoxes in the transition to the digital mindset.

Q: How do you begin to connect the digital dots between functional departments?

A: Clearly, the old BLS departments are in transition from independent entities to integration. BLS management needs to guide this transition by building collaborative bridges. Here is a three-step process for doing so:

1. Invite all department leaders to cooperate in addressing a challenge of mutual interest (e.g. moving the customer through the *Digital Involvement Cycle*). Request that each participant prepare three documents for the meeting:

    - Suggestions to augment BLS' marketing strategy in order to move more customers through the *Cycle* to purchase and product advocacy.
    - A short presentation highlighting their department's best digital practices and case examples.
    - Recommendations for collecting data from potential and current customers moving through the *Cycle*, and suggestions for how this data can be effectively used to achieve specific goals.

2. Have the group identify two or three initiatives that are linked to the goals and expected outcomes of the *IDM* strategy and tied to quantifiable metrics.

3. Offer weekly trainings on topics requested by the group. Each session should include a collaborative task.

Q: As we build a team to implement our IDM strategy, what competencies do we need to develop internally or look for externally when hiring new team members?

A: To better understand the leadership competencies required to become a *Digitally Integrated Organization*, it's useful to review the findings of a research study conducted by General Electric (GE). The study compiles interviews of many GE officers, mostly digital immigrants, from different businesses and regions to develop a model for "social media-leadership," although the model translates to digital leadership as well.[6]

The study describes such leaders as having six overlapping roles and capabilities (Figure 11.3).[7]

Role	Skill	Competency
Producer	Create compelling content; hone technical skills	Inspire strategic creativity
Distributor	Sustain body of social followers	Leverage communication and dissemination dynamics
Recipient	Use intelligent filtering for timely responses	Manage communication flow
Adviser	Raise digital media literacy of staff and stakeholders	Drive strategic digital media utilization
Architect	Leverage diverse digital tactics and tools	Balance accountability with collaboration
Analyst	Anticipate and respond to the next paradigm shift	Monitor digital trends and innovations

Figure 11.3: Roles, Skills, and Competencies of Social/Digital Leadership

Building digital literacy within the organization is critical to competitive advantage. Here are a few ways today's emerging digital leaders can accomplish this:

- Require a collaborative skill set to bridge siloed departments.
- Blend strategic and tactical approaches.
- Stay focused on the next disruption and on creating new business models.
- Be efficient in attracting better talent and tapping into the capabilities of current employees (e.g. integrate various roles not currently combined).

"Creativity is essential to drive innovation, as is courage, risk taking, and reinvention. This is not limited just to how Coke goes to market. It means having to reinvent the company and the way it's it is structured and networked internally and externally. It is our ability to adapt, to participate in, and even lead in culture, that will allow us to achieve our business goals."[8]

John Tripodi, CMO and COO of Coca-Cola

Q: How do we encourage innovation?

A: For BLS to continue to develop into a *DIO*, we need to facilitate ongoing innovation. Here are a few insights from Terry Jones, former CEO of Travelocity and now Chairman of Kayak.com, on how to use innovation to spur company growth in today's digital environment:

- Free-up Channel Communication – Jones suggests that we remove the middle management layer, or "Bozone" Layer, that stifles innovation by using smaller, more effective teams to encourage new ideas to move up the channel. Most innovation comes from the bottom, from those who are talking to customers.[9]

- Hire the Right People – Jones believes in hiring people who don't fit the mold. If everybody is cut from exactly the same cloth, then you probably are not going to get a lot of unorthodox thinking; you're just going to keep doing what you did, and if you do that, you're going to have the same result you had before.[10]

- Encourage Innovation, Take Risks – According to Jones, 20% of everything you see on the Kayak website is a test; he encourages testing and does not punish failure. He believes companies should "kill projects, not people." Certainly, there are different levels of risk with respect to how much innovation an organization can tolerate, but it's important to create a culture in which people are encouraged to come forward with their ideas, and where those ideas are accepted; where, if the idea is bad, the idea is punished, not the person.[11]

Q: We seem to have a clash of cultures among the three generations that make up our organization. How do we address disparities in digital literacy?

A: First, organizational culture is the biggest hurdle to the adoption of a digital mindset and digital integration. People and their cultures are difficult to change. There are four archetypes of organizational culture, each with different leadership styles, values, and beliefs about effectiveness.[12]

1. Internally-focused, hierarchical cultures: focus is on control-based systems.
2. Internally-focused, collaborative cultures: focus is on interpersonal relationships.
3. Externally-focused, market cultures: focus is on customer service and competitiveness.
4. Externally-focused, innovation-based cultures: focus is on the future and managing discovery.

Bill, you need to understand the members of your management team and see how their leadership styles, values, and beliefs contribute to the organizational culture of BLS. These must be acknowledged and then agreement made as to how your team can blend them together to create a single overarching culture that reflects the organization's core values and business goals.

To foster effective communication between generations, sometimes referred to as generation collaboration, you need to find bridges that engage and inspire everyone.[13] Here are some ideas:

- Employ Familiar Processes – Use project management tools familiar with older generations and accepted by younger generations.
- Level the Playing Field – Use internal online forums to crowdsource new opportunities and challenges; this will democratize the exchange of ideas. Working groups that include multiple generations will facilitate cooperation.
- Transparency is the Standard – Open, transparent communication will allow all employees to understand and appreciate the contributions of others. Transparency increases trust and collaboration, which are both vital to competitive advantage in the digital age.
- Reverse Mentoring – Connect digitally-savvy Millennials with senior leaders to discuss the latest technologies and social buzz. This GE Leadership University practice exposes leaders to the digital mindset, encouraging experimentation and relationships with future managers. Nick Tran, head of social media at Taco Bell, supports this approach: *"Our method is hiring Millennial-minded individuals because they live and breathe social media. The digital natives entering the workforce today are passionate about social; by having them dispersed throughout our teams, we are staying on the forefront of trends...then everyone in the organization contributes to this sort of "think tank," or social center of excellence."*[14]
- Be Flexible – Offer flexible, "work from anywhere" options to bridge generations. Mobile technology is about freedom, efficiency, and innovative solutions. (e.g. working mothers can contribute from home).

"One of the things we look at is our holistic media plan that is online and offline and how they work together, because they do.... Everybody must be aligned with the same goal, which is something we do. If people don't have common goals, sometimes they unintentionally work against one another. La Quinta has the same revenue goals across the whole team. We have individual goals by functional area but they all ladder up to the number one goal and what we are trying to accomplish."[15]

Julie Carey, Chief Marketing Officer, La Quinta Inns and Suites, from *The Integrated Marketing Playbook*, IgnitionOne

Q: Rosa, the real question is, how do I manage change and chaos?

A: Bill, in our continually evolving, digitally integrated environment, your title of CEO has expanded to that of chief entrepreneurial officer. As your title has morphed, so too have the old definitions of leadership, competitive advantage, and ROI. The digital landscape is a sea of constant change and chaos, a state of perpetual flux. There is not one model or answer for managing a digital organization. *Fast Company's*' article, *Generation Flux*, reflects this sentiment, featuring interviews with a new breed of CEOs who share their approaches to reinventing their products and organizations. The answer to your question is embedded in their comments:[16]

- *"There's so much chaos all around; you can't prevent the chaos, only respond to it...quickly."*
- *"Traditional organizational structures no longer seem sufficient."*
- *"YOU HAVE TO BUILD AN ORGANIZATION THAT IS CAPABLE OF ACTING LIKE A STARTUP BUT CAN OPERATE AT LARGE SCALE SIMULTANEOUSLY."*

Here are six recommendations for managing digital transformation supported by national studies of CEOs from businesses[17] and non-profits:[18]

Be involved in shaping and driving your organization's digital goals and strategy. Successful programs require clear leadership and strong governance from the top.

2 Maintain regular contact with your team; they need your feedback and support.

3 Expand digital beyond marketing and communications; it can transform every aspect of your business model.

4 Budget digital as a long-term investment; as infrastructure, not as marketing media.

5 Adopt flexible budgeting. Reserve some 5-15% of your project budget to fix or optimize functions that don't perform; seize dynamic opportunities; reinvest in things that work.

6 Focus on digital literacy. Your team needs to have the mindset, knowledge, and confidence to make business-critical decisions about digital investments.

For insight into applying digital transformation best practices within your organization ->

Social Literacy for Competitive Advantage

"Social-media engagement will confront leaders with the shortcomings of traditional organizational designs. Leaders who address these shortcomings will learn how to develop the enabling infrastructure that fosters the truly strategic use of social technologies. When organizations and their leaders embrace the call to social-media literacy, they will initiate a positive loop allowing them to capitalize on the opportunities and disruptions that come with the new connectivity of a networked society. And they will be rewarded with a new type of competitive advantage."[19]

McKinsey and Company study

- Constant change, chaos, and disruption are the CEO's new reality; as organizational leaders, CEOs need to embrace change, seeing it as a strategic opportunity rather than a threat.

- Traditional organizations were not designed to reflect the core values of the digital culture; this new reality requires new structures and approaches.

- The *DIO* requires constant inputs of data generated from various touch points (e.g. employees, partners, customers, online, and social media).

- Business leaders need to anticipate and leverage this data and the forces of change to create new strategic opportunities.

- In today's continually evolving, digitally integrated environment, the title of CEO has expanded to that of chief entrepreneurial officer.

CHAPTER 12: STRUCTURAL INTEGRATION

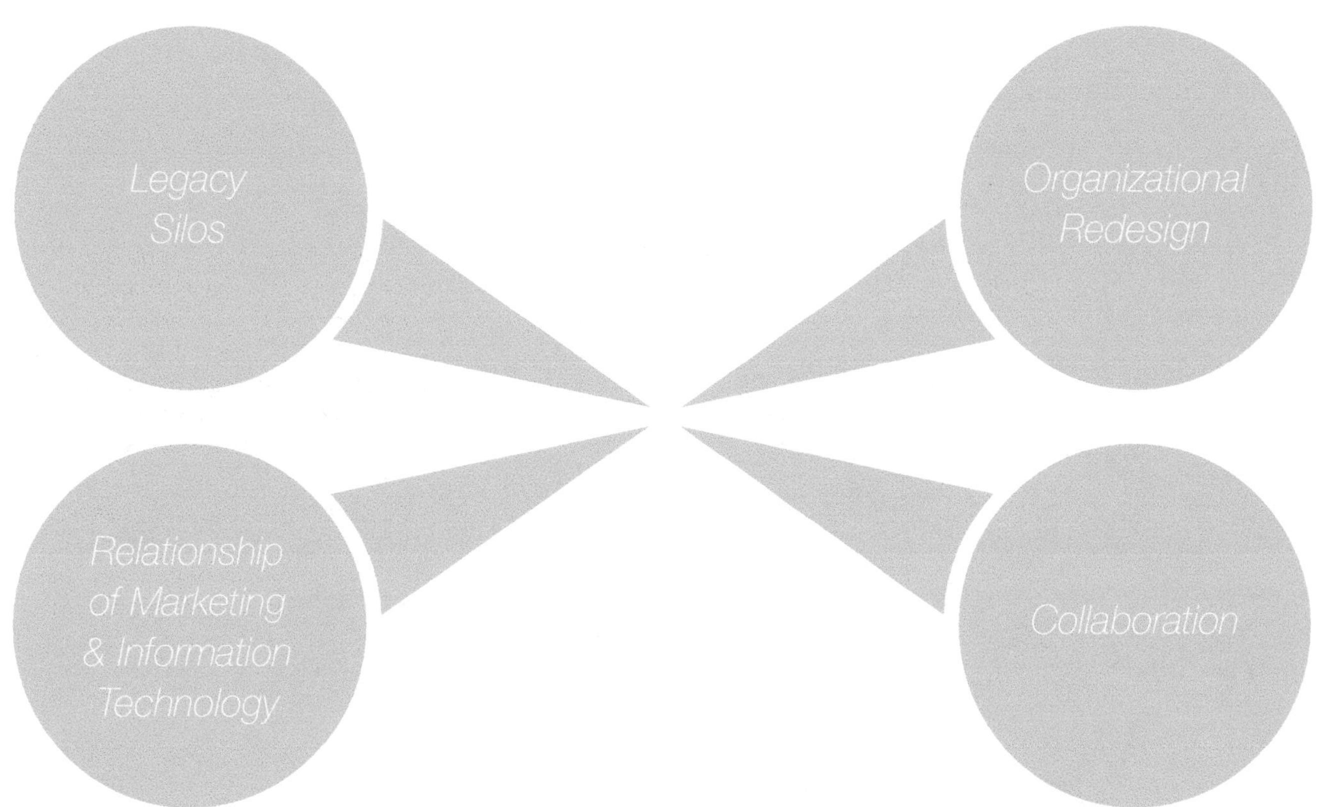

In chapter 11, we examined the organizational buy-in, preparedness, leadership, and culture necessary for digital alignment and transformation. Acting as a catalyst for digital transformation, digital alignment governs not only the external activities, but also the internal functions, of an organization. In this chapter, we will review how organizational structure and policy can encourage – or inhibit – digital alignment and transformation; ultimately, it is the internal processes of an organization that define their success or failure.

Specifically, this chapter will address the following three questions:

1: *Why is organizational structure, a topic traditionally addressed in the human relations department, integral to the future of marketing?*

Because marketing is no longer a siloed function, but instead a process that is integrated throughout the organization.

In a compelling piece entitled, "We're all marketers now," a team at McKinsey and Company provided some insight into this important question: *"[Customers] don't separate marketing from their in-store or online experience—it is the experience. In the era of engagement, marketing is the company.... Companies of all stripes must not only recognize that everyone is responsible for marketing but also impose accountability by establishing a new set of relationships between the function and the rest of the organization.... As that transformation happens, the marketing organization will look different: there will be a greater distribution of existing marketing tasks to other functions; more councils and informal alliances that coordinate marketing activities across the company; deeper partnerships with external vendors, customers, and perhaps even competitors; and a bigger role for data-driven customer insights.... CMOs and their C-suite colleagues must collaborate intensively to adapt their organizations to the way customers now behave and, in the process, redefine the traditional marketing organization."*[1]

Furthermore, digital communications manifest both internal and external to the organization, and digital technologies necessarily cut across and impact all independently run silos. If legacy structures block innovation, change, internal communication, and collaboration, then movement along the *Path to Digital Integration* is severely compromised.

2: *Digital is transforming many traditional marketing practices. Why, then, do most marketing departments and business organizations basically look the same as they did 20+ years ago?*

Simply put, because they have retained the same structure.

Each organization's unique structure reflects the way decisions are made, communications are sent and received, innovations are processed, rewards are dispensed, and ultimately, the speed and extent of digital integration. John Kotter, an expert in leadership and strategy at Harvard Business School, expands on this idea: *"Almost all companies organize people in a hierarchy.... The hierarchical organization that we see today was invented in the last century...it opposes change, strives to standardize processes, solve short-term problems, and achieve stopwatch efficiency within its current mode of operating.... The hierarchy ignores new opportunities that require transformation because these don't align with its core purpose of maintenance and optimization. A market opportunity for tablet computers, for example, is more of a distraction than an opportunity to the hierarchy of a giant PC manufacturer focusing on this quarter's earnings targets."*[2]

3: How can the "organizational paradox" of digital be resolved?

Throughout the globe, C-suite executives expect new digital technologies will transform their businesses, but more than 50% note that existing organizational structures and IT systems are not designed to meet their digital business priorities.[3]

This causes stress, reduces innovative thinking, and inhibits the adoption of the mindset needed for digital transformation.

Bill faces the same organizational paradox at BLS as he attempts to guide his company toward digital integration. To clarify the challenges, he's invited a digital integration consultant to work with his management team. After an organizational audit, the consultant noted four major areas of focus:

- Legacy Silos
- Organization Redesign
- Relationship of Marketing and IT
- Collaboration

Bill and his team (including the CMO, CIO, CFO, and director of digital marketing) brought their questions and concerns to the meeting; the consultant shared some new perspectives and recommendations. The following is an outline of their dialogue.

LEGACY SILOS

Our hierarchical, top-down organizational structure seems inefficient and slow to respond in the digital age. We know we need to make changes but don't know where to begin.

As a company, you must first define BLS' objectives and expected results before you can make any changes in organizational structure.

Accordingly, the team brainstormed a number of objectives and expected results (Figure 12.1).

Objectives	Expected Results
Facilitate employee collaboration and communication; encourage innovation	Improve product offerings and customer experience
Create an enjoyable work environment	Attract better talent
Reduce departmental competition	Become more competitive
Boost agility and speed of decision	Increase efficiency
Connect with customers and partners	Enhance the bottom line
Promote organization-wide digital integration	Build a *Digitally Integrated Organization (DIO)*

Figure 12.1: Structural Change: Objectives and Expected Results

Many of your objectives begin with integration; it is the currency of the *DIO*. It is also the key component in addressing your objectives and realizing your expected results. The *DIO* integrates

- planning processes across cross-functional teams.
- digital and traditional strategies.
- independently operating departments.
- communication between management and employees, the organization and consumers, and the organization and the community.

Integration is the foundation of BLS' future digital agility and structural change. It utilizes digital technologies, blending different approaches to challenges and opportunities to realize optimal solutions. It is built on the core values of the digital culture: trust, openness, and equality – all requirements for internal organizational change.

The integration of existing silos can be approached in two ways: by fundamentally changing the relationships and communication patterns between silos, or by eliminating existing silos altogether.

In either case, successful structural change requires an internal shift in organizational mindset on seven dimensions:

1. *Loyalty* – Silos are often organized as separate entities with their own agendas, deliverables, and budgets. This mindset has to change: loyalty to the organization must necessarily come first, creating a shared consciousness. Silos and personal agendas must be set aside; employees should be loyal to the organization's mission, as it unites effort, expertise, and resources.

2. *Empathy* – It is impossible to change an organization from within unless both the management team and the employees feel the pain and understand the necessity for change to sustain the organization.

"Creating an organization where the best ideas win starts with instilling what he [General Stanley McChrystal] calls a 'shared consciousness.' Leaders want the best ideas, but they want to ensure that everyone across the organization understands its goals and strategies. How else can you ensure that your people will act as you would like, even when you are not there?"[4]

Fast Company, The Secrets of Generation Flux

3 *Relationships* – The autonomous silo, formerly the core unit of the organization, needs to be replaced with relationships based on two-way communication between management and employees, department heads, and employees of different functional groups. Relationships based on loyalty to the organization need to bridge existing silos.

4 *Transparency* – At the center of these two-way relationships, stakeholders must let go of the traditional impulse to control or hoard information and encourage a culture of openness and trust. Transparency reveals opportunity.

5 *Trust* – Trust is four-sided. The management team must trust the employees with vital information; department heads must trust each other to share challenges and collaborate, not compete; the organization must share information and ideas with partners and suppliers across digital channels; and finally, the organization must deal honestly with its customers, developing trust.

6 *Commitment and Consistency* – The adoption of a broad-based strategic plan such as that of digital integration must be committed to and implemented consistently across all silos and departments.

7 *Proactivity* – The organization needs to proactively incorporate change and disruption, recognizing them as strategic opportunities instead of obstacles. Being proactive translates to being vigilant about industry innovation, acting on data related to user experiences, and designing responses that lead, instead of follow, the competition.

If you choose to facilitate collaboration to help your organization move beyond traditional silos, here are five questions for a focus group of your department heads:[5]

1. What priorities do you, or your department, have that are not aligned with another department?
2. Put yourself in the place of another silo. What would make that silo realize your need is a priority, that it has value?
3. What information do you or your department have that could be useful to others?
4. What information or assistance do you need from another silo that you are not getting?
5. In what ways would increasing inter-departmental collaboration and reducing individual autonomy be more beneficial to the organization?

ORGANIZATIONAL REDESIGN

What kind of organizational redesign do you suggest for BLS?

As you know, traditional organizational structures are hierarchical, with downward flow of communication and influence. The CEO and the management team sit at the top of the hierarchy, managing a series of silos (e.g. marketing, sales, human relations, IT, public relations, finance, R&D, operations, and customer service), each designed to independently achieve specific business goals. This structure is controlling by design – coveting information, inhibiting communication, and promoting competition.

There are many alternatives to consider. Here are perhaps the two most critical questions: Does the new design reflect your management style and company culture? Does it reflect your vision for BLS as a DIO?

Dr. John Kotter proposed the dual operating system,[6] a complementary structure that integrates the best features of the Hierarchy and Network systems (Figure 12.2). The Hierarchy system is focused on optimizing and managing work, while the Network system is more team-oriented, egalitarian and adaptive; it co-creates the future, fostering change through collaboration. Kotter asserts that by using the Network system, an organization can more easily recognize opportunities and adapt accordingly.[7]

Hierarchy and Network

Figure 12.2: Hierarchy and Network – Video[8]

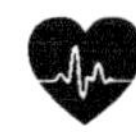

Can you see Hierarchy and Network structures working within the same organization?

- What adjustments would be required?

Organizations with a strong digital focus design Network structures that reflect the inherent integration of digital. They organize for responsiveness, speed, and strategic alignment. Creating a corporate "culture of inclusion" can even affect employees' view of the company's future economic performance. According to a recent Cisco IBSG survey, 55% of respondents from companies with inclusive business environments are "very confident" about their organizations' future revenue outlook, while only 35% from non-inclusive companies expressed this same level of confidence.[9]

There are many examples of technology firms creating Network structures that break down traditional silos to open up communication channels and collaboration throughout the organization. One such firm, Electronic Arts (EA), has established cross-company virtual communities that provide the benefits of coordinated decision making while preserving the independence required for creativity and innovation. These communities are supported by a unique governance structure and a fun and engaging technology platform. This new internal structure is an homage to the community of gamers that often stimulated product innovations.[11] Brian Neider, COO of EA Labels, commented, *"The key is to create a spirit of collaboration and communication... for ensuring that we're aligned on our company's objectives."*[12]

There is No One Answer!

Intuit succeeds by embracing the inconsistencies of today's market - the need for hierarchy and the need for openness to ideas from anywhere, the need for vision and the need to adjust on the fly.

Brad Smith, CEO at Intuit, built the "network effects platform," to help "end users and developers make our products better while we sleep." Smith tapped an internal network of 170 staffers trained as "innovation catalysts." Distributed throughout the company, they spend about 10% of their time propagating new ideas and educating the rank and file about initiatives such as the network effects platform.[10]

Fast Company, The Secrets of Generation Flux

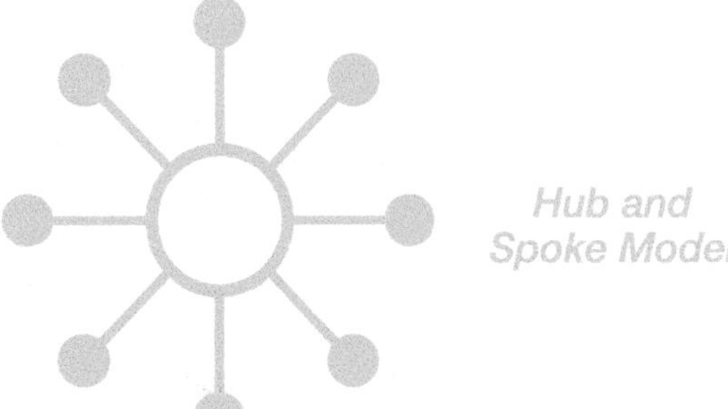

Hub and Spoke Model

Figure 12.3: Hub and Spoke Model[13]

Over the past few years, the Altimeter Group has surveyed a number of organizations to determine their maturity as a social business. Most continue to experiment with many different models to manage their social media activities. The Hub and Spoke model (Figure 12.3), which features a centralized, cross-functional team as the source of guidance and support for the social campaigns of various departments or business units, is the choice of some 35% of organizations.[14]

Can you suggest a plan to help us transition to a *DIO* structure?

Here is a five-step model for transitioning to a new organizational structure that supports long-term digital integration.[15]

1

Agree on the Organization's Goals with Digital – Initially, your management team and department heads must agree on goals and move-forward strategies. Open employee forums are powerful venues that can reveal challenges and opportunities. The team must be prepared to deal with whatever comes up in these forums. Selected focus groups within each department can open the dialogue in a more limited fashion. Here are some questions that need to be addressed:

- *How does your organization currently manage digital?*
- *In what ways can digital help your organization maintain a focus on the CX?*
- *How well do your digital channels (web, email, social media, mobile) perform against your competitors?*
- *Can you innovate and respond fast enough?*
- *Is digital focused in one silo of the organization, or does it permeate all silos?*
- *Do internal departments feel well supported by organization-wide digital efforts?*
- *Does the organization have an agreed upon digital strategy?*
- *Is there resistance to change?*

2 *Launch a Digital Innovation Project (often referred to as a Skunkworks project)* – Launching a *Digital Innovation Project* requires the least amount of change and political confrontation, yet it can produce a significant impact. This type of project creates a small, and nimble division placed outside of the existing organizational structure. It reports directly to a C-level executive, and is tasked with creating cutting-edge digital products and solutions that support customer and business needs; it is in charge of the company's entire digital footprint.

3 *Implement Digital Innovation Unit* – This requires a hand-picked group of digital experts, including some of the individuals from the *Digital Innovation Project*, to develop and implement an organization-wide digital infrastructure unit designed to meet both customer and business needs. It is a fully accountable business unit with its own performance objectives; it has the authority to influence company-wide operations. Its main focus is to get non-digitally savvy employees to use digital tools to advance business goals. Upon completion of its objectives, key members of the *Digital Innovation Unit* should be reassigned to relevant departments throughout the company to further aid digital integration.

Integrate Media – The next step is to integrate the online and offline functions of a particular area of the organization. For example, a single customer-service group should handle issues via telephone, email, and social media, and a retail merchandizing group should manage products in both offline and online stores. The result is an organization organically structured around each stage of the relationship with the customer.

Launch DIO – The most progressive organizations design their structure to reflect the Network: they distribute digital staff across key departments, and leveraging a core group of experts to lead key initiatives. Some digital projects are launched by business units and others by the *Digital Innovation Unit*. This type of distributed leadership model (Figure 12.4) reflects one potential structure of the *Digitally Integrated Organization*.

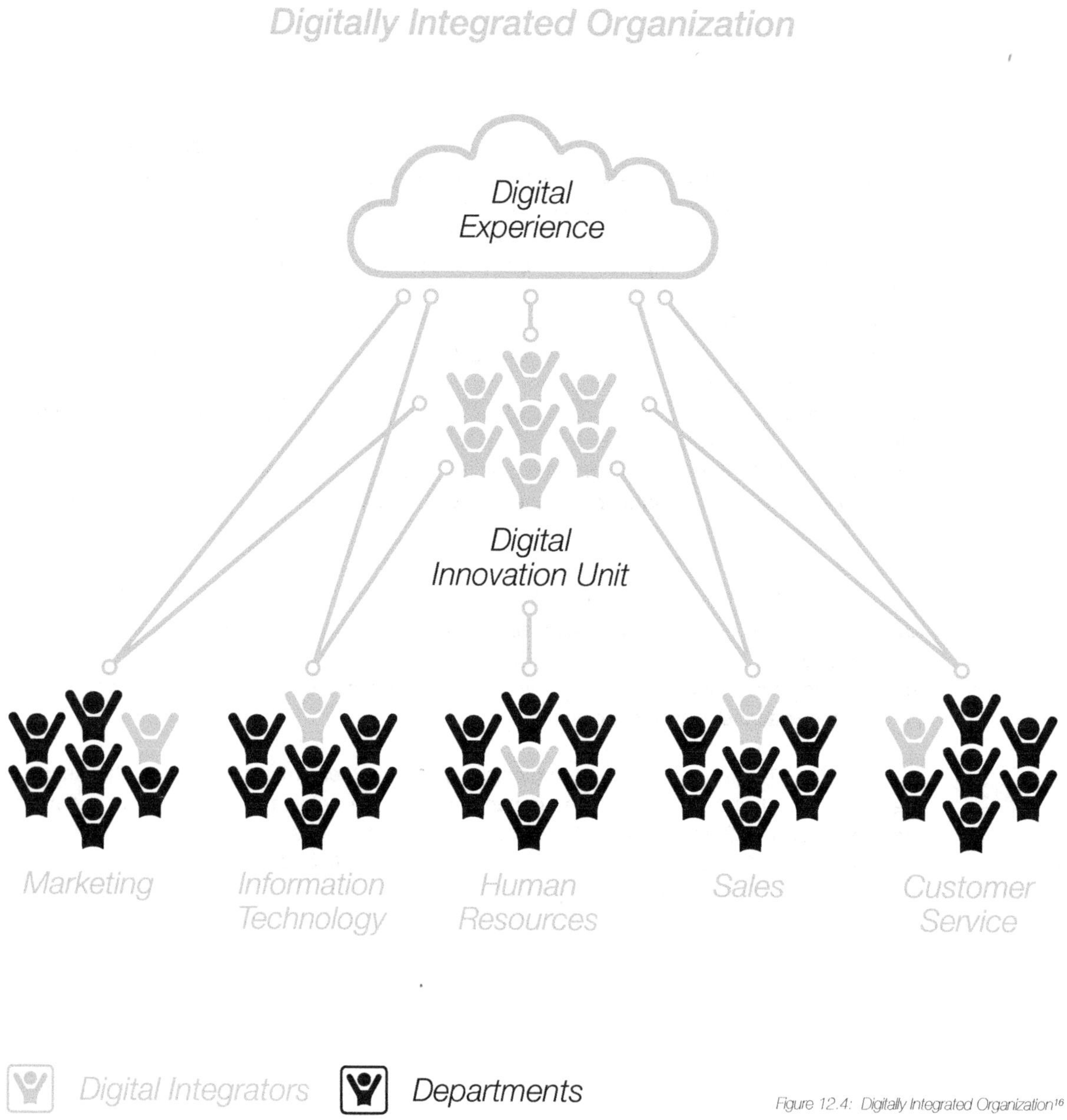

Digitally Integrated Organization

Digital Experience

Digital Innovation Unit

Marketing

Information Technology

Human Resources

Sales

Customer Service

 Digital Integrators  Departments

Figure 12.4: Digitally Integrated Organization[16]

RELATIONSHIP OF MARKETING & INFORMATION TECHNOLOGY

Now let's address the relationship of Marketing and IT in digital integration.

Both our CMO and CIO handle aspects of digital at BLS. Who should take the lead?

Bill, this is one of the seminal questions facing CEOs. Harmonizing the relationship between marketing and IT will determine the future sustainability of the organization. *"By 2017, the CMO will spend more on IT than the CIO,"* notes Gartner analyst Laura McLellan.[17] This projection defines the potential conflict and highlights the necessity for a strategic partnership between the CMO and CIO; it signals an evolution of both roles and demands for collaboration to sustain future organizational growth.

First, let's get on the same page with respect to the two positions. Traditionally, the chief marketing officer (CMO) directed a siloed effort to get attention in the marketplace, acting as "chief interrupter." This has all changed. The CMO is now faced with the necessity of transitioning to a digital mindset and managing technologies for which he/she is not totally prepared.

This notion is supported by the findings of a 2013 Forrester/BMA survey of B2B CMOs:[18]

- Nearly 100% of respondents say marketing must do things it hasn't done ever before to be successful.
- 90% say they have more responsibility without any growth in their budgets.
- Nearly 70% say that the pace of change is making planning a serious challenge.

It is also reflected in the bottom line of IBM's Global CMO Study, *From Stretched to Strengthened*, where the report concludes that CMOs the world over are experiencing unpreparedness for managing their expanding digital marketing responsibilities, including the data explosion, social media, growth of channel and device choices, and customer collaboration and influence.[19]

By contrast, the chief information officer (CIO) anticipates technological trends in the marketplace and navigates these trends through expert guidance and strategic IT planning that is aligned to organizational strategy and goals. The CIO's responsibility for the flow of information and the collection and analysis of big data interfaces with the CMO's use of digital technologies, both internal and external to the organization.

Jennifer Beck, Vice President, Gartner, describes "a sense of urgency" among businesses to break down the historical barriers between marketing and IT, two disciplines that are sometimes said to speak different languages. In fact, Gartner's research supports the emergence of a hybrid role within organizations. In 2012, 70% of companies surveyed reported having a Chief Marketing Technologist. One year later, that figure had risen to 80%.[20]

PepsiCo's Chief Digital Officer is an example of an executive without line responsibility who drives the application of best practices across the beverage group's global digital efforts.[21] Similar intersecting roles have surfaced in recent years, including chief data officer and chief convergence officer. The emergence of these positions underscores the struggle to redefine the relationship of marketing and IT in the digital age.

Bill, it is clear that the roles of CMO and CIO are rapidly changing. BLS needs to allow this new position to develop organically. There is no need to create a new position in lieu of digital integration. The focus should remain on fostering new forms of collaboration within the organization.

To learn how other organizations are fostering collaboration between marketing and IT ->

Where is the Chief Marketing Officer?

Marketing has changed and so has the role of the Chief Marketing Officer ("CMO"). Current and future customers leave data behind from every interaction they have with a brand: walking into a store, visiting a website, redeeming a daily deal, making a purchase, and so on. Smart marketers are crossing functional domains and going beyond just attracting customers to analyzing how and why people interact with a brand. They are not focusing on marketing, but on the brand experience.

For the most part, management teams within large organizations have not adapted to these changes; Marketing and Information Technology are beginning to come into conflict.

Enter the new CMO. Sometimes called something like the Chief Experience Officer or Chief Exchange Officer (CXO), the new CMO listens to and advocates for current and future customers. She finds meaning from data they leave behind to tell a story. To consumers, her stories drive a desired behavior: buying their products, raising awareness of a social issue tied to the brand, or learning more about the company and its culture, to name a few. To colleagues, her stories help them understand the brand experience consumers expect and why they expect it. This helps align executives and ensures the voice of the customer resonates throughout the organization.

Avery Fisher, CEO, Remedify

COLLABORATION

How do we to collaborate to identify, evaluate, and implement emerging opportunities?

Collaboration requires a detailed plan to bridge cultures with different values and ways of thinking. Siloed managers often have a static skill set, as they are in control of their teams and don't frequently interact with different points of view. On the other hand, collaborative teams interface with different agendas and expertise daily. In today's fast-moving digital environment, decisions require a constant infusion of fresh knowledge and insight to design creative solutions and address emerging opportunities.

To illustrate this point, I suggest we look at how BLS can encourage collaboration between the CMO and CIO. Here are five best practices to fostering inter-departmental collaboration:

Receptiveness – You must begin by reflecting on the existing culture at BLS. How strongly entrenched are the CMO and CIO silos, how strained is the communication? How prepared are both department heads to shift loyalty from their functional area to a "BLS first" approach?

Patient Implementation – Digital Integration is a threatening and emotional subject. It involves letting go of entrenched habits, established control and authority, and, to an extent, your personal identity as a department head. Implementation must be patient and focused on mutual benefit.

- *Internal Communications* – BLS needs to open communication channels up and down the organization. A core value of the digital culture is equality, which levels the playing field and democratizes communication. Jack Dorsey, co-founder of Twitter and CEO of Square, follows a policy of "responsible transparency" within his organization.[23] Information and opportunities are not coveted in departments; there is open sharing. This approach fosters idea generation and innovation.

- *Efficiency* – By eliminating competition and improving communication, coordinated effort stimulates creative solutions, improves workflows, and reduces costs. Furthermore, the budget is a collaborative effort that reflects the optimal use of funds. In a very competitive marketplace, marketing and IT have no choice but to work as strategic partners to realize efficiencies and drive value for BLS.

3 *Education* – BLS needs to educate their management team on the following:

a. The benefits of a strong partnership between marketing and IT; it is a win-win for both, and critical to the sustainability of BLS.

b. The new responsibilities of both the CMO and CIO.

c. The new skills required to effectively manage their areas.

d. Collaboration goes beyond marketing and IT; it's about integration across the entire organization.

4 *Cross-Functionality*

- *Cross-Functional Team* – Launch BLS' language learning app as a *Digital Innovation Project*, which will include representatives from product development, operations, customer services, sales, marketing, communications, IT, and business development. Give each team member a stake and role in the launch and outcome of the *Project*. This *Project* team reports directly to Bill, your CEO.

- *Holistic CX* – Cross-functional collaboration will eliminate the siloed approach to managing the customer experience (data analytics, media strategy, and customer service). It facilitates engagement between the BLS brand and the consumer, creating a holistic CX.

- *Integrated Data* – BLS needs systems for data collection, analysis, and targeted distribution which integrate the needs of marketing and the expertise of IT to deliver customer insights and real-time analytics.

- *Security* – Marketing the BLS app across multiple web, social, and mobile platforms increases the need for tight technical oversight to manage security, and reduce risk. Marketing and IT must collaborate to proactively address potential threats.

5 *Feedback* – When a customer interacts digitally, he or she is interacting with the entire organization. Feedback needs to be shared in real time across the organization. Every team member needs to be made aware of the benefits of this integrated approach. Given that the *Project* is a testing ground for the collaborative model, every team member should be encouraged to suggest adjustments as the *Project* becomes part of the BLS organizational culture.

Collaboration is the Path to Digital Connection

"Companies have crept to the edge of the new. There's no longer any question that marketers can forge a deep relationship with customers and prospects by participating, convening, aggregating, syndicating, and publishing relevant and credible content across multiple channels. But to reap the biggest benefits of the digital relationship requires a new way of working – one that puts partnership, collaboration, and shared success front and center."[22]

Jeff Pundyk, Vice President, Content Marketing and Strategy, The Economist Group

We have differing opinions on the BLS digital media use policy. Do you have any suggestions?

This question is often the most controversial, as it exposes cross-cultural differences (between digital natives and immigrants), and requires a redefinition of productivity (should employees spend valuable company time on social media?) and trust (will employees get distracted with non-business-related activities?).

To answer this question, it may be helpful to first identify the general uses of digital media in the modern-day organization, and then examine various policy considerations.

Digital Media Uses:

- *Productive Communications* – Digital media is poised to become an office productivity tool, with a $1.3 trillion untapped value in improved communications and collaboration within and across enterprises.[24]
- *Trusted Outreach* – Employees are often the most passionate and knowledgeable boosters of an organization's product or service. Employee outreach to prospects and consumers is a win-win, as employees instill brand confidence and trust.
- *Expanded Networks* – Employees have their own social networks. By using their trusted access to targeted communities, they can spread the organization's message for little expense.

The Challenge:

- 81% of companies believe social media is a corporate security risk, yet 69% of them say they don't have a social media policy in place.[25]
- A digital media policy is essential for all organizations. It can be created and mandated or collaboratively designed and agreed upon. The design of the policy should reflect the organization's culture.

Policy Considerations:[26]

- *Be Prepared for the Unknown* – You can't control digital, so have a plan and expect to modify it.
- *Manage Risk and Uncertainty* – Create a cross-functional group to respond to challenging posts.
- *Agree on Digital Cultural Values* – Design processes that emphasize training, support and evaluation.
- *Consider Legal and Compliance* – Be proactive toward your industry's regulations.
- *Design Two Social Media Policies* – One for on-the-job and another for personal use.

Do not reinvent a digital media policy for BLS. Learn from the mistakes and build on the successes of other organizations. Craft a digital media policy that reflects the values, goals, and unique culture of your organization.

Let's re-address the lead question in this chapter:

> *Why is that which worked "half of the time" 20 years ago still the standard for most marketing departments and business organizations?*

Pixar founder Ed Catmull addressed this question when relating the company's success with an open, non-hierarchical environment. This structure, he noted, encourages all employees to offer ideas across functional disciplines and up and down communications channels. Feedback is direct; there are no stars at Pixar.[27]

When companies like BLS attempt to infuse a digital framework that is open and dynamic into an organizational structure that is hierarchical and static, they are inviting impasse. To avoid this, they need to develop an incremental adoption plan that recognizes the goal of becoming a *DIO* and outlines a clear process to bring the organization, step-by-step, along the *Path to Digital Integration*.

> *"Now think about the typical corporate marketing organization, with often adversarial relationships between departments, partner agencies and suppliers, glorified turf wars and personality cults. Clearly we need a new paradigm."*[28]

Fast Company, The Secrets of Generation Flux

- Organizational structure and policy can encourage – or inhibit – digital integration and transformation.
- Traditional organizational structures are not designed to meet the requirements of digital integration.
- In many companies, silos are run as separate entities with their own agendas, deliverables, and budgets; this needs to change to foster digital integration.
- Organizations with a strong digital focus restructure to reflect their core values of the digital culture; they restructure for openness, responsiveness, strategic alignment, and sustainability.
- The evolution to a strategic partnership between the CMO and CIO is a necessity; it demands changes in both roles and requires collaboration to sustain future organizational growth.
- The challenges of inter-departmental collaboration necessitate a detailed plan that involves receptiveness, patient implementation, education, cross-functionality, and feedback.
- A digital media policy is essential for all organizations. It can be created and mandated, or collaboratively designed and agreed upon.

CHAPTER 13: EVALUATION AND ROI

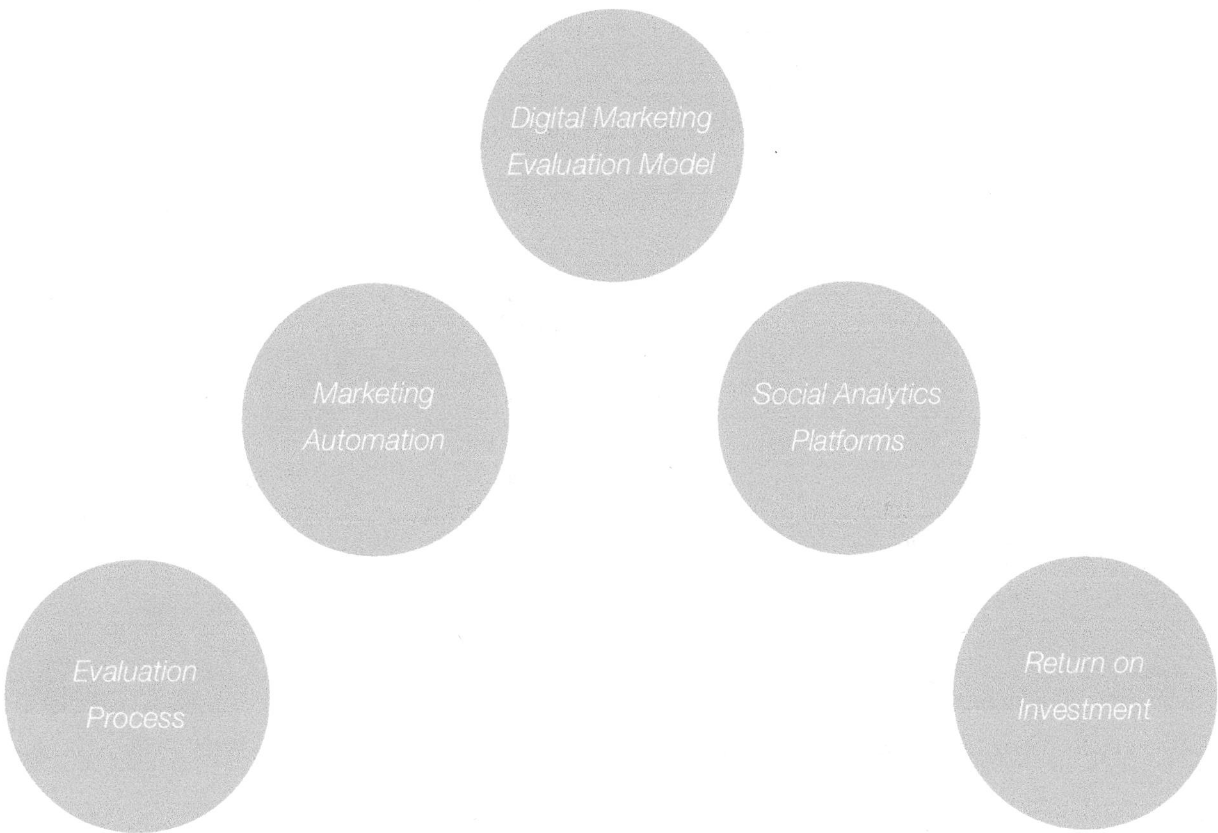

Throughout this book, we have documented the dramatic impact of digital transformation on consumer behavior and purchase decision. In an ironic twist, today's marketing practitioners are feeling overwhelmed by the sheer volume of consumer-generated data available to them. They recognize the need for a coordinated approach to measure and evaluate this flood of information, and appreciate the expertise required to relate it all to strategic objectives and organizational goals. According to research from iStrategy, the integrated marketing conference for CMOs, monitoring, measurement, and tracking collectively represent the number one priority for CMOs in 2014-2015.[1] In this chapter, we will review various methods and tools your organization can use to accurately measure and evaluate marketing ROI.

After their last series of meetings with the digital integration consultant, Bill and the BLS management team realized that the collection, analysis, and integration of data will be critical to the company's movement along the *Path to Digital Integration*. They did some research and came up with a number of alarming statistics that reflect the challenges of measuring and evaluating digital media:

- Only 20% of companies surveyed in 2013 have a strategy that ties data collection and analysis back to business objectives.[2]
- 81% of survey respondents do not measure the ROI of their web analytics efforts, which is one of the easiest ways to link efforts to outcomes.[3]
- 57% of marketers see measuring ROI as a primary challenge when using digital media.[4]

At length, the team decided they needed some clear direction in order to formulate an efficient approach to measurement and evaluation. They generated the following agenda to discuss in the follow-up meeting with the consultant:

- *Digital Marketing Evaluation Model*
- *Marketing Automation*
- *Social Analytics Platforms*
- *Evaluation Process*
- *Return on Investment*

DIGITAL MARKETING EVALUATION MODEL

For many years, measurement and evaluation (M&E) have been treated as afterthoughts in the development of business plans and marketing campaigns. Enter digital technology and its dramatic effect on the marketplace. Now measuring and evaluating the ROI of digital campaigns have become strategic and tactical imperatives.

To address these challenges, we need to work from a common measurement and evaluation model. Doing so will help shape the way in which BLS implements M&E.

"To increase the business value of information, we need data from various angles. In addition to sales data, we need to know why sales increased. We need to know how and where we are influential."[5]

Life Sciences Industry CEO from Japan, from the IBM CEO Study, *Leading Through Connections*

Measurement is the yardstick by which organizations are judged. Nurturing a culture of measurement allows businesses of all sizes to leverage data to accomplish their goals. When this use of data becomes rooted within the culture of an organization, the benefits of making data-driven decisions become immediately apparent.[6]

Legendary management consultant Peter Drucker often said, *"you can't manage what you can't measure.... if you can't measure it, you can't improve it."* Thus, to define success, we need to set tangible, measurable goals. The first step is to develop an M&E model that consistently tracks metrics such as return on investment (ROI) and key performance indicators (KPIs) to quantify organizational performance.

EVALUATION MODEL

The *Digital Marketing Evaluation Model* combines the five-step Digital Marketing & Measurement Model developed by social analytics expert Avinash Kaushik[7] and the social analytics metrics designed by John Lovett and the *Web Analytics Demystified Group*.[8] An important planning tool, the *Digital Marketing Evaluation Model* needs to be developed before launch. Each of its five steps builds upon the previous to provide an actionable organizational framework for M&E:

1. *Identify Business Objectives* – Set the broadest parameters for the project. This is critical, as it establishes the context for the M&E strategy.

2. *Identify Outcomes* – Pinpoint goals or outcomes for each measurable business objective. These are the specific aspects of the marketing plan you want to evaluate.

3. *Identify Key Performance Indicators (KPIs)* – These are the metrics that help you gauge your organization's performance in relation to its objectives. KPIs are the tools you use to measure the performance of projected outcomes. They could be industry or organization specific, but must be consistent. For each KPI, the project supervisor determines the method of calculation and sets the parameters of success upfront. Here are four sample metrics based on the work of the *Web Analytics Demystified Group*:[9]

   - ***Counting metrics*** are the most available and easiest to collect. These tend to be quantifiable volume measurements such as social media likes, fans, check-ins, and mentions, as well as website traffic, lead and conversion rates, and web and social analytics. Many companies collect some or all of these data, but they need to be understood and integrated into other measurements to contribute to the evaluation process.

   - ***Foundation metrics*** are building blocks to develop other metrics. They are calculated as follows:

     - Interaction = conversions/activity
     - Engagement = visits x time x comments x shares
     - Influence = volume of regular content x comments x shares x reach
     - Advocacy = influence x positive sentiment
     - Impact = outcomes/(interactions + engagement)

- ***Outcome metrics*** reflect the stages of the *Digital Involvement Cycle* (see chapter 4) and the metrics that define each stage:

    - *Awareness* – reach, media mentions, virality, publication activity.
    - *Interest* – new visitors, referrals, links, active users, user growth rate, trending brand topics, keywords.
    - *Involvement* – time spent, pages viewed, contests entered, apps downloaded, messages sent, comments submitted, content downloaded.
    - *Commitment* – number of conversions (e.g. event registrations, in-store/online purchases, trial offers).
    - *Loyalty* – return visitors, recent visits, visit length and frequency, satisfaction score, positive review ratio.
    - *Advocacy* – content syndication, likes, mentions, social shares, bookmarks, links, influence (Klout), referrals.
    - *Champion* – social media advocacy, user-generated reviews and other supportive content, referrals.

- ***Business value metrics*** align digital marketing activities with results for the satisfaction of stakeholders:

    - *Revenue* – projects income received from the sale of products and services.
    - *Market Share* – determines the percentage of total market revenue generated by your products and services.
    - *Profit* – reflects the effect of digital marketing performance on the bottom line.
    - *Brand Awareness* – measures brand recognition by prospects and customers.

- *Customer Loyalty* – measures how well a customer's needs are met or exceeded. This is directly linked to referrals.

- *Customer Retention* – tracks if a user continues to be a customer. Satisfied customers spend more, refer others, and share the product with their network. A decline in retention indicates issues with CX (e.g. service, logistics, quality).

- *Employee Productivity* – measures hours worked and absentee rates and relates them to sales volume and production. Productivity directly impacts efficiency, sales, and profitability.

- *Sustainability* – measures performance based on a comprehensive assessment of long-term economic, environmental, and social criteria affecting local communities and the world (e.g. Dow Jones Sustainability Indices).

4 *Identify Targets* – Set indicators of success for each objective (e.g. number of visits/month, percentage increase in likes/week). Targets can be determined from historical performance or from other campaigns. The *Integrated Media Matrix* (Figure 13.2) helps the team identify such targets.

5 *Identify Segments* – Once targets have been determined, identify the most important segments to focus on to accomplish each goal. Identify the sources of traffic and types of people desired (e.g. attributes, behavior, expected business outcomes), and the tools needed to attract and convert them. Building detailed buyer personas will help to focus your efforts.

Take a Deep Breath, Analytics will Change Again

Digital media is evolving very quickly, yet the analytics are becoming more complicated and fragmented; each form of media requires its own analytics and many of the metrics aren't compatible, making a 360 degree converged view of brand marketing effectiveness problematic. Marketing frameworks and customer journeys are helpful in understanding the voice of the customer, but few organizations are able to utilize such constructs to hone marketing effectiveness. In fact, most organizations are unaware of the full extent of marketing analytics and research resources that are available or how to apply the information in a context meaningful to their use case.

In the next 36 months marketing analytics will drastically change. For one, what is called "moving data" or "the internet of things" will converge and create a new set of data metrics that will be much more actionable. Marketers will finally have access to the information they have always wanted but was out of reach. The next set of applications will have the data and context integrated and geo-located.

Marshall Sponder, author, Social Media Analytics

When considering each step of the *Digital Marketing Evaluation Model*, you need to use the following three criteria as a filter:

1. *Acquisition of Traffic* – How do you expect to drive traffic (paid, earned, owned media), and to where (corporate website, social platform(s), microsite, landing page)?

2. *Expected Behavior* – Are there certain actions the user is expected to take when arriving (e.g. spend x amount of time on y page(s), download an ebook, watch a video, click on a contest)?

3. *Outcomes* – What actual outcomes signify value to the bottom line of the organization (e.g. sales, registrations, qualified online leads, email promotion signups, return customers)?

To better understand how this all works on a practical level, I suggest you build a *Digital Marketing Evaluation Model* for the BLS language learning app.

The team is shown a graphical depiction of the *Digital Marketing Evaluation Model* (Figure 13.1) with each of the five steps identified:

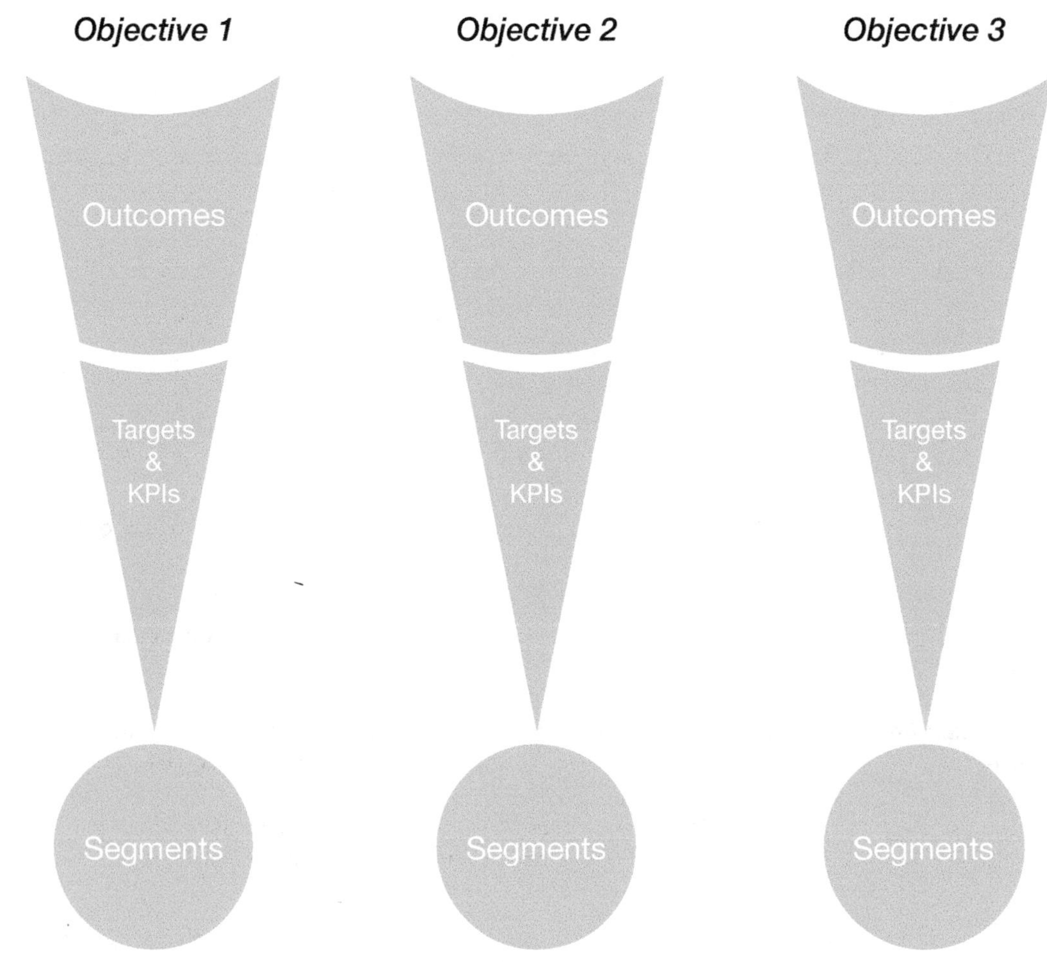

Figure 13.1: Digital Marketing Evaluation Model[10]

The team discusses each step, referring to the *Digital Involvement Cycle* to determine objectives and outcomes. They then fill out the *Integrated Media Matrix* (Figure 13.2) to clarify the media tactics and tools needed to operationalize the *Digital Marketing Evaluation Model* for BLS' language learning app. (see Figure 13.3 for sample *Model*).

Media	Budget	Campaign Objective		Campaign Objective	
		Outcome 1 (e.g. Increase awareness/exposure)	Target 1 (e.g. Increase website traffic by 15%)	Outcome 2 (e.g. Increase downloads/ conversions)	Target 2 (e.g. Increase purchases/ registrations by 25%)
Flyers/brochures					
YouTube - Video					
Facebook					
Twitter					
Email blast					
Blog					
Social bookmarks					
Pinterest					
Instagram					
TV/radio					
Infographic					
Newspaper (print)					
Posters					
Newsletter (online)					
Personal networks (friends, family, orgs)					
Local businesses					
WOM friends					
Events					
Past participants/buyers					
Partner organizations					

Figure 13.2: Integrated Media Matrix

EVALUATION MODEL

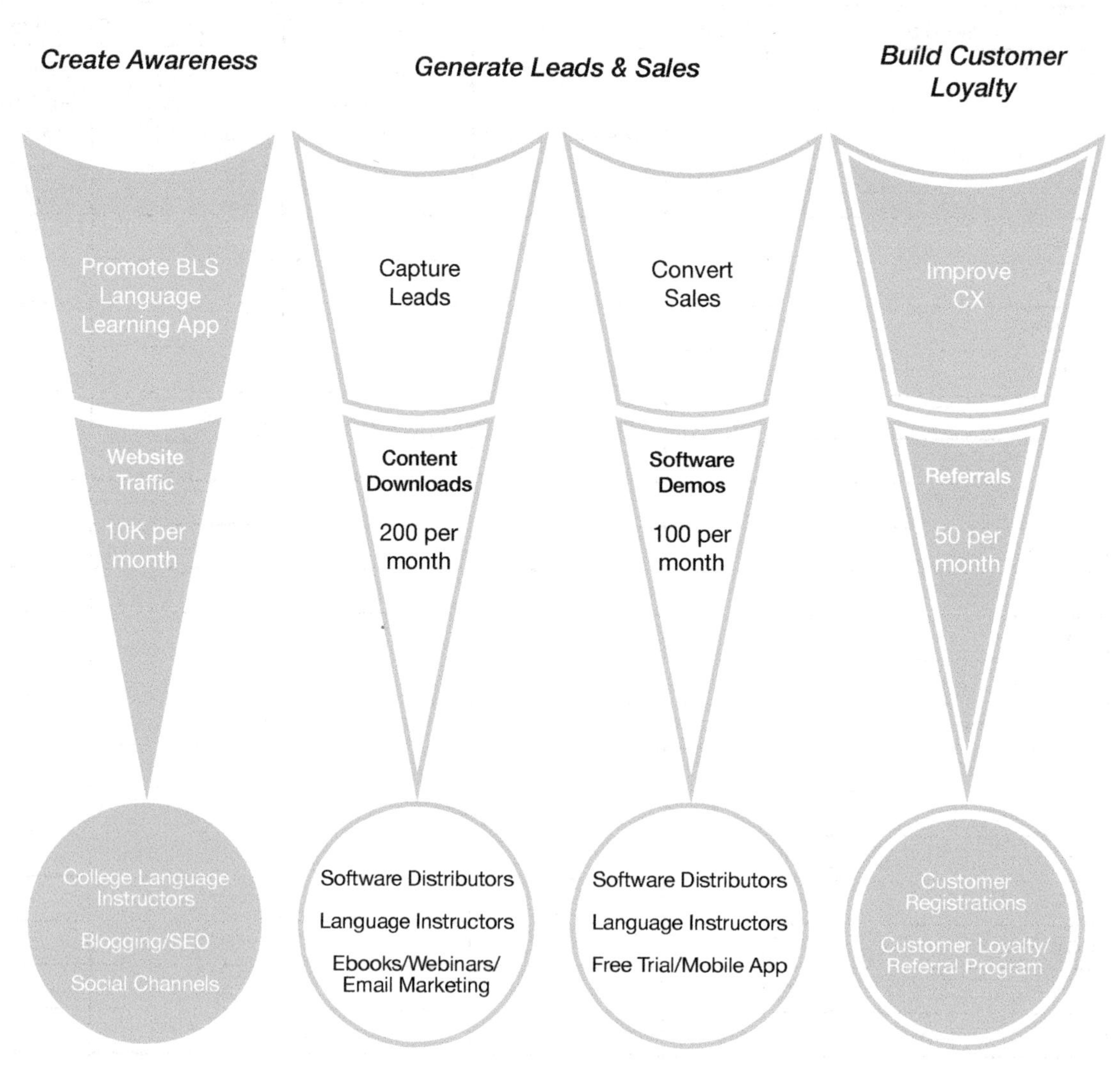

Figure 13.3: Evaluation Model for BLS Language Learning App

MARKETING AUTOMATION

Now that we have built the *Digital Marketing Evaluation Model* and completed the *Integrated Media Matrix,* is there an efficient way to consistently measure and evaluate metrics and outcomes?

In your old sales model, you would launch a new variety of Spanish language flash cards by way of direct mailings, sales outreach, and trade shows, and then monitor the results of your efforts on a whiteboard or an Excel spreadsheet.

Today, you have access to a number of digital technologies to attract and engage customers in new ways, and then measure and evaluate results. Chief among them is marketing automation software, which helps organizations like BLS transform their sales and monitoring process. With marketing automation, your team can connect with new prospects and existing customers and maintain and nurture relationships; better still, nearly everything is measureable, so you can optimize the efficiency of your marketing efforts. This type of software is not just for Fortune 500 companies: some vendors offer packages beginning at $200/month for startups and small and midsize businesses.

What functionalities does marketing automation software typically offer?

Marketing automation is an umbrella concept that includes tools for both initiating and monitoring, all under one roof:

- *Demand Generation*, including traditional and pay-per-click advertising, SEO, and inbound and social media marketing.

- *Website Optimization*, including web analytics and visitor analysis software that tracks visitors, their location, and interests.

- *Lead Generation*, including all lead qualification, nurturing, and management associated with content marketing/thought leadership activities (e.g. blogging, ebooks, newsletters, case studies, etc.).

- *Sales Process*, including the contacting of potential and existing customers via email, digital channels, or phone, as well as post-purchase customer interaction and CRM.

- *Ongoing Campaign Analysis*, including sales effectiveness tracking and sales intelligence.

- *Marketing Budgeting and Forecasting*

A comprehensive marketing automation software suite offers a variety of tools, some that you can add on and grow into as your needs expand. These tools drive traffic to your website by helping you create and manage search-engine optimized web and social content, design CTAs and landing pages to turn this traffic into viable leads, and build customized, segmented email campaigns that help you engage prospects as they proceed through the *Digital Involvement Cycle*. Further, at each step along the sales process and customer decision journey, your team is provided with analytics and metrics to allow for mid-course campaign adjustments and real-time results monitoring. Some of the more advanced marketing automation software lets you segment your content and messaging to better connect with different buyer personas, make on-the-fly adjustments to messaging and targeted offers, and observe response metrics such as lead conversations generated, all in real time.

This market is growing each year, so before you commit, make sure to dive deeply into the features of each product and analyze how it might integrate with your current software. As a reference, here are VentureBeat's top 10 "superheroes of marketing automation:"[11]

1. *HubSpot* – Simplicity, accessibility, and power, all in one package.

2. *Marketo* – Experiencing explosive growth; offers a wide range of tools.

3. *Eloqua* – The power of the enterprise and the usability of a modern startup, nicely married.

4. *Salesforce* – A CRM/marketing automation hybrid; its functionality is popular with sales teams.

5. *SAS* – Powerful but pricey; perhaps the most user-friendly enterprise-level solution.

6. *IBM* – Power to spare, but be prepared to integrate and train and launch.

7. *InfusionSoft* – Built-in e-commerce, drag-and-drop campaigns.

8. *LoopFuse* – Very affordable starting pricing.

9. *MindMatrix* – Strong focus on sales, with vertical solutions.

10. *Silverpop* – Amazing for email.

SOCIAL ANALYTICS PLATFORMS

Once you have selected the appropriate marketing automation software, you need to align business objectives to KPIs and select the social analytics platforms and vendors that best match your requirements (see Figure 13.4). Note, as this area continues to expand, various marketing automation software packages are now incorporating social analytics. Given the profusion of choices, choosing the right social analytics platform(s) can be a complex process; your management team will need to collaborate in order to fully evaluate all options. Here is a sample checklist of criteria to look for when doing so:

- ✓ *Quality (features and functionality)*
- ✓ *Operating system*
- ✓ *Process efficiency*
- ✓ *User experience (usability, speed, clarity of dashboard)*
- ✓ *Deliverables (metrics, reports)*
- ✓ *Real-time integration with social networks*
- ✓ *Interactivity with customers*
- ✓ *Internal communications platform*
- ✓ *Social analytics (e.g. tracking leads through the Digital Involvement Cycle)*
- ✓ *Technical support*
- ✓ *Installation and training*
- ✓ *Enhancements/upgrades/fixes*
- ✓ *Cost*

The size of your organization, its business objectives and required KPIs, as well as the above criteria will help to filter your options. For example, smaller companies (or their staff that want to gain initial exposure to a basic suite of social analytics tools might consider Sproutsocial.com or Hootsuite.com.

Business Objective	Key Performance Indicator	Social Analytics Platforms
Foster Dialog	Share of Voice	Alterian SM2, Radian6, Scout Labs, Statsit, Trendrr, Visible Technologies
	Audience Engagement	Coremetrics, Webtrends, Radian6, Scout Labs, Converseon, Filtrbox (Jive), Visible Technologies
	Conversation Reach	Alterian SM2, Radian6, Scout Labs, Social Radar, Statsit, SWIX, Trendrr, Visible Technologies
Promote Advocacy	Active Advocates	Biz360, Filtrbox (Jive), Radian6
	Advocate Influence	Cymfony, Filtrbox (Jive), Lithium, Radian6, Razorfish, (SIM Score), SAS, Telligen, Twitalyzer, Visible Technologies
	Advocacy Impact	Coremetrics, Lithium, Omniture, Webtrends, SWIX, Telligent
Facilitate Support	Resolution Rate	Filtrbox (Jive), RightNow Technologies, Salesforce.com, Telligent
	Resolution Time	Filtrbox (Jive), RightNow Technologies, Salesforce.com, Telligent
	Satisfaction Score	ForeSee Results, iPerceptions, Kampyle, OpinionLab
Spur Innovation	Top Trends	Alterian SM2, Cymfony, Filtrbox (Jive), Radian6, SAS, Scout Labs, Social Mention, Social Radar, Trendrr, Visible Technologies
	Sentiment Ratio	Alterian SM2,Converseon, Cymfony, Filtrbox (Jive), Radian6, SAS, Scout Labs, Social Radar, Trendrr, Visible Technologies
	Idea Impact	Biz360, Cymfony, Filtrbox (Jive), LugIron, Radian6, Scout Labs, Visible Technologies

Figure 13.4: Objectives, KPI's, and Social Analytics Platforms[12]

EVALUATION PROCESS

At this point, the campaign is implemented and the measurement tools are in place, each one generating basic counting and foundation metrics, as well as more complex outcome and business value metrics, with the aid of selected marketing automation and social analytics software platforms.

Utilizing the *Digital Marketing Evaluation Model* as a framework, the BLS team must continually gather and measure data to evaluate actual campaign performance against projected outcomes and targets. By doing so, your team can use hard data to determine if the campaign is fulfilling its objectives or if adjustments are needed.

Finally, results are reported to your stakeholders.

RETURN ON INVESTMENT

The next step in the evaluation process is the determination of return on investment (ROI). For marketers, there is a more refined metric – return on marketing investment (ROMI), defined as "the contribution attributable to marketing (net of marketing spending), divided by the marketing 'invested' or risked."[14]

"Establishing a ROI Digital Marketing strategy is the top challenge among executives"[13]

CMOs support the use of ROI to determine effectiveness, but there is no consensus as to the measurement and evaluation methodology. Should ROI be measured and evaluated against standard industry benchmarks? Organizational expenditures (of time, effort, and money)? C-level expectations? Depending on the measurement used, it is possible to extrapolate vastly different ROIs from the same data.

Managing marketing ROI can be even more elusive. According to data from an IBM study, 63% of CMOs surveyed think ROI will be regarded as the principal measurement by 2015, but 56% feel ill-prepared to manage ROI.[15] This concern is supported by evidence from a Bazaarvoice survey, in which only 12% of companies acknowledged being able to track the effectiveness of their social media efforts against revenues.[16]

How can we be proactive and strategize to realize a strong digital marketing ROI?

Here are some best practices to accomplish this:

Clarify goals – Marketers often have trouble clearly defining goals for their digital marketing efforts. Some goals, like brand affinity, are hard to quantify; others, like measuring leads and sales conversions, are much easier. As inbound marketers HubSpot point out, "the challenge is that too often social media goals reflect the core functionality of the channel rather than the core needs of the business."[17]

First-click attribution – Adobe found that using first-click attribution instead of last click resulted in social media ROI that was nearly twice as high (88%). In last-click attribution, social channels tend to engage people at the top of the sales funnel rather than right before they buy, thus reducing ROI.[18]

Be where they shop – Go beyond connecting with potential customers via information sites; this does not deliver real ROI. According to data from an ODM Group study, 74% of shoppers rely on social networks to guide their purchase decisions. Establish separate channel benchmarks for key response and conversion metrics, especially those which can be measured in real time.[19]

Map user-generated content (UGC) – The higher the volume of user-generated content, the greater the direct effect on marketing ROI.

Measure the effectiveness of channel KPIs – Establish a baseline for every web and social channel; test different content and messaging; measure the impact of each on traffic and other KPIs at the point of transaction.

Target each stage of the Cycle – Use relevant metrics and strategies to evaluate marketing ROI at each stage of the *Digital Involvement Cycle*.

Re-examining ROI for the Digital Age

Even as digital continues to transform the marketing function, many of us are still using traditional ROI models to measure and evaluate our marketing efforts. As one digital agency put it, *"in a multichannel nonprofit fundraising environment, the old methods of measuring return on investment begin to fall apart."*[20]

ROI Reflects your Key Objective

The question most frequently posed by management to social media proponents is, 'what will be my ROI?' It assumes short-term ROI, but social media is designed for the mid and long term.

Let's ask the question in reverse: What is the negative effect (return) on not having an appropriate level of social media marketing? For most companies, their competition is already using social media.

The next question is – what level of usage is sufficient? First, we need to decide the key objective – Is it to create awareness, commitment, or advocacy?

Once the objective is determined, then a plan can be developed to determine if the objective has been achieved. Since social media efforts are for the long haul, it is rare to see immediate sales increases. By measuring social media's effect on the key objective, much more focused, realistic expectations can be determined. The key point is that the ROI of social media cannot be a cookie-cutter approach; it needs to reflect a targeted objective in the sales funnel and the specific digital tools employed.

Bob Bengen, former Director Market Research, Microsoft

To meet the challenges of marketing in the digital age, perhaps we need to change the term ROI to *Digital ROI (DROI)*. As we know, ROI stands for "return on investment." In today's emerging digital business framework, our understanding of "return" should be expanded beyond financial metrics. From an executive's point of view, "social net worth" is a measure of the power of the brand, above and beyond assets and liabilities (similar to Mark Schaefer's *"return on influence"* metric noted in chapter 4). Like social net worth, *DROI* is not necessarily linked to a specific time frame or set of initiatives, but rather to the strength of the brand built up over time.

To measure *DROI*, we need to look at how the organization is improving the overall value of its brand. Here are five proposed inputs:

Brand health is comprised of loyalty, authenticity, and reach. Social Brands 100 determines brand health using three social KPI's: win-win relationships with customers, employees, and supply chain; active listening to comprehensively serve customers' needs; and social behavior that is compelling, truthful, authentic, and open with each community.[21]

2 *Customer quality* goes beyond traditional metrics like percentage of repeat customers. It measures the user-generated content, influence, and reach of advocates and champions. For example, how willing are your customers to interact with you? How extensive are their social networks and communities? What is the quality and reach of these networks and communities? How many users are having conversations about your brand? How many are active advocates or champions of your brand? How many are sharing posts about your company?

3 *Added value* is the benefit (in addition to the engagement) your organization receives through its presence on digital networks. For example, what is the added value of using Twitter for customer service, Facebook for product introductions, or LinkedIn for recruitment?

4 *Digital footprint* is a measure of your visibility and influence throughout the digital universe. It reflects the overall impact of your organization's digital efforts over web, social, and mobile. Your brand can measure its digital footprint in a number of ways, including changes in search engine rankings, social influence, mobile app downloads, and social mentions. An increase in an organization's digital footprint contributes to brand health.

5 *Competitive position* is the net effect of your *Integrated Digital Marketing* efforts; the end product of your ability to connect with new prospects and existing customers, to drive deeper interaction with website, social, and mobile channels. Competitive position can be evaluated in a number of ways, including top-of-mind brand recognition, touch points to your brand's web and social assets, and responses to social engagement.

How do you measure the ROI of both traditional and digital efforts?

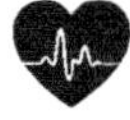

- How do you link marketing campaigns to outcomes?
- How do you evaluate your objectives for a campaign?

In this chapter, we have reviewed various methods and tools your organization can use to evaluate marketing ROI, a necessary aspect of digital integration. However, to create the enduring brand value characteristic of the *DIO*, your organization must move beyond ROI and focus on broader relationships with customers, stakeholders, and the greater community. For this, we turn to chapter 14.

- Measurement and evaluation (M&E) for digital marketing is not a well-developed discipline; in a recent survey, only 12% of companies were able to track the effectiveness of their social media efforts against revenues.

- The *Digital Marketing Evaluation Model* is an effective planning tool that provides the organization an actionable framework for M&E.

- The *Integrated Media Matrix* is a useful tool to determine the appropriate media for a specific objectives, outcomes, and targets.

- Marketing automation software is a cost-effective way for most organizations to find customers, maintain relationships, and optimize the efficiency of their marketing efforts.

- Relevant metrics and strategies should be used to evaluate marketing ROI at each stage of the *Digital Involvement Cycle*.

- *DROI* expands on the traditional definition of ROI to examine how the organization is improving the value of its brand.

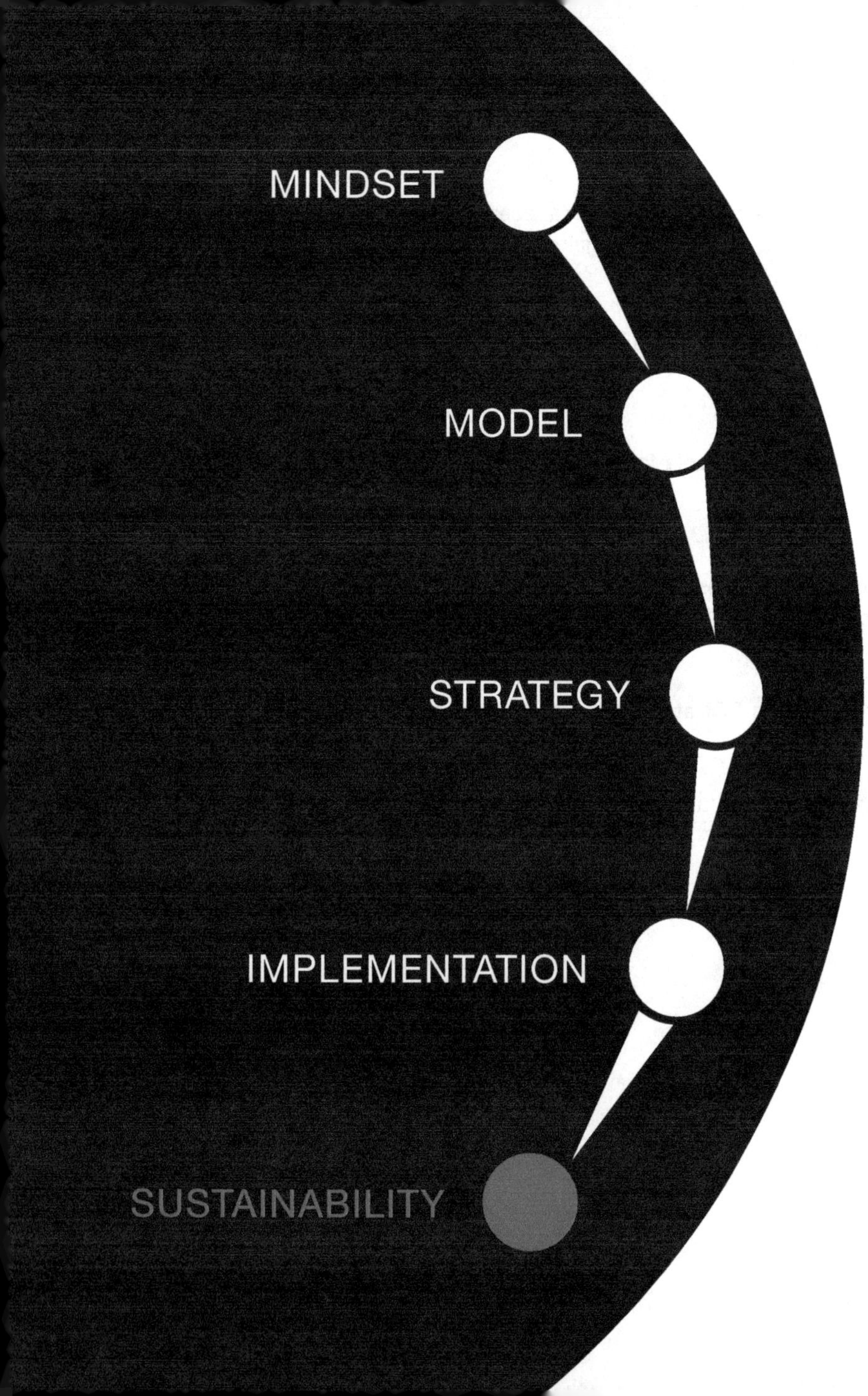

MINDSET

MODEL

STRATEGY

IMPLEMENTATION

SUSTAINABILITY

Chapter 14: Building Shared Value

Chapter 15: From Social Business to Digitally Integrated Organization

Each organization moving along the *Path of Digital Integration* is faced with many new challenges, including how to grapple with a new mindset and strategic model (*Integrated Digital Marketing*), as well as how to properly implement the strategies, tactics, and tools necessary to bring forth the digital transformation characteristic of the *DIO*. As the organization reflects on the time and resources required to fully commit to digital integration, it must also conceive of a plan for continued sustainability.

At the heart of organizational sustainability is building shared value. To achieve this, the organization must first agree on a set of core values that serve to define and drive its efforts. It must then leverage these to create measurable value by addressing the social issues relevant to both the organization and the greater community. Finally, it must follow organizational sustainability best practices to complete the evolution to a *DIO*.

As a reminder, you can access in-depth information, videos, and updates from our *Digital Marketing Resource Center* (www.dmresourcecenter.org) wherever you see this icon.

CHAPTER 14: BUILDING SHARED VALUE

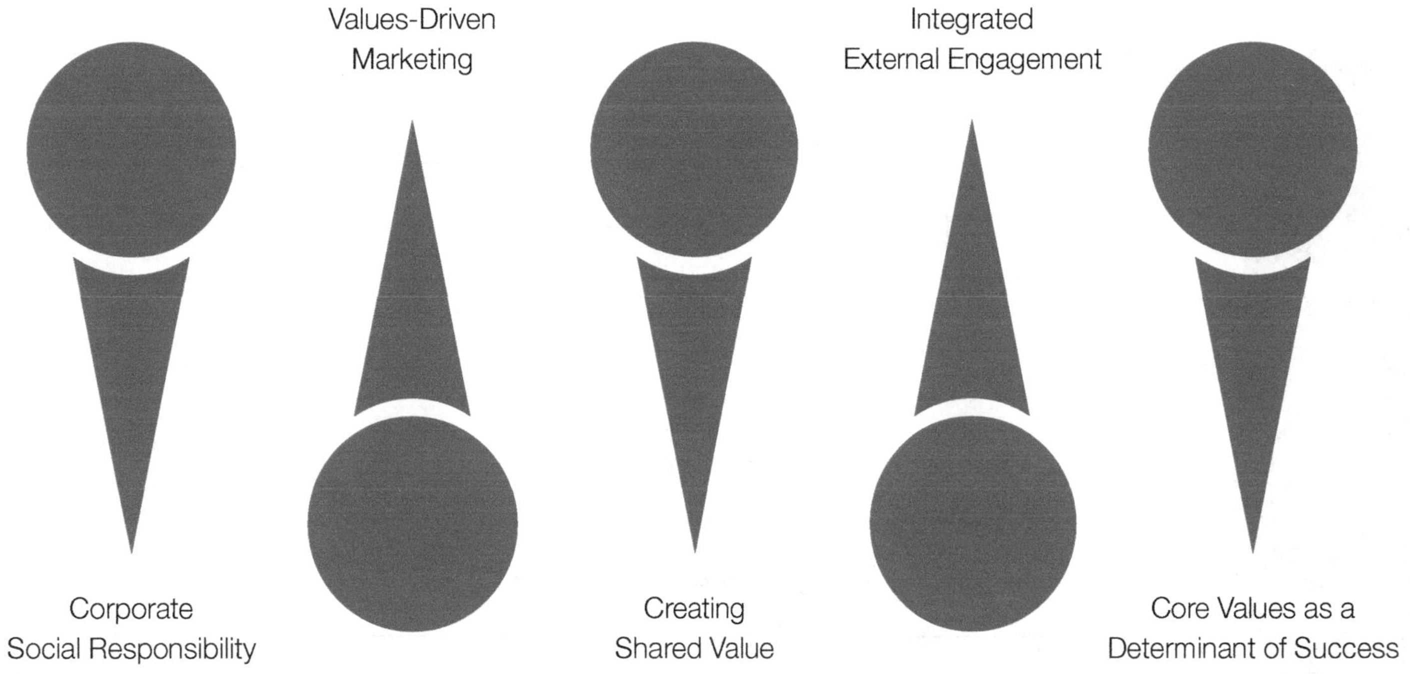

Traditionally, most businesses have focused on optimizing short-term profitability (ROI) as a key determinant of success. Any long-term impact of their actions, whether on the part of their customers or the local and global community at large, has been of secondary consideration at best.

During the last 20 years, however, the gap between economic and societal development has begun to bridge, as the C-suite demonstrates a sincere and growing commitment to collaborate with non-governmental organizations (NGOs) and governments, dedicating resources and discovering new venues for mutually beneficial and sustainable solutions. Paralleling this trend has been the growth of the Internet and other digital technologies, which have begun to shatter long-existing hierarchies and open up communications between C-suite executives and their customers and employees. Consequently, the transformation to sustainable corporate planning serves as both a pillar of the *DIO* and a powerful force for competitive advantage.

The following graphic (Figure 14.1) briefly illustrates the evolution of the integration of economic and societal development within the organization. It also suggests some ways in which sustainable corporate planning will play a crucial role in redefining the future of business.

Concept	Organizational Focus
Traditional Capitalist Venture	*Optimize short-term profits, shareholder value*
Triple Bottom Line (TBL)	*Balance between profits, people, and planet*
Corporate Social Responsibility (CSR)	*External response to community with philanthropy, project resources, and PR*
Creating Shared Value (CSV)	*Internal allocation of resources toward shared business and social objectives*
Integrated External Engagement	*Integrate engagement into strategy at all levels*

Figure 14.1: Integration of Economic and Societal Development within the Organization

In the mid-1990s, the first major breakthrough in sustainable corporate planning occurred as John Elkington developed the triple bottom line (TBL), a new framework to measure sustainability performance in corporate America.[1] It went beyond optimizing short-term profits, return on investment, and shareholder value to consider comprehensive environmental and social impact. Through his efforts the 3P's – profits, people, and planet – were born. TBL became an accounting tool to support sustainability for a number companies, including General Electric, Unilever, Proctor and Gamble, and 3M.[2]

CORPORATE SOCIAL RESPONSIBILITY

Over time, TBL grew into a new consciousness that took companies beyond the sole focus on profit to consider other factors. Corporate social responsibility (CSR) was now to have an input in executive planning.[3] In many ways, CSR represented a grassroots attempt to work with the community in developing collaborative efforts to mitigate local challenges. It addressed four levels of responsibility: economic (make profits), legal (obligation to comply with laws), ethical (do the right thing because its right) and philanthropic (go above and beyond to give back to the community).

Unfortunately, aside from creating a number of beautiful public relations annual reports, a bit of philanthropy, and some collaborative community projects, CSR – one of the great business buzz-terms of the 1970-1990s – failed to deliver. This is because CSR, in fact, lay external to corporate strategy and investment. Substantive social change can only occur as companies allow societal and community concerns “inside” the board room and the solutions are integrated into their corporate plans, investments, and value-add to shareholders.

Figure 14.2: Corporate Social Responsibility

VALUES-DRIVEN MARKETING

Professor Phillip Kotler, considered by many the "guru of modern marketing," proposed that marketing has evolved to a new level focusing on human aspirations, values, and spirit. In Marketing 3.0., he argued that companies are now focused on contributing to a triple bottom line: their profits, their people, and the planet; they want to appeal to the human spirit and make a difference in issues affecting all of our lives.[4]

Within the context of values-based principles, Professor Kotler has noted, "The best way to create shareholder value is to create stakeholder value. US business people made a mistake when they said that companies should maximize shareholder value. That led to very short run gains. Shareholders are not that loyal to a company. Many just buy and sell stock. The company that wins long-run profits does it by building a set of loyal stakeholders, who all gain from the performance of the company. By rewarding the stakeholders fairly, the company will be able to maximize long-term shareholder value."[5]

Professor Phillip Kotler, S. C. Johnson Distinguished Professor of International Marketing, Kellogg School of Management, Northwestern University

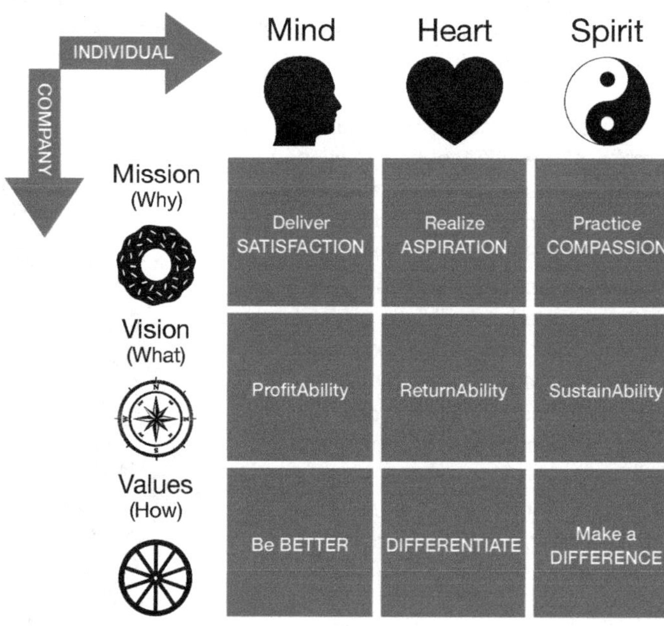

Figure 14.3: Kotler's Values-Based Matrix[6]

Accordingly, Kotler designed the values-based matrix (Figure 14.3) to analyze the values-driven marketing efforts of an organization. It explores how brands can impact societal challenges (e.g. public health, environment) as well as employees and channel partners. The matrix has two dimensions: the vertical axis defines the overarching corporate strategy, including Mission (Why), Vision (What), and Values (How – standards of behavior); the horizontal axis defines how the corporate strategy impacts the individual (e.g. current and future consumers). Corporate strategy is first targeted to the individual's Mind (cognitive thoughts), then to the Heart (affect, emotions) and finally to the Spirit (values). In this way, brands are able to connect social responsibility for global issues (e.g. environment, hunger, poverty, human rights, health and wellness, etc.) with different levels of the human experience.

To serve as an example, the values-based matrix of S.C. Johnson (Figure 14.4) is reflective of its core values, which are clearly outlined in the FAQs section of the company's website:

"What does it mean to be a family company? Being a family company also means we put core values – such as integrity, respect, fairness and trust – above everything else. Being privately held enables us to focus on doing what's right for the next generation, not just the next quarter's earnings report."[7]

	Mind	Heart	Spirit
Mission *Contributing to the community well-being as well as sustaining and protecing the environment*	*Household and Consumer Product Lines*	*Promoting reusable shopping bags*	*Targeting Base of the Pyramid*
Vision *To be a world leader in delivering innovation solutions to meet human needs through sustainability principles*	*For SC Johnson creating sustainable economic value means helping communities prosper while achieving profitable growth*	*The Ron Brown Award for Corporate Leadership*	*Sustaining Values: SC Johnson Public Report*
Values Sustainability *We create economic value We Strive for environmental health We advance social progress*	*We believe our fundamental strength lies in our people.*	*One of the 100 best companies for working mothers*	*The chance to do what's right for the environment and social sustainability*

Figure 14.4: S.C. Johnson's Values-Based Matrix[8]

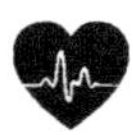

Evaluate your organization's current efforts to integrate economic and societal development by completing the values-based matrix. This will help your team gain insight into whether your mission, vision, and values are consistently aligning with those of your target audience. It will also reveal areas of potential improvement.

For S.C. Johnson, these values translate into a triple bottom line – the economic value of its employees, environmental health of its customers, and social progress of its community. To address the individual's needs, the company targets the Mind by providing value to the community through the strength of its products and employees; it targets the Heart through the company's responsible environmental practices as well as its progressive policy toward working mothers; it targets the Spirit by living its commitment to sustainability in the local and global community.

As S.C. Johnson illustrates, brands that live their mission, vision, and values are more likely to align with the interests of their consumers and stakeholders, consistently projecting their internal values throughout all external touch points, including their products and services, media content, and customer service initiatives. Both traditional and digital media serve to transmit these values-driven messages which, in turn, influence consumer behavior and advocacy.

CREATING SHARED VALUE

Digital technology has allowed organizations to add the fundamental attributes of access, openness, and transparency to their roster of core values. As a 2013 McKinsey and Company article points out, *"Digital Communication has enabled individuals and nongovernmental organizations (NGOs) to observe almost every activity of a business, to rally support against it, and to launch powerful global campaigns very quickly at almost zero cost. High expectations and scrutiny are here to stay. Successful companies must be equipped to deal with them."*[9]

The demands of the digital age quickly underscored the inability of traditional CSR to deliver additional value for businesses or solutions to major societal challenges. A new approach was needed that truly demonstrated economic and social value while incorporating digital technologies.

In 2011, creating shared value (CSV) was proposed by Porter and Kramer to measure *"economic and social value or new benefits that exceed the costs for the business and society to engage the scale and innovation of companies to advance social progress."* CSV has gained global attention because of its differentiation from CSR, where the focus is on the external factors of reputation and responsibility for doing good deeds by virtue of societal pressure.[10]

In contrast to CSR, CSV is internally generated and therefore is not confined to financial budgets. CSV encourages organizations to reconsider their vision for sustainable growth. Using CSV best practices, many leading companies have doubled down on their commitment to social responsibility, including S.C. Johnson, GE, Google, Nestlé and Cisco, to name a few.

Shared value is a management strategy focused on companies creating measurable business value by identifying and addressing social problems that intersect with their business. The shared value framework creates new opportunities for companies, civil society organizations and governments to leverage the power of market-based competition in addressing social problems.

Nestlé – Living by Example

Nestlé has taken the lead in redefining its global corporate strategy through its "Nestlé and society" CSV initiative.[11]

"We define CSV as a strategic way to achieve triple bottom line sustainability. In other words, be financially, environmentally and socially sustainable. At the end of the day, Nestlé seeks to create shared value in those areas where we can make the most impact and that are material to our business. CSV focuses our engagement on critical topics and asks the whole company to see what can be improved for society and ourselves."[12]

Heidi Paul, EVP Corporate Affairs 

Nestlé's 5 Steps to CSV Implementation:[13]

1. Governance – CSV is a companywide effort lead and supervised by the CEO. It includes an external advisory board of experts to assess progress and discuss challenges.

2. Measurement – Nestlé's CSV programs are externally measured by international standards and reporting, and performance is transparent. In addition, the company collaborates on the design of new measures for CSV performance.

3. Stakeholder Engagement – A vast global stakeholder network identifies emerging issues, shapes their responses, and drives performance improvements.

4. Public Policy – All policies and practices are fully transparent. Nestlé works with governments and local authorities to develop public policies in line with their CSV, sustainability, and compliance commitments.

5. Partnerships – Complex social challenges such as those taken on by Nestlé require collaboration from multiple sectors to incorporate *"best human resources knowledge, technical expertise, as well as financial support to help such projects reach their objectives and, more importantly, amplify their impact."*

Nestlé's commitment to CSV has invited scrutiny from all quarters. Nestlé Waters, the number one bottled water company worldwide, has been constantly challenged. As one Nestlé executive retorted, *"If bottled water isn't available, people routinely purchase another packaged drink, one with calories and with a heavier environmental footprint."*[14]

Walmart is another company that has made a commitment to sustainability through the brand's environmental and social justice initiatives. However, evidence suggests WalMart's words may not be matching its deeds. The Institute for Local Self-Reliance examined the retail giant's environmental impact and found that the results are falling far short of the company's promises. According to senior researcher and author Stacy Mitchell, *"Walmart's sustainability campaign has done more to improve the company's image than to help the environment."*[15]

Nestlé in Society

Figure 14.5: Nestlé in Society: Creating Shared Value and Meeting our Commitments – Video[16]

Even though a number of brands have embraced CSV, it is still in an embryonic stage of mainstream adoption. Broader acceptance will require management teams to be in sync with the interests and priorities of their customer base and recognize how external relationships align with changing social mores to enhance business value.

The growing shift from shareholder value to sustainable value is the natural outcome of a new external business environment characterized by declining natural resources, radical transparency, and rising consumer expectations. Thus the sustainable value framework directly links the societal challenges of global sustainability to the creation of shareholder value on the part of the organization.[17]

Taken as a whole, all of these approaches to corporate sustainability served to anticipate the next evolutionary step in the integration of economic and societal development, integrated external engagement (IEE).[18]

Integrated External Engagement

IEE takes a holistic approach to managing the organization's engagement with the external world (e.g. employees, consumers, regulators, potential users, social media activists, and legislators). With IEE, decisions made at all levels of the organization must be integrated consistently with its core values, as they affect the relationships with the external world and impact its shared value.

> *"Cisco Culture is driven by high standards of corporate integrity and by giving back using our resources for a positive global impact. Through corporate philanthropy and public/private cooperation we are building strong and productive global communities in which every individual has the means to live, the opportunity to learn, and the chance to give back."*[19]
>
> John T. Chambers, President and CEO, Cisco Systems Inc.

Most executives agree and support these objectives in theory, but admit that they do not know how to achieve them in reality. This raises a fundamental question:

How can you integrate external considerations into decision making across all levels of the organization?

Going back to our ongoing BLS case study, let's view how Bill and the management team at BLS can incorporate IEE into their corporate strategy to build a sustainable *DIO*. Adapted from McKinsey and Company's research,[20] here are seven steps:

1 *Define What You Contribute* – A company contributes much more than the product or service it offers. Organizations must be explicit about how fulfilling their internal purpose benefits external society. In the case of BLS, its cutting-edge language learning software helps people with advanced study, opening up new commercial and job opportunities.

2 *Clarify Your Core Values* – Though by definition all core values are important, in order to make them actionalbe, certain ones may necessarily take priority over others. As an example, organizations may want to divide their core values into two groups: a limited number of action values, which serve as immediate drivers of change, and aspiring values, which are deemed important but are part of a longer-term sustainability strategy.

3 *Know Your Audience* – Understand your stakeholders as rigorously as you understand your consumers. Knowing stakeholder preferences, expertise, and networks can often open doors to innovative partnerships and solutions.

4 *Apply Progressive Management* – This seems like a given. Effective managers must be able to integrate TBL and IEE best practices into each decision and action. They need to uphold the same standards for external engagement as internal management, to the extent that these standards become the cultural DNA of the organization.

5 *Establish Consistent Processes* – Each strategy, initiative, and task needs to consider the consequences for the business and the impact on its stakeholders. Consistency in the ways an organization hires, fires, rewards, and recognizes employees can be seen as a direct expression of its values.

6 *Measure Outcomes* – Measure in terms of quantifiable value added to the business; this exacting standard is upheld by less than 20% of global executives.[21]

7 *Engage Passionately* – Communication to the external world is an ongoing activity and must be proactive, not an afterthought. Passionately engage and share; don't sell. This is a fine line that the inspired marketing director will often exceed, sometimes turning away his or her target audience. Communication is not monolithic. Collaboration does not always rule; sometimes respectful but direct confrontation is the optimal strategy.

Core Values Direct Our Actions

The mere articulation of universal values, which are culturally sensitive vis-a-vis how they are articulated, is not sufficient. It is necessary for those values to be part of a symbolic template that reflects personal beliefs and principles, as they will affect processes from product design and hiring new employees to evaluating performance and customer communications.

The idea that core values direct our actions as well as our future intentions itself has value. Marketing to and serving such values is a respectful affirmation of the integrity of the people you are serving. Many years ago, I realized that a warranty was a promise of quality and affirmation of trust, but over time it became a disclaimer of liability. It is now time to realize that the open source, transparent and accountable digital world might just be the way back to quality of product and integrity of service. To me this has implications far beyond business; it is a means to generate sustainability, a foundation for education, and a way to affirm in practice what already is manifest in intent.... a more globally coherent, albeit, significantly independent and diverse, set of moment-to -moment interests and needs.

J.E. Rash, Founder and President, Legacy International

Core Values as a Determinant of Success

Values are often portrayed as soft, immeasurable inputs into a business model, sometimes even regarded as "flaky" or "touchy-feely." In reality, sustainable values are beliefs and behaviors that produce the inspiring self identity and group knowledge flow that help people within the organization thrive individually and collectively.[22] They are universal values that have been promoted and practiced by spiritual leaders and philosophers throughout history, and include notions like wisdom, courage, humanity, justice, moderation, and transcendence – universal values that are also reflected in the values of the digital culture.

In truth, many of the same core values of the emerging global digital culture (as outlined in chapter 1) are integral to running a sustainable, social business – a precursor of the *DIO*. Organizations that adopt and consistently live their sustainable values enjoy superior performance on a number of levels, including employee engagement, productivity, innovation, and strategic alignment.[23]

In keeping with this, the "war for talent" among technology companies has gone beyond salary, sign-on bonuses, and work environment. Sustainable values are increasingly defining the norms and processes of many of these organizations as C-level executives begin to leverage the core values of the digital culture to help their teams carry out the company's vision. Deliberately shaping the cultural DNA of your organization enables you to attract talented people who reflect your core values and who want to work for a company that focuses on the bigger picture.[24] As MIT Sloan Management Review notes, building a strong talent pipeline requires "integrating stated core values and business principles into talent management processes." Many progressive companies, including IKEA and IBM, "consider corporate culture as a source of sustainable competitive advantage."[25]

Feedback from the largest demographic in US history seems to confirm this notion. In a 2013 online survey, a sampling of over 2,000 Millennials was asked what is non-negotiable when selecting an employee. Twenty-nine percent responded, "a corporate culture that aligns with my beliefs," while twenty-three percent said "the community, environment, and future is important."[26] Talented digital natives want to contribute in a meaningful way to a work environment with shared values that integrates social responsibility programs into strategic initiatives. In this way, values-driven talent helps to perpetuate sustainable corporate planning within the *DIO*.

For a detailed treatment of how your organization can leverage its core values for competitive advantage ->

TAKEAWAYS

- The transformation to sustainable corporate planning serves as both a pillar of the *DIO* and a powerful force for competitive advantage.

- Three strategic imperatives for the organization to evolve into a *DIO* are progressive management, shared values and culture, and dynamic strategy.

- Substantive social change can only occur as companies allow societal and community concerns “inside” of the boardroom, and the ensuing solutions are integrated into their corporate plans, investments, and value-add to shareholders.

- Many of the same core values of the emerging global digital culture (as outlined in chapter 1) are integral to running a sustainable, social business – a precursor of the *DIO*.

- For many progressive companies, corporate culture is a source of long-term competitive advantage. Values-driven talent will help drive sustainable corporate planning within the *DIO*.

CHAPTER 15: FROM SOCIAL BUSINESS TO DIGITALLY INTEGRATED ORGANIZATION

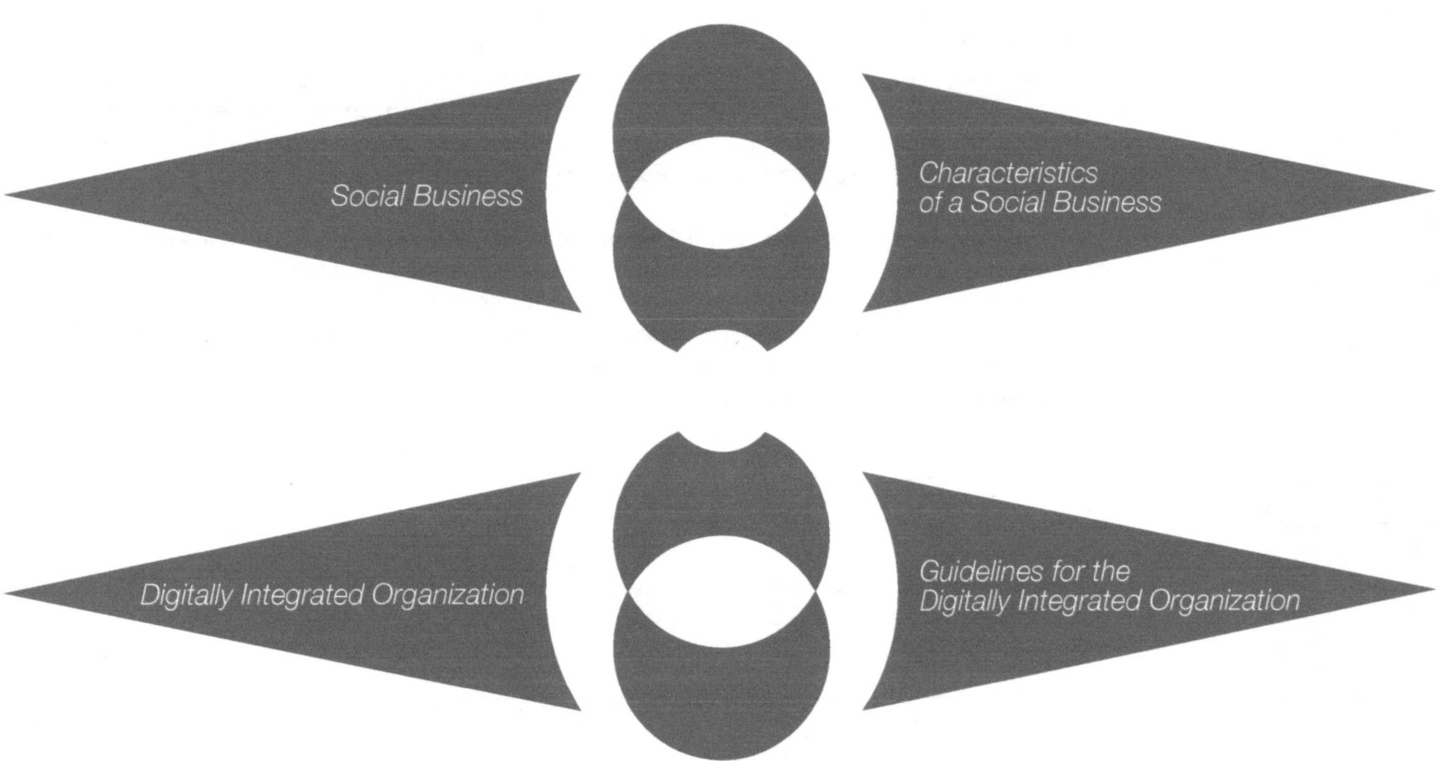

We are now a few hundred pages into preparing you and your organization to weather the ongoing and ever-changing *Digital Tsunami*. The last chapter discussed how many of the same core values of the emerging global digital culture are integral to creating shared value and running a sustainable, social business.

This chapter walks you through the final steps of your journey along the *Path to Digital Integration* by examining the organization's evolution from the social business into the *Digitally Integrated Organization*.

At the outset, we outlined the ways in which the *Path to Digital Integration* brings the organization into alignment with its core values and reveals the actionable strategies and tactics required for it to evolve into the *DIO*. In chapter 4, we noted how the very idea of marketing has its roots in the village marketplaces of old, where one could buy, sell, or exchange a product or service with another in a climate of open engagement and equivalency. During the era of mass media everything changed, as consumers began to sacrifice the personal intercourse and service of the local marketplace for greater product selection at lower prices.

The technologies of the digital culture have helped us rediscover this village marketplace model by creating a climate where businesses that value trust, respect, responsiveness, honesty, and social communion can prosper. The village has now expanded to the global community; its marketplace has been replaced by the Internet and social media; its local conversations and relationships have grown across communities and nations; its singular notion of family subsistence has evolved into those of shared value and sustainability for the organization and the greater community to which it is intrinsically connected.

Are we in the middle of a marketing revolution or is it something even more surprising?

Two technologies – widespread access to high-speed Internet and the availability of free, easy-to-use publishing tools like Facebook, blogs and Twitter – have not so much revolutionized marketing as returned us to our roots. These technologies have democratized influence and placed customers at the power center of commerce, where they had been for a thousand years.

Before the Internet, before advertising or mass media, we bought from people we knew and trusted. Business was human. We needed to fiercely protect our reputation and provide good products because a negative word in our community could destroy a business. And, there was a social aspect to buying at the village market. It was fun.
Does this sound familiar?

The qualities that have always been at the heart of business – a trusted human presence, responsiveness, honesty, and social communion – are at the heart of the social media strategy. We lost sight of these qualities for 100 years – the advent of mass media. We are not so much experiencing a revolution as a return to the way people have always wanted to do business with us.

Mark Schaefer, Marketing Consultant, College Educator and Author of *Return On Influence*.

SOCIAL BUSINESS

Where are we now?

In 2006, Professor Muhammad Yunus was granted the Nobel Peace Prize for creating and launching the microfinance organization Grameen Bank as a social business. He defined social business (aka social enterprise) as a non-dividend company created to solve a social problem. Like a non-governmental organization it has a social mission, but like a business, it generates its own revenues to cover its costs and is financially sustainable.[1]

During this same period, digital technology emerged as a potent force shaping society and business. Companies began to make a distinction between the application of social media marketing as a tactical tool not tied to organizational goals and a social business, or an organization that deeply integrates social media and social methodologies throughout the company to drive real business impact.[2]

Though the two interpretations of social business differ in emphasis, with the former more applicable to the non-profit arena and sustainable values and the latter to profit-driven corporations and business impact, both reflect many of the core values of the digital culture. This is no coincidence, for it is through the merging of these two interpretations of the social business that sustainable organizational models such as the *DIO* emerge.

Within the context of digital marketing, social businesses are organizations that align their digital media strategies with their goals. They are both inward and outward focused, deeply integrating digital technologies across the entire organization to drive business impact internally and externally.

However, a 2013 online survey of social media strategists and executives from a number of mid-size and large corporations conducted by Altimeter Group suggests that for many organizations, the road to social business transformation is a rocky one full of surprising paradoxes.[3]

Digital transformation is maturation process. Only 17% of organizations surveyed are truly strategic in the execution of their social strategies. Moreover, with a lack of clear leadership, organization, and strategy, many companies experience a kind of "social anarchy" of siloed, uncoordinated social efforts.[4]

The Altimeter Group survey found that, while social initiatives are now commonly deployed throughout a number of business units, including customer service, product development, HR, and advertising, only 26% are integrated holistically throughout the organization. As companies become more socially mature (moving toward a social business), they transform their organizational structure to be less hierarchical (24% are now using the Multiple Hub and Spoke model (see chapter 12). Nearly half of the companies surveyed were expecting to invest more in social media management systems and training in the short term; however, only 52% of executives were informed, engaged, or aligned with their company's social strategy.[5]

Why Social Business Works

"When you inspire your workforce to innovate and collaborate more productively, you create tangible business value. When you anticipate needs and deliver exceptional experiences, you delight your customers and create advocates. When you integrate your business processes with the right social tools, you secure a competitive advantage and pioneer new ways of doing business."[6]

IBM Social Business

CHARACTERISTICS OF A SOCIAL BUSINESS

Here are seven characteristics that define a social business:

1 C-Suite Buy-in – The movement to social business integration (involving the entire organization) requires executive buy-in and ongoing involvement. Research from MIT Sloan Management Review and Deloitte shows the importance of building a social business is rapidly growing among executives. In 2012, 36% of executives felt "social business is important today" (an increase of 100% from 2011); 54% of the same executives projected this importance in 2013.[7]

2 Brand Refocus – Most organizations are external-focused – on the social brand and the engagement of customers and prospects. To transition to a social business, the brand must incorporate the needs of various internal and external groups, including its customers, employees, and other stakeholders. An example of such a transition in the marketplace can be found in the reordering of the rankings for the "Most Valuable Brand."[8] In 2013, Apple replaced Coca-Cola as the #1 brand, the position Coke held for 13 consecutive years. Samsung moved up to #8 with a brand strategy that included "a greater focus on social purpose." This underscores research which indicates that American consumers are willing to switch their brand loyalty to "one that was associated with improving people's lives."[9]

3 Digital Crosses Departments – In the traditional, hierarchical organization, business functions were for the most part managed in independent, siloed departments. Social business proposes a massive disruption of this model by integrating digital throughout all internal and external functions of the organization. Digital technologies are now used externally to connect customers with the social brand (e.g. marketing, communications, PR, sales) and internally to increase the efficiency and integration of organizational functions (e.g. HR, IT, customer service, product development, operations). In a larger sense, we are only at the beginning of this process of digital integration. Many organizations see digital strategies initiated and implemented only in the marketing function, inhibiting cross-departmental collaboration.

Deloitte addressed this challenge by developing the "MILO" framework: marketing, innovation, leadership and operation; this initiative supports the executive's vision to expand the impact of digital across other functional areas.[10]

4 Collaboration – Social business fosters collaboration between departments to more effectively realize business goals. Collaboration is not always viewed as a win-win strategy by all involved; it takes more time and effort and requires a sharing of the spotlight to find success. Organizations need to provide internal incentives to drive collaboration. Here are some suggestions:

- Integrate tasks where each person produces what is needed for the next person's job.
- Offer shared goals and rewards for cross-departmental collaboration.
- Provide technologies that encourage and facilitate collaboration.
- Restructure the organization, replacing silos with cross-functional working teams.
- Clarify accountability for the tasks assigned and goals to be achieved.
- Encourage input from outside experts to address more complex solutions.

Enterasys Networks, a mid-size network infrastructure and security company, has 80% of management and employees using Salesforce's Chatter platform to collaborate and share across organizational functions. This technology has opened-up external communications between Enterasys and its customers, and enabled the internal functions of customer service, sales, engineering, and senior management to better solve customer problems. Enterasys Networks provides a great example of cross-departmental integration and collaboration centered on delivering an excellent customer experience.[11]

5 Training – The majority (70%) of businesspeople agree that social business practices can fundamentally change the way their organizations work.[12] According to research conducted by the Altimeter Group, the key ingredient for social business success is a highly trained staff; however, less than one-third of companies offer formal digital media training.[13] Social business requires higher-order social skills than digital media proficiency; the challenge goes beyond technical training to include collaboration. For the successful social business, the employee onboarding process and transition to the new work environment requires thoughtful training.[14]

6 Investment and Reward in Social Technology – Social business requires a new level of technology management for both external and internal applications. On the external side, IT must integrate social initiatives with content management and the growing consumer demand for mobile, tablet, and composite devices. On the internal side, McKinsey Global Institute finds that twice as much potential value lies in using social tools to enhance communications, knowledge sharing, and collaboration within and across enterprises; organizations have an opportunity to raise the

productivity of interaction workers – highly-skilled knowledge workers, including managers and professionals – by 20 to 25 percent.[15]

> *"To transform a vision into a reality, executive leadership must guide middle management on the value of being a social business and build companywide support for the use of social practices across organizational functions."*[16]
>
> Kevin Custis, VP, Social Business and Mobility Services, IBM Global Business

Data-Driven Strategy – Social business aggregates multiple sources of solicited and unsolicited information (e.g. user feedback, reviews, social data) to drive strategic decision making. Here are some uses for this information:

- Determine actionable insights.
- Define trends and competitive positions.
- Relate data to KPIs (key performance indicators).
- Adjust the customer experience.
- Provide insights to product development.
- Drive strategic changes.

The following example aptly illustrates this point. T.M. Lewin, a large UK clothing retailer, decided it had two goals: to grow the brand's social presence while increasing ROI. To accomplish these goals, the company used a data analysis solution to centralize and segment customer data to determine the effectiveness of its digital efforts. The result was an increase in revenue directly attributable to the company's email campaigns, as well as a 1000% increase in Facebook engagement. T.M. Lewin's success was attributed to targeted communications that complemented its efforts to unify digital media and email in order to drive engagement and increase the size of its email database.[17]

Altimeter Group describes the last stage of social business maturity as "converged social business" – a singular business strategy process where social merges with digital and holistic customer experiences are created using converged media, forming a social culture.[18] Altimeter's State of Social Business 2013 report noted that only 3% of the companies surveyed had achieved this level of maturity.[19]

THE DIGITALLY INTEGRATED ORGANIZATION

Beyond social business is the *Digitally Integrated Organization (DIO).* It combines digital technology and digital marketing strategy with core human values to generate abundance for all stakeholders – its employees, shareholders, customers, and community. It is differentiated from social business in terms of its intentions and projected results. Social business is focused on impacting both the internal efficiency as well as the external environment of the organization. The *DIO* considers both internal and external efficacy, but also organizational values and long-term sustainability, as the guiding criteria of all actions. Social business uses digital technology to drive business goals (e.g. operating cost reduction, revenue growth, brand integrity, employee engagement) while the *DIO* builds on the work of the social business. With a mandate that reaches beyond just a social mission, the *DIO* integrates digital technology and marketing strategy with core values to drive organizational goals that lead to sustainable outcomes for both the organization and its stakeholders, including the greater community to which it is connected.

> *"I would say the internal drivers are 80% responsible for our sustainability efforts, benefits include operating costs, revenue growth, brand integrity and employee engagement."*[20]
>
> Bill Morrissey, Vice President, Environmental Sustainability, Clorox
> MIT Sloan/BCG Sustaninability Global Executive Survey

The *DIO* is a learning organization, facilitating an interconnected way of thinking, collaborating, and innovating, continuously transforming itself to meet new challenges. Integration is the currency of the *DIO*. Structural integration paves the way for the organizational innovation and efficiency necessary to be competitive in the digital age.

The *DIO* is an *Integrated Digital Marketing* organization, especially as the role of marketing continues to expand beyond its silo to impact other business functions. John Hayes, CMO of American Express, suggests marketing is *"responsible for establishing priorities and stimulating dialogue throughout the enterprise as it seeks to design, build, operate, and renew cutting-edge customer-engagement approaches."*[21]

This notion extends into the boardroom as the C-suite begins to recognize the power of the consumer and of digital marketing to affect brand and corporate outcomes.[22]

For further insight into the *Digitally Integrated Organization* ->

The necessity of the *DIO* is highlighted in two recent studies that reflect the challenges, practices, and projections of CEOs, non-profit directors, and thought leaders from around the world as they grapple with the impact of digital technologies and sustainability on the future of organizations. The findings and suggested best practices of these two studies offer an outline of the strategic imperatives for organizational sustainability and the *DIO*.

Here is a brief overview of the studies' findings.

Leading Through Connections: IBM CEO Study[23]

An interview of 1700 CEOs in 64 countries examining the convergence of digital technologies and its effect on customers, values, and partnerships. Three initiatives were noted as essential for companies to outperform other organizations:

Empowering Employees Through Values

- Organizational openness offers tremendous upside potential; as rigid controls loosen, organizations need a strong sense of purpose and shared beliefs to guide decision making.
- Allow the organization to collectively compose its core values. Employees must internalize corporate culture and embody and live the organization's values and mission.

Engaging Customers as Individuals

- 73% of CEOs are making significant investments on gaining new insights into their customers, including understanding individual customer needs, seeing customers as part of a holistic environment interacting with the business and rest of the world.

Amplifying Innovation with Partnerships

- Nearly 70% of CEOs are aiming to partner extensively to increase the speed of innovation and to gain competitive advantage.

MIT Sloan/BCG Sustainability & Innovation Global Executive Survey[24]

A survey of 4,700 executives, managers, and thought leaders from around the world looking at the integration of sustainability as a business goal.

- 37% of respondents report profiting from sustainability.
- Approximately 50% of companies have changed their business models as a result of sustainability opportunities.
- Companies report translating sustainability opportunities into business value adds to their bottom line and can boost market share, energy efficiency, and competitive advantage.

Douglas Conant, former CEO, Campbell Soup Company, made sustainability a company focus. He advanced "abundance mentality," challenging people not only to create shareholder value but to do it in a way that simultaneously helps build a better world.[25]

What efforts has your organization made to integrate sustainability into its long-term goals?

- What data and resources would your organization require to adopt sustainability as a part of its DNA?

The goals and intentions of the *DIO* are reflected in various sustainable enterprise initiatives gaining currency in the marketplace:

- Social Enterprise Alliance is a growing organization in North America that defines social enterprises as *"businesses whose primary purpose is the common good. They use the methods and disciplines of business and the power of the marketplace to advance their social, environmental and human justice agendas."*[26]

- B-Corps (Benefit Corporations) offer a positive vision of a better way to do business by voluntarily meeting higher standards of transparency, accountability, and performance. With over 1,000 certified B-Corps from 34 countries having joined the global movement at the time of writing, these unique entities encourage all companies to be the best for the world, resulting in greater economic opportunity while addressing challenging environmental problems. The idea behind the B-Corps is simple: more people will find fulfillment by bringing their whole selves to work.[27]

- Innovating for Shared Value is a study by Harvard Business Review of 30 global companies that consistently rely on five mutually reinforcing elements to succeed in building shared value, whose optimal form and balance depend on the particular culture, context, and strategy of each organization. For example, Nestlé's chairman worked for two decades to transform his company to living shared value at all levels. He found the link between the essence of Nestles' business and rural agricultural communities, water resources, and consumers. *"Today every country manager is expected to create a business plan that makes progress on those issues as well as profits for its shareholders."*[28]

GUIDELINES FOR THE DIGITALLY INTEGRATED ORGANIZATION

The *DIO Action Matrix* (Figure 15.1) summarizes various guidelines for the *DIO* and how they translate into results.

Guidelines	Results
Gain strong support from C-suite executives	Leadership, involvement, direction
Think integration first	Collaboration between siloed departments; culture of innovation
Make customers, employees, and partners the central focus	Two-way conversations, holistic decision-making
Foster a learning organization	Flexible, interconnected, adaptive mindset
Introduce sustainability as a shared value	Investments in a positive future for the organization, community, and world
Modify hierarchical organizational structure	Open and transparent environment; encourages loyalty and innovation
Build cross-functional teams	Collaborative, efficient, responsive solutions
Adopt the *New Marketing Normal*	Digital mindset permeates all marketing components
Develop an *IDM* Strategy	All marketing components augment each other; digital media converge to create optimal impact
Align *IDM* strategy with values, goals, and infrastructure	Technology, people, and processes seamlessly integrate
Build relationships with customers, stakeholders, and the greater community	Enduring brand value; long-term sustainability
Hire the right talent	Caring, sustainable organization poised for innovation

Figure 15.1: DIO Action Matrix

Each of these guidelines is critical to the success of the *DIO*, but the most essential guideline is *Hire the Right Talent*. The *DIO* is people centered; the digital integrators that will lead the *DIO* must combine strong technical and analytical skills with deep-seated values and ethics. Visionary, collaborative professionals who are committed to sustainable solutions and who live the mission of their organization will become the standard for the *DIO*.

The *DIO* is at the innovator stage of the adoption curve, with only a small percentage of organizations having reached such high levels of digital integration. As the findings of the two studies referenced earlier in this chapter suggest, the number of *DIOs* is expected to increase dramatically in coming years.

So what does this mean for a midsize company like BLS, just starting its journey down the *Path to Digital Integration*?

"Connectedness is the hallmark of our era - and the driver of numerous possibilities. But what will CEOs do with this defining characteristic? How will they create value from it – for their customers, their employees, their partners and, by extension, their organizations? Individually, those choices will dictate the success of their organizations. Collectively, they will inspire our future."

Leading Through Connections: IBM Global CEO Study[29]

BLS has committed its organization to digital integration. For Bill and his management team, the *Path to Digital Integration* offers a series of guideposts leading to the *DIO*, providing direction, inspiration, best practices, and case studies for them to draw from throughout their journey.

Much like BLS, the vast majority of organizations the world over are only at the beginning of the historic process of digital integration. The takeaways are clear for anyone willing to listen – digital is a strategic and tactical imperative for those who want to survive, compete, and sustain in today's disruptive, global business environment. The *DIO* provides organizations a framework for achieving competitive advantage in the digital age.

In a deeper sense, the *DIO* represents the living embodiment of the core values of the digital culture. By doing so, the *DIO* reflects the essence of the human experience on both an individual and a collective level: one of unity, integration, and connectedness.

Thus, the *Digitally Integrated Organization* completes the circle that has been slowly drawn through millennia of individual achievement and cultural attainment: people, and the organizations they create, are turning to digital to more efficiently express their intrinsic humanity.

The Digitally Integrated Organization: A Look Into the Future...

I think the "Digitally Integrated Organization" is going to look structurally very different from what we have today. It may take 10 years, but eventually it will happen. We will have more intelligent companies that use data as a common currency; more collaborative companies able to mix different skill sets to solve problems; more orchestrated companies able to work globally in a seamless way without losing control; and more open companies able to leverage the power of crowds of customers, partners and independent brains to innovate. In the end, you will have companies that have productivity levels that far exceed what has been seen in the current models of organization. Some of the basic underlying assumptions we've made about how organizations work will be fundamentally challenged by digital.

Didier Bonnet, Senior Vice President and Global Practice Leader, Capgemini Consulting

The DIO: Transforming Your Organization

Figure 15.2: How-To-Video – The DIO: Transforming Your Organization

- Social business integrates both internal and external communications. *DIO* integrates sustainability as a standard for all actions.

- Social business is about engagement with employees and customers. The *DIO* is about engagement and core values.

- Social business uses digital technology to drive business goals. The *DIO* integrates digital technology and marketing strategy with core values to drive organizational goals that lead to sustainable outcomes.

- Social business is measured by organizational change. *DIO* is measured by the sustainability of the organization, and the greater community of which it is a part.

- Social business investments are focused on internal communities, social technologies, and training. *DIO* investments are focused on sustainable business models.

- Social business and the *DIO* share a common intention: to create value for all stakeholders – customers, the organization, and the community.

DIGITAL TRANSFORMATION AND MARKETING DEVELOPMENT *[Afterword]*

After completing the manuscript, we noted a number of organizations are practicing the values and strategies that lie at the foundation of digital transformation. We decided to include this Afterword to give various digital marketing thought leaders the opportunity to share their insights and experiences as to how the integration of digital marketing with core values and sustainable outcomes facilitates the development of ***Digitally Integrated Organizations***.

We chose participants from different sectors and organizations to reflect varied points of view. Each participant interviewed was asked the same set of questions; their responses are shared in the pages that follow.

Didier Bonnet *Senior Vice President and Global Practice Leader, Capgemini Consulting*

Jeffrey L. Cohen *Distinguished Lecturer Marketing, Miller College of Business, Ball State University; Author,* Social Media Marketing for B2B

Beth Comstock *Senior Vice President, Chief Marketing Officer, General Electric*

Doug Conant *Chairman, Avon Products; Chairman, Kellogg Executive Leadership Institute; Founder & CEO, Conant Leadership; Former President & CEO, Campbell Soup Company*

David Edelman *Partner & Co-Leader, Global Digital Marketing Strategy Practice, McKinsey & Company*

Susie Faries *CEO, SciMed Partners, Associate Faculty, Mission College (Silicon Valley)*

David Ferguson *Director of Center for Digital Marketing Advancement, Ball State University*

Scott Inks *Director of the HH Gregg Center for Professional Selling, Associate Professor of Marketing, Miller College of Business, Ball State University*

Anthony Marshall *Global CEO Study Program Director and Strategy and Transformation Leader, Institute for Business Value, IBM*

Marnie Webb *CEO, Caravan Studios (Division of Tech Soup Global)*

Why do you think the following two paradoxes are so prevalent in today's business landscape?

- Digital is being adopted at an exponential rate by consumers, but less than half of CMOs admit they are technically or analytically prepared to address this opportunity.
- Executives expect digital to transform their companies, but their organizations are not structurally or technologically prepared for the speed of change.

Anthony Marshall

It is very clear that digital is not simple. That's because it is not about doing one thing; it is about doing everything together. So the full power of digital is about the synergies that come with the intersection of a variety of technologies. It is about the evolution of economic systems and about the formation of eco-systems; the changing role of customers within that environment and also of changes in business economics. The whole will be far greater than the sum of the parts. You have exponential benefits that will drive the creation of compelling experiences in what ultimately will become a seamlessly integrated digital-physical environment.

Like many things, creating a unique digital experience is all about demand and supply. Customers are being trained to expect more – to demand compelling experiences and to have things integrated and individualized for them – to no longer be the integrator or last resort. They are putting pressure on organizations to deliver those seamless personalized experiences. On the supply side, it is now possible to begin delivering these types of seamless experiences through technologies such as cloud and analytics and mobility. There is already major pressure on organizations to grow and evolve, and this pressure will continue.

Digitization is not a trivial concept; making things simple and compelling for customers is highly complex and challenging. It is all pretty profound.

Didier Bonnet

Digital fundamentally challenges how we work, how we organize, how we innovate and how we do marketing because it is very cross-functional. For that reason, it needs to be driven hard, it needs to force through the organization something that is fairly unnatural, because different functions, different P/Ls, different geographies need to collaborate and work together to a common goal. This is why, in all cases of successful digital transformation that I have seen, top-down leadership was a key criteria for success.

Secondly, every time we mention digital, people start thinking about the technology first. But like every transformation process, there is a strong people element. If you treat these programs as purely technology programs, you are focusing more on the "deployment" of technology, at the expense of business adoption. Unfortunately, the return on investment is actually based on the adoption not on the deployment.

Doug Conant

The issues of the digital age, much like the dilemmas of any age, are centered around people. The three primary challenges we face are not about technology. They are about people.

The first challenge to be aware of is people's capacity for large-scale change. We've seen the workplace transform dramatically in recent years. The speed at which work is done has increased exponentially. The unrelenting wave of information and "interruptions" – emails, text messages, phone calls, knocks at the office door – can be overwhelming. Knowledge workers feel chronically awash in information and requests. There is a palpable fear that no matter how frantically one tries to address every incoming issue, they will never have enough time to get everything done. This feeling is exacerbated by the fact that the massive changes in technology that have revolutionized the way we do business have often carried with them the implicit expectation that requests will be responded to immediately.

The second challenge is the burgeoning complexity of the workforce. For the first time, we have 5 (soon to be 6) different generations at work at the same time, all with different perceptions, norms, agendas, and skills. We are also experiencing unprecedented gender diversity, ethnic diversity, geographic diversity, and lifestyle diversity in the workplace. The advent of diversity in the workforce is exciting, and should be celebrated on many levels, but it also requires that leaders and workers be evermore committed to working with each other to navigate the changing business landscape effectively. With the growing volume of digital communication, increased complexity in the workplace, and an omnipresent time management issue where more and more is expected to be done "on-demand" – in my opinion, there is unprecedented stress for today's contributors to manage. And this does not even take into account the additional pressures people face at home with their families and their communities.

It is no surprise then that there is some dysfunction with how people are reacting to the digital age. Intellectually, they *want* to embrace digital because of its undeniable benefits. But emotionally, there is a feeling of being suffocated by the onslaught of technology, and this sense of onslaught unmistakably tempers acceptance. Clearly, the workplace is struggling to evolve at the same lightning pace as technology and the expectations of the marketplace.

The third challenge is leadership. It takes remarkable skill for today's leaders to create the conditions for people to meaningfully learn, grow, and contribute with technology in a useful way. Many executives grew up in a hierarchical corporate world. They adhered to a traditional model of ascending the corporate ladder: you did what you were told to do, learned your way, and then secured a position where you in turn told others what to do. That doesn't work anymore. Things change too fast. Unfortunately, we don't yet have the leadership skills in place to manage the change process – not in the corporate world or in the public and non-profit sectors. That is where the challenge lies – creating a new cadre of leaders who have the capacity to develop an organization that successfully accepts and grows with the pressures of technological change.

What has worked to facilitate the adoption of digital?

Didier Bonnet

I encourage my clients to focus on employee engagement and building specific strategies for *capability building*. There is no single silver bullet to solve the capability gap. You need to deploy a panoply of tactics, like recruitment, training, organizational development, partnering, incubating, and the like. Nestlé's Digital Acceleration Team (DAT) is a good example. The DAT is developing global digital ambassadors who are seconded from the brands for a limited period of time. It fulfills two objectives – grow individual skills as fast as possible on real projects, and help to develop coherence by harmonizing Nestlé's global approach to digital and social. It is a very effective model if you can scale it up. Building capabilities faster than your competitors has become a real source of advantage.

Beth Comstock

You have to create "proof points" to create some of these experiments that prove out the hypothesis, so you can show your colleagues, "Hey, this worked." You can engage them in the planning on doing it as a team – you need IT, you need sales, you need technology. So you become a convening force through these proofs, these pilots. You get your customers and other partners engaged; people see it working. Then they say, how can we do more of it.

I'm a total believer in the Skunkworks model, but it does not always have to be hidden. Skunkworks sometimes is done best in a very quiet, separate way. Sometimes you want a lot of visibility because it is really a cultural imperative. I am a big believer of putting in a fast, nimble team and being very visible about it. We've done that with our digital media and marketing team, just saying, "Go for it, go figure out new models, how do you tell the story using digital?" Their job was to be first and innovative and try things out and then somebody in the business would grab it, translate it, and make it scalable for them. For me that is what good marketing leadership is, seeing something, translating the opportunity into your company and creating the kind of proof and momentum behind it so other people find it valuable for them.

David Edelman

You've got to start with "pilots." Most companies are doing something in the digital space; they just might not be gaining the full potential of what digital can offer. They are still approaching it in a sort of campaign-push kind of way. I know one bank that basically every two weeks has a different campaign that they put up on their website or put out on display, that's not the way digital works. You've got to show them benchmarks, of what is possible, in terms of victory rates and conversions and then start piloting things.

You've got to get senior support in doing a pilot, in their environment. We frequently work with companies taking a particular product line, or a particular geographical area, and say let's together do it right. Let's take advantage of all the data we have, let's push the content management personalization system that you have as far as it will go, without having to invest in any new technology.

The pilot is a chance to "hit the 'rethink' button" and show a different way of operating. It's hands-on and a complete immersion with their products. The pilot shows how a campaign can be different, from the set-up in the first place, incorporating multiple cells and designing them to have measurement, and optimization. You are going to change the working process with the agency so that you are getting reports back daily, and you are adjusting the buy daily, at least. You are thinking creatively about a much wider variety of segments. Then there are two things you do, one is that you show that it can be done, but second is that you understand what the restraints are in the company, both technologically and operationally, so that you can start addressing them. Otherwise you are just in theory land, and until you get on the ground and actually do a pilot, you are just talking, you are not doing. Inevitably you start to see results that are 2x, 3x what you have before, and so the organization starts getting religion. Nothing breeds change like success. The main thing is that you have to prove it to them that it can work.

Marnie Webb

Many non-profits are going to just keep up with digital, but they are not being transformative. That has its pluses and minuses. They are making changes, they are moving forward, but they are never going to make an enormous shift. One of the things non-profits provide is access to shelter, food, healthcare, and knowledge. *In almost every instance those things are going to get cheaper and easier to do without the non-profit*. So organizations need to look at digital as a way to transform what they do, not just marketing.

That kind of transformation is hard and will be painful. They have to face the fact that they have been asking for money for the last 20 years, but because of digital, this is no longer needed by anyone. For example, in organizing a beach cleanup, the big thing non-profits did was organize names, bring people together. Facebook does it better than that non-profit. The non-profit has to say, "My value is not that I can get the 200 people to turn up to do beach clean-up; my value has to be something else – where do I find that." It is threatening to see it coming, now they have to figure it out, using digital to reinvent themselves.

David Ferguson

Some companies can step into a new digital mindset more easily than others; and it may be that it is because they are closer to their roots. A lot of start-ups launch with a strong orientation to the team and to the customer, then over time with the natural growth of a corporation, that gets a little too stilted; they end up having lost touch with the those fundamentals. I look at a company like Exact Target (Salesforce); they have a culture, they named it "Orange." It starts at the top with Scott Dorsey, the CEO. As I have observed him, he has worked harder at upholding that culture, the closeness, the camaraderie, the sense of the individual, the higher transcendent purpose that you are there for, than most anything else he has done.

Some C-Suite folks either have been able to fight for that fundamental or can recapture it, and others are going to be lost at sea, and they will have to figure out who they are again. In the digital, transparent world, you can't fake it.

Anthony Marshall

In transforming their organizations, executives and other leaders should recognize that the new technologies are just the beginning point, not the end point – they need to add new functions, processes, and skills; in addition, you've got cultural change that's required. We talked in the 2012 CEO Study about "future-proofing" employees because it is such a complex environment. It becomes very difficult to plan ahead, for example it gets harder and harder to accurately conclude, "I require these types of skills for that type of job," because some of the skills that will be essential in the future may not even exist today. The idea behind future proofing employees is evolving with growing complexity and digital disruption. While you may not be able to plan ahead with complete accuracy, you can help employees become better predictors of what skills will be required, and support them in their pursuit of their own continuing education, professional adaptation, and personal growth.

How do you see the role of marketing changing to meet the opportunities and challenges of the digital business environment?

Beth Comstock

I'm a big believer that marketers are the conveners in an organization and they are the ones understanding where the world is going. They have to see that and define it for their companies. And if not them, who? I think marketers need to understand they have a cultural mandate. Yes there is a growth mandate; you have to grow the top line of the company and hopefully the margins by showing value. Marketing has a role there, but there is a cultural piece. Marketing has to pull more of the pieces of other disciplines into what they do. Change management is a big part of marketing; we are the anticipators, the warners – "Hey, the world is changing and we've got to get ready"

As CMO with a big team across the company, I've tried to redefine marketing as a development function. "Market development" takes trends and where the world is going and translates them into action. For example, affordable healthcare. The world needs affordable healthcare. OK, what are we going to do in my company to deliver on affordable healthcare? What's the value? What are the technologies, who are the partners that we need inside and outside? How are we going to know we are successful? How do we make money on it? In every company there are little bits of players who have pieces of that, but no one who brings it together, usually. I think that is *a call for Marketing*.

Digital has had to be a part of that. Marketing has been the one to say, "Hey, digital is happening." It is a way for us to connect with our customers, with outside partners, a way for us to connect with ideas outside the company that can speed us to market. So very early on we said to our marketers that digital has to be part of what you do. We created pilots and examples that they can take to their organizations and say, "See what we can do; now imagine how we can scale this."

Marnie Webb

At many non-profits when a new tool comes out, they think, "Oh, that's going to fix my marketing problem." For example, "I'll put a QR code on this flyer." But the QR code takes you to a website that is not mobile friendly. There is this huge disconnect between what's current in marketing and what it takes to get engagement. I think what digital does is it pushes our need to be authentic in real time, to drive engagement, which means that it gets exponentially harder and everybody in the organization has to be a marketer.

David Edelman

Data that is available now, either through new forms of market research or from getting feedback from behaviors in the marketplace, gives marketing incredible insight into who the customers are, what are they saying, what are they doing, what are they seeing. This intelligence is the currency marketing brings to drive influence within the organization. It is really about being the steward for insight into the customer, their hesitations, their behaviors, and translating that into innovation, operations, service, and of course marketing itself.

Top executives at the senior table should be bringing new kinds of insights. In one of the companies I'm working with, a financial services firm, the executives get together every sixth week for customer feedback. They are getting customer feedback from all the different channels – what are people saying when they call into the call center, when they see something online. All of the data and marketing orchestrates that. So the CMO is the one who is pulling information from all the different functions, plus from their own insights groups. Then they determine what will have to be done differently, some of which will be in marketing, some of which will be in other functional areas. But they are the stewards of that insight, and that is where a big chunk of their influence and power derives.

Scott Inks

While the *role* of marketing will continue to be revenue generation, brand building, and positioning, marketing communications strategy (including advertising, personal selling, direct marketing, public relations, sales promotion, interactive digital) will change significantly in the face of a growing digital business environment. Organizations will need to rethink resource allocation, shifting resources from more traditional components such as advertising to interactive digital communications tools. Ultimately, marketing as a discipline and business function will need to evolve such that "digital marketing" becomes so integrated into marketing thought and practice that it becomes traditional marketing.

Susie Faries

Marketers will be forced into the digital age – some screaming and resisting – others embracing the change. I am hopeful that we do not swing so far into digital as to delude ourselves that digital will replace the classic marketing strategies and execution. Instead of replacing classic tools, strategies, and tactics, the CMO must consciously integrate digital as one of the core pieces.

In what ways do you think a businesses' core values (e.g. integrity, openness, sustainability) should be integrated into its digital marketing strategy and business planning?

Beth Comstock

I love your diagnostic, *Digitally Integrated Organization*; I think you picked the right components – technologies, digital marketing, and core values. I don't think you can separate them.

If you aspire to be more transparent as part of your belief and integrity, digital is going to get you there faster and more meaningfully. If you want to engage with your stakeholders and partners, digital allows you to share more openly, faster, and track your results.

As we set-up customers' communities, they are able to iterate product development much, much faster using digital. We are able to open those up with those people who know nothing about any of our industries and ask them to help us innovate. In some ways, it puts a finer point on your values as a company, because if you really believe in transparency, if you really believe in community and engaging, there is a certain set of rules you have to believe in. In a sharing world you have to learn what is share-able, and for competition what you are not going to open up as much – not everything falls into that category.

At GE the *"Key to business success is innovation, innovation is driven by understanding and responding to the worlds needs."* One of our goals is to make the company a leader in transparency.... In that context, digital and sustainability cannot be separate silos, they have to be integrated.

Doug Conant

Core values must be pervasive. Your values should be represented clearly and meaningfully in every aspect of your business including all of your marketing, advertising, and promotional efforts. You have to essentially become "one" with the message. And, the message should powerfully and authentically tap into the humanity of all of your stakeholders. This should extend to the employee value proposition – your corporate behaviors will attract, develop, and retain the employees who will execute your strategy. It is imperative they have a clear understanding of what you stand for. People should be evaluated against these kinds of expectations, and given feedback so they can continuously improve in this direction. The more we become enamored with technology, the more we benefit from "leaning in" to our humanity and leveraging our human capital. It is not one or the other. It is, emphatically, both. That is the new paradigm....

Didier Bonnet

Transparency and openness are really important. First, digital drives transparency everywhere. Organizations are becoming fairly transparent on all sorts of dimensions: reporting, customer data, performance metrics, benchmarks and so on. Transparency is one of the key outcomes of a truly digital business. Second, digital also drives openness. You cannot effectively connect to your ecosystem, engage with your customers, access skill sets you don't have, or leverage external sources of innovation without a strong open culture and a business model to suit.

The other value that is really important to me is "authenticity." This is a big paradox. Despite digital marketing becoming more scientific, I believe it has also become much more human than it used to be. The broadcast medium is a very impersonal and blunt instrument. When you start doing personalized marketing and social media you engage with customers in a very meaningful way. In addition, consumers have become very sophisticated; they can "read" through your programs and assess the value you bring to them as individuals. In that context, authenticity becomes really important because marketing becomes about human interactions. This is a big culture change for many organizations.

David Edelman

Today's transparent marketing environment opens up a window into everything that a company does, whether or not employees or consumers can talk about it. It is very hard to keep secrets or to operate in a way that at all times is appropriate, knowing it will become public. So for many of our clients, we turn it around using transparency as strategy for our client's advantage. We become proactive by doing the kind of things that make our employees and customers feel good; we "get everyone to love us" at no loss to their bottom line.

The result – many companies are re-thinking their whole social media strategy and its effect on their overall goals. Some are changing out of necessity, being "forced" by transparency; others because it is the right thing to do; and others still because they want to make their employees feel good about working for a company that really has an impact on the community.

The world is too competitive to have pure idealism; it's more like "enlightened self-interest." The focus on core values will become more important to companies over time; but for now, many companies are backing into it out of necessity.

Anthony Marshall

Characteristics or qualities like sustainability and integrity are 100% correlated with the forces of openness and transparency. Openness and transparency means that you are going to be scrutinized 100% of the time, and all organizations make mistakes – organizations comprise people and people make mistakes. When mistakes are made, really the only defense you have is your integrity and the trust that customers and others have in your organization – the perception that at least you are trying best to do the right thing. Sustainability and other issues that are important to customers will become even more important. Good faith will be critical, the trust and reputation. In our studies of Millennials these themes of integrity and sustainability are even stronger. And CEOs recognize this trend – for them, values remain a very high priority, as are personal and organizational ethics.

Jeffrey L. Cohen

Values are one of the most important pieces driving digital. The digital technologies are really wrapped up in the idea of transparency and sustainability. It is a combination of these ideas that is driving consumers to expect certain things from the companies they deal with, buy from, and work for. Not only do companies need to present these core values in everything that they do, but they have to believe them and act upon them. If the officers of the company honestly don't care about these sorts of values, and you say that you do, people are going to see through you. Certainly one of the best examples is the BP oil spill, when the CEO said how much they cared and how much they were going to do to correct things. It didn't work out because you got the sense that he was being told what he had to say, but at his core, there was not as much concern, and these company values did not really exist at the executive level.

Scott Inks

I suppose that depends upon the extent to which organizations want to be identified by their markets as having particular core values. Core values that enhance the marketability of a company and/or its brands should influence business planning and digital marketing strategy development. Perhaps the most important component of the relationship between an organization's core values and its marketing efforts is the monitoring of social media networks to ensure those core values are interpreted correctly and valued by the market. After all, it doesn't really matter what core values an organization wants to project, it is the markets' perception of the core values an organization possesses that define it in the marketplace.

Marnie Webb

Transparency means much more to the non-profits; the executive wants to be the guardian of the ideal. Non-profits are having a hard time fostering real-time, authentic conversation that doesn't just come from the Executive Director. So how do I empower my team to be able to talk well about the organization, or volunteers about the kind of work we are doing. That is a much harder step for non-profits, because they are letting go of the "control" of their mission.

How do values help to align shareholder goals with stakeholder expectations?

Doug Conant

Evidence increasingly suggests that corporations must seek greater harmony between their business agenda and the societal agenda. Flying in the face of societal expectations will not cut it – and it's clear the two agendas are not yet sufficiently aligned. You can't work single-mindedly for your shareholders alone. All stakeholders must be considered – your employees, your customers, your communities, and your shareholders.

Taking this leap to more fully align the organization requires more transparency. To do this, companies have to effectively become "one" with society just as they must become "one" with their message. Pressure for increased transparency is only going to rise. While improving transparency will undoubtedly be a messy process for many organizations, it's a crucial measure to ensure better alignment. Embracing transparency can be a daunting process for boards and corporate leaders in the short term as their efforts are likely to be met with criticism (i.e. "well, why weren't you transparent before"?) but they will emerge from the messiness in an immeasurably better place.

Beth Comstock

Hopefully shareholder goals and stakeholder expectations all come together. I'm a firm believer that if you solve your customers' problems first, the shareholders get rewarded. Employees feel empowered because you are on a mission to solve world problems through your customers. Energy utilities, hospitals, and airlines face big challenges; so once you understand that digital is really an "operating system," a way of organizing, and try to bring the right partners and the right examples. To me leadership is really about examples that others can follow. Any marketer who wants to lead in these areas needs to identify which examples are important and proselytize about them.

Anthony Marshall

Ethics and values are something that CEOs seek to perpetuate throughout their organizations. Collaboration is becoming ever more important for the organization, with customers, with partners, and as ecosystems of activity become increasingly commonplace, with any number of other individuals or entities. As organizations become more open, individual employees will be making more and more direct decisions that might impact the reputation and the perception of the organization to the outside world. So how do you, as an organization, as a leader help your employees make the right decisions at the right time, in the right way? You need to give the cultural guidelines – cultural cues and norms. Ethics and values, integrity and honesty are absolutely critical to helping your employees to achieve the outcomes you want. You cannot be 100% prescriptive in an open environment. As an executive, you need to trust your people, but you need to help them do the right things in the right way.

Didier Bonnet

I struggle with sustainability. I think it is massively important of course, particularly as the next generation of consumers, Millennials, is putting much more emphasis on social responsibility than older generations. But many corporations are still taking a narrow view of sustainability, or worse, treating it as a marketing slogan.

Too many of the corporate social responsibility (CSR) programs that I've seen are driven by corporate communications people who feel they have to do it. It doesn't really filter through the core of the corporation; I think that's a mistake. If you are going to approach this topic seriously it really needs to filter through everything that you do. Your products and services, your marketing actions, your operations and the way you communicate and engage with communities. This is where authenticity plays a key role – the way you portray your achievements, but also the way that you apologize when you do make a mistake. It's what I call *sustainable values*. It needs to be led.

You need to worry about solving people's problems and care how your company can help these people get a better life. I've seen companies doing this really well, really focusing on how to help customers solve their everyday problems. Sometimes it is about basics, like not having electricity or water, or sometimes it can be about enhancing their experience in more subtle ways. But you need to care. Selling your wares becomes much more meaningful and authentic in that context.

6 What is the next step for digital transformation in organizations?

Beth Comstock

To me it is all about the mission. That is why I work at GE, this is a mission-based company. We have a mission to our investors, but the only reason it works for investors is because we have a mission to make the world better; it is that simple. The colleagues that I have been fortunate enough to work with share that sense of mission. So that's what I think is sustainable. How are you going to get there? How are you going to accomplish it? You are going to use the best digital tools, you are going to connect with the brightest minds possible, both inside and outside your company. If that is not clear, you don't have a story, you don't have a value proposition. You don't have people following, so I think it comes back quite quickly to marketing.

David Ferguson

Transparency is causing the C-suite to have to understand what their real values are, and capture those, and cast that vision. At the same time, there is an enhanced need to listen to the company itself at the grassroots level, and coalesce that identity as clearly as possible. Vision becomes one of the major shifts/drivers in the context of the shifting business environment. Actually, the vision has to be grounded in understanding the nature of societal change that is going on. It is both sweeping and ongoing; it is a new landscape or setting – the re-envisioning of each company as it finds itself in a new digital world

Jeffrey L. Cohen

Digital transformation relates to the shift in culture; the shift in the importance of societal values; and the idea of customer-centric companies. The old adage, *"the customer is always right,"* has never really been paid attention to by lots of companies. If you were to update that to the current culture, it needs to be, *"the customer always needs to be heard,"* it is a different way of thinking. Companies really need to pay attention to what customers are talking about. The idea of customer-centric is driving this transformation.

Doug Conant

Next steps should be focused around developing high-character organizations. Transformations should be anchored in what you stand for and executed by doing precisely what you say you are going to do – and doing so in a very human and integrity laden way.

Corporate-speak like, "enlightened self-interest" should be avoided. As you embark on a transformational journey, the endeavor needs to be legitimately selfless. The more selfless you become, the more the world embraces you. Alternatively, the more you use buzz terms like "enlightened self-interest" the more you lose credibility and public perceptions of your organization become jaded.

While I was CEO of Campbell Soup Company I found that the more our company tried to take care of the world, the more the world cared about our company. It's a valuable lesson. You can lean into these concepts so that you achieve a competitive advantage in the marketplace while also better aligning your company with societal interests. To me, if you are just trying to just manage risk, the motivation is inadequate. As with everything, an earnest effort begins with making things better for other people and springs outward from there. Embracing digital, as with all initiatives, comes back to the people. It is truly all about the people.

Didier Bonnet

The future is not so much figuring out what's the next technology that is going to be disruptive. It is about your ability to effectively use existing technologies for business advantage. Getting your employees to work more effectively, improving the productivity of your operations, giving a better experience to your customers and so on. This is what will generate a better return for your shareholders, customers, employees, and partners. Digital transformation is all about getting organizations ready to face this exponential wave of technological innovations and how to leverage their power for improved business outcomes.

I would go even further. It definitely requires a mindset change, as I believe that leading digital organizations in the future will be fundamentally different and will require new managerial tools. It is hard to predict today what the exact shape of the digital organization of the future is going to look like. That is why I think your *"Digitally Integrated Organization"* concept is directionally useful. What are the implications of digital on the way we lead and manage organizations? This is an important question. And one we need to answer to be able to guide organizations on their path to transformation. Defining potential endgames, what likely target operating models look like, will be crucial for consultants, academics, and business leaders alike, as we are all striving to navigate this new digital world.

END NOTES

PREFACE

[1] Tim Moran, "Adobe Study: Half Of Marketers Losing Sleep Over Digital," CMO.COM, September 23rd, 2013, accessed December 3rd, 2013, http://www.cmo.com/content/cmo-com/home/articles/2013/9/22/adobe_study_half_of_.html.

[2] "Digital Distress, What Keeps Marketers Up All Night?" Adobe Corporation, accessed December 3rd, 2013, http://wwwimages.adobe.com/www.adobe.com/content/dam/Adobe/en/solutions/digital-marketing/pdfs/adobe-digital-distress-survey.pdf.

[3] Moran, "Adobe Study."

[4] YuYu Chen, "Technology, Integration & Disparate Data Top Marketing Challenges [Study]," ClickZ, November 27th, 2013, accessed December 3rd, 2013, http://www.clickz.com/clickz/news/2307528/technology-integration-disparate-data-top-marketing-challenges-study.

[5] "Digital Distress."

[6] "Digital Distress."

[7] Dorie Clark, "The End of the Expert: Why No One in Marketing Knows What They're Doing," Forbes, November 11th, 2012, accessed December 3rd, 2013, http://www.forbes.com/sites/dorieclark/2012/11/11/the-end-of-the-expert-why-no-one-in-marketing-knows-what-theyre-doing/.

[8] "EVRYTHNG in 77 seconds," Vimeo.com, accessed December 3rd, 2013, http://vimeo.com/51878487.

[9] Peter Weill and Stephanie Woerner, "Is Your Organization Ready for Total Digitization?," Harvard Business Review (HBR) Blog, July 24th, 2013, accessed December 3rd, 2013, http://blogs.hbr.org/2013/07/is-your-organization-ready-for/.

CHAPTER 1

[1] Eric Qualman, "#Socialnomics," accessed August 16th, 2014, https://www.youtube.com/watch?v=zxpa4dNVd3c.

[2] Penny Power, "What is a Digital Mindset?" your Business Channel, November 21st , 2010, accessed September 13, 2013, http://www.youtube.com/watch?v=UsN_-zz8TzM.

[3] "Digital," Webopedia, accessed August 21st, 2013, http://www.webopedia.com/TERM/D/digital.html.

[4] "Rupert Murdoch Quotes," Evan Carmichael, accessed August 22nd, 2013, http://www.evancarmichael.com/Famous-Entrepreneurs/640/Rupert-Murdoch-Quotes.html.

[5] Todd Wilms, "CMOs of Cisco, Adobe, and SAP Discuss Leading a Social Transformation…and a Few Surprises," Forbes, June 18th, 2012, accessed August 22nd, 2013, http://www.forbes.com/sites/sap/2012/06/18/cmos-of-cisco-adobe-and-sap-discuss-leading-a-social-transformation-and-a-few-surprises/.

[6] Wilms, "Social Transformation."

[7] "Digital Transformation," Digital Business Forum, AT Kearney, accessed August 21st, 2013, http://www.atkearney.com/web/digital-business-forum/digital-transformation.

CHAPTER 2

[1] "Marketing to Millennials: A Social Approach for a Socially Savvy Generation," Social Chorus, accessed November 21st, 2013, http://www.socialchorus.com/author/gina-melani/.

[2] Brian Solis, "What's the Future of Business?" Slideshare, April 10th, 2013, accessed November 21st, 2013, http://www.slideshare.net/briansolis/official-slideshare-for-whats-the-future-of-business.

[3] "Millennials in the Workplace," Bentley University study, July 2012, accessed December 3rd, 2013, http://www.bentley.edu/centers/center-for-women-and-business/millennials-workplace.

[4] "Millennial Innovation Survey," Deloitte, January 2013, Slideshare, accessed December 3rd, 2013, http://www.slideshare.net/fred.zimny/deloittes-millennial-innovation-survey-2013.

[5] "Millennials and the Future of Work," oDesk, Spring 2013, accessed December 3rd, 2013, https://www.odesk.com/info/spring2013onlineworksurvey/.

[6] "Quarterly Digital Intelligence Briefing: Digital Trends for 2013," eConsultancy/Adobe, January 2013, accessed December 3rd, 2013, http://www.tsbc.com/Downloads/whitepapers/Digital%20Trends.pdf.

[7] "Digital Integration," accessed January 27th, 2014, http://en.wikipedia.org/wiki/Digital_integration.

[8] "From Stretched to Strengthened: Insights from the Global Chief Marketing Officer Study," IBM, October, 2011, accessed December 3rd, 2013, http://public.dhe.ibm.com/common/ssi/ecm/en/gbe03433usen/GBE03433USEN.PDF.

[9] "From Stretched to Strengthened."

CHAPTER 3

[1] Marshall Sponder, "The Converged Digital Industrial Economy and the Internet of Things," ClickZ, October 21st, 2013, accessed December 27, 2013, http://www.clickz.com/clickz/column/2301744/the-converged-digital-industrial-economy-and-the-internet-of-things.

[2] Andy McAfee, "Digital Transformation – We Haven't Seen Anything Yet," Capgemini Consulting, April 30th , 2013, accessed December 27, 2013, http://www.youtube.com/watch?v=AZ5ePL36BbU.

[3] Dan Farber, "Google Search scratches its brain 500 million times a day," C/NET, May 13th, 2013, accessed December 27, 2013, http://news.cnet.com/8301-1023_3-57584305-93/google-search-scratches-its-brain-500-million-times-a-day/.

[4] Farber, "Google Search."

[5] Farber, "Google Search."

[6] Farber, "Google Search."

[7] "Quarterly Retail, E-Commerce Sales – 3rd Quarter 2013," U.S. Census Bureau News, November 22, 2013, accessed December 27, 2013, http://www.census.gov/retail/mrts/www/data/pdf/ec_current.pdf.

[8] "Quarterly Retail, E-Commerce Sales."

[9] Seth Fiegerman, "Report: U.S. Mobile Commerce to Hit $114 Billion This Year," Mashable, May 12, 2014, accessed June 30, 2014, http://mashable.com/2014/05/12/mobile-commerce-sales/.

[10] "50 Must-Know Mobile Commerce Facts and Statistics," Mobify, July 03, 2013, accessed December 27, 2013, http://www.slideshare.net/mobify/50-mustknow-mobile-commerce-facts-and-statistics.

[11] "50 Must-Know Mobile."

[12] "50 Must-Know Mobile."

[13] "Experian Marketing Services reveals 27 percent of time spent online is on social networking," Experian, April, 16, 2013, accessed December 27, 2013, http://press.experian.com/United-States/Press-Release/experian-marketing-services-reveals-27-percent-of-time-spent-online-is-on-social-networking.aspx.

[14] "Experian Marketing Services."

[15] Tara Walpert Levy, "The Engagement Project: Connecting with Your Consumer in the Participation Age, Google Think Insights, May 2013, accessed December 27, 2013, http://www.google.com/think/articles/engagement-project-new-normal.html.

[16] John Glenday, "IAB study finds 90% of consumers back brands after interacting via social media," The Drum, July 4, 2013, accessed December 27, 2013, http://www.thedrum.com/news/2013/07/04/iab-study-finds-90-consumers-back-brands-after-interacting-social-media.

[17] "Engaging consumers where it matters most," Wildfire, accessed December 27, 2013, http://go.wf-social.com/Customer_Lifecycle_Report_Req.html.

[18] "Engaging consumers."

[19] Allison Schiff, "Q&A: Flora Caputo, VP and ECD, Jacobs Agency," Direct Marketing News, July 1st, 2012, accessed December 28, 2013, http://www.dmnews.com/qa-flora-caputo-vp-and-ecd-jacobs-agency/article/246897/.

[20] Joshua Brustein, "Walter Isaacson on Crowdsourcing His New Book," Bloomberg Businessweek, December 30, 2013, accessed January 4, 2014, http://mobile.businessweek.com/articles/2013-12-30/walter-isaacson-on-crowdsourcing-his-new-book.

[21] David Moth, "10 interesting digital marketing stats we've seen this week," eConsultancy, October 18th, 2013, accessed December 28, 2013, http://econsultancy.com/blog/63606-10-interesting-digital-marketing-stats-we-ve-seen-this-week-58.

[22] Moth, "10 interesting."

[23] Greg Sterling, "Mobile Close To 20 Percent Of Internet Traffic Globally," Marketing Land, September 4th, 2013, accessed December 28, 2013, http://marketingland.com/mobile-close-to-20-percent-of-internet-traffic-globally-58015.

[24] "Adobe 2013 Mobile Consumer Survey Result," Adobe, 2013, accessed January 4, 2014, http://success.adobe.com/en/na/programs/products/digitalmarketing/offers/june/1306-35508-mobile-consumer-survey-results.html?s_osc=701a0000000mynJAAQ&s_iid.

[25] "Mobile Devices Empower Today's Shoppers In-store and Online," Nielson, December 4, 2012, accessed January 4, 2014, http://www.nielsen.com/us/en/newswire/2012/mobile-devices-empower-todays-shoppers-in-store-and-online.html.

[26] Nick DiMarco, "Location recognition applications filter the noise of social media," abc2news.com, October 16th 2013, accessed January 4, 2014, http://www.abc2news.com/dpp/news/region/baltimore_county/location-recognition-applications-filter-the-noise-of-social-media#ixzz2qDSGLPOx.

[27] Ingrid Lunden, "Senator Charles Schumer, Location Analytics Firms Unveil Code Of Conduct For Tracking Shoppers By Cellphones," TechCruch, October 22nd, 2013, accessed December 28, 2013, http://techcrunch.com/2013/10/22/senator-charles-schumer-location-analytics-firms-unveil-code-of-conduct-for-tracking-consumers-by-cellphones/.

[28] "Our Mobile Planet: United States," Google Think Insights, May 2012, accessed December 28, 2013, http://www.google.com/think/research-studies/our-mobile-planet-united-states.html.

[29] Mitya Voskresensky, "Nielsen Research: Mobile consumer report 2013," Nielsen Research, March 27, 2013, accessed December 28, 2013, http://www.slideshare.net/duckofdoom/mobile-consumerreport2013-17748641.

[30] Simon Khalaf, "Flurry Five-Year Report: It's an App World. The Web Just Lives in It," Flurry, April 3rd, 2013, accessed December 28, 2013, http://www.flurry.com/bid/95723/Flurry-Five-Year-Report-It-s-an-App-World-The-Web-Just-Lives-in-It#.U7GXjvk7uSo.

[31] "Adobe 2013 Mobile."

[32] Abhijit Naik, "How Does SMS Work?" Buzzle, September 27th, 2011, accessed December 26, 2013, http://www.buzzle.com/articles/how-does-sms-work.html.

[33] Marc Knoll, "Mobile Payment Overview: Definition, Trends And Payment Systems, TrendBlog.net, December 4, 2012, accessed December 28, 2013, http://trendblog.net/mobile-payment-overview-definition-trends-and-payment-systems/.

[34]"Mobile Augmented Reality- The 8th Mass Medium," Juniper Research, November 2013, accessed December 29th, 2013, http://www.juniperresearch.com/shop/whitepapers/mobile_augmented_reality.

[35] Raul F. Chong, "Changing the World: Big Data and the Cloud," The Atlantic, January 2013, accessed December 28, 2013, http://www.theatlantic.com/sponsored/ibm-cloud-rescue/archive/2012/09/changing-the-world-big-data-and-the-cloud/262065/#ixzz2qDp1xhSb.

[36] Brett King, "Too Much Content: A World of Exponential Information Growth," Huffington Post, January 18th, 2011, accessed December 28, 2013, http://www.huffingtonpost.com/brett-king/too-much-content-a-world-_b_809677.html.

[37] Ciara Byrne, "Lessons From A Crash Course In Data Science," Fast Company, April 21st, 2013, accessed December 29, 2013, http://www.fastcolabs.com/3008620/lessons-crash-course-data-science?partner=rss&utm_source=feedly&utm_medium=feed&utm_campaign=Feed%3A+fastcompany%2Fheadlines+(Fast+Company).

[38] "Understanding the Cloud Computing Stack: SaaS, PaaS, IaaS," Rackspace, October 22nd, 2013, accessed December 29, 2013, http://www.rackspace.com/knowledge_center/whitepaper/understanding-the-cloud-computing-stack-saas-paas-iaas.

[39] Eric Griffith, "What Is Cloud Computing?" PC Magazine, March 13, 2013, accessed December 29, 2013, http://www.pcmag.com/article2/0,2817,2372163,00.asp.

[40] James Kaplan, Chris Rezek, and Kara Sprague, "Protecting information in the cloud," McKinsey & Company, January 2013, accessed December 29, 2013, http://www.mckinsey.com/insights/business_technology/protecting_information_in_the_cloud.

[41] Kaplan, "Protecting information."

[42] Kaplan, "Protecting information."

[43] "Understanding the Cloud Computing Stack."

[44] "Understanding the Cloud Computing Stack."

[45] "Understanding the Cloud Computing Stack."

[46] Graham Charlton, "Q&A: Andy Hobsbawm on the 'internet of things,'" Econsultancy, June 3rd, 2011, accessed December 29, 2013, http://econsultancy.com/blog/7591-q-a-andy-hobsbawm-on-evrythng.

[47] Michael Fitzgerald, Nina Kruschwitz, Didier Bonnet, and Michael Welch, "Embracing Digital Technology," MIT Sloan Management Review and Capgemini Consulting, October 2013, accessed December 29, 2013, http://sloanreview.mit.edu/projects/embracing-digital-technology.

[48] Fitzgerald, "Embracing Digital."

[49] Didier Bonnet, "Do You Have the IT For the Coming Digital Wave?" Harvard Business Review, August 26th, 2013, accessed December 29, 2013, http://blogs.hbr.org/2013/08/do-you-have-the-it-for-the-com/.

[50] Fitzgerald, "Embracing Digital."

CHAPTER 4

[1] "Definition of Marketing," AMA, accessed September 3rd, 2013, http://www.marketingpower.com/AboutAMA/Pages/DefinitionofMarketing.aspx.

[2] "John Battelle on making advertising 'inherently valuable,'" Bazaarvoice: Connected Perspectives, accessed September 3rd, 2013, http://connectedperspectives.com/videos/john-battelle-on-making-advertising-inherently-valuable/.

[3] "The Break Up," Microsoft Advertising, uploaded to YouTube by Geert Desager, May 16th, 2007, accessed September 3rd, 2013, http://www.youtube.com/watch?v=D3qltEtl7H8. Client: Microsoft Digital; Contact Client/Trade Marketeer: Geert Desager; Agency: Dallas Antwerp (www.dallas.be); Creatives: Stef Selfslagh, Stijn Gansemans; Account Manager: Mathias Delmote; Production: Caviar Films LA; Director: Ben Zlotucha.

[4] "About Marketing 2.0," Marketing Medley, accessed September 4th, 2013, http://www.marketingmedley.com/marketing_2.php.

[5] Philip Kotler, Hermawan Kartajaya, and Iwan Setiawan, "Marketing 3.0: From Products to Customers to the Human Spirit," New Jersey: Wiley, 2010.

[6] Philip Kotler, "Thriving with Marketing 3.0," Slideshare, November 10th, 2010, accessed September 5th, 2013, http://www.slideshare.net/giudicebr/kotler-marketing30.

[7] Lauren Johnson, Razorfish Exec: Brands Need to Get Smarter on Mobile Segmentation," Mobile Marketer, December 6th, 2013, accessed December 10th, 2013, http://www.mobilemarketer.com/cms/news/content/16741.html.

[8] Chad Pollitt, "Embrace Digital Personas Now Before It's Too Late," Social Media Today, October 27th, 2013, accessed December 10th, 2013, http://socialmediatoday.com/index.php?q=cpollittiu/1810251/embrace-digital-personas-now-it-s-too-late.

[9] Greg Satell," The Brand's New Open Architecture," Digital Tonto, July 25th, 2012, accessed December 10th, 2013, http://www.digitaltonto.com/2012/the-brands-new-open-architecture/.

[10] Jemima Gibbons, "The Tale of the Social Brand," Fresh Business Thinking, April 28th, 2011, accessed September 5th, 2013, http://www.youtube.com/watch?v=qFw63Y5T3vs.

[11] Social Brands 100: The Report 2013," Headstream, May 22nd, 2013, accessed December 10th, 2013, http://www.rankingthebrands.com/PDF/Social%20Brands%20100%20ranking%20report%202013.pdf.

[12] John Goodman and Karl Friedman, "Show Me The Money! Focusing Lean SS on Enhancing Top Line Revenue," March 8th, 2010, accessed December 10th, 2013, http://asq.org/conferences/six-sigma/2010/pdf/proceedings/d1.pdf.

[13] Dave Carroll, "United Breaks Guitars," Dave Carroll Music, uploaded on YouTube July 6th, 2009, accessed via YouTube December 10th, 2013, http://www.youtube.com/watch?v=5YGc4zOqozo.

[14] "'United Breaks Guitars:' Did It Really Cost The Airline $180 Million?" May 5th, 2011, accessed December 10th, 2013, http://www.huffingtonpost.com/2009/07/24/united-breaks-guitars-did_n_244357.html.

[15] "Oracle CX Overview," Oracle, February 4, 2013, accessed December 10th, 2013, http://www.oracle.com/in/corporate/events/oracle-cx-portfolio-overview-1986648-en-in.pdf.

[16] "2011 Customer Experience Impact Report," Right Now Technologies, Jan 10th, 2012, accessed December 10th, 2013, http://www.slideshare.net/RightNow/2011-customer-experience-impact-report.

[17] "2011 Customer Experience Impact Report."

[18] "American Customer Satisfaction Index," accessed December 10th, 2013, http://www.theacsi.org/the-american-customer-satisfaction-index.

[19] "Net Promoter Score," accessed December 10th, 2013, http://www.netpromoter.com/why-net-promoter/about-net-promoter/.

[20] "Customer Effort Score," accessed December 10th, 2013, http://www.executiveboard.com/exbd/sales-service/customer-effort/index.page.

[21] Adapted from David Wood, "How to Build a Sales Funnel (Part One)," accessed September 6th, 2013, http://workwithdavidwood.com/how-to-build-a-sales-funnel-part-one/.

[22] "Basics of Influence Marketing," Appinions, December 20th, 2012, accessed September 6th, 2013, http://www.slideshare.net/appinions/basics-of-influence-marketing-appinions-dec2012.

[23] Mark Schaefer, "Return on Influence: The Rise of the Citizen Influencer," May 5th, 2012, accessed September 6th, 2013, http://sparksheet.com/return-on-influence-the-rise-of-the-citizen-influencer/.

[24] Mark Schaefer, "Return On Influence: The Revolutionary Power of Klout, Social Scoring, and Influence Marketing," New York: McGraw Hill, 2012.

[25] Jonah Berger, "Contagious: Why Things Catch On," New York: Simon & Schuster, 2013.

[26] Lydia Dishman, "Why Ideas and Products Become Contagious: The Jonah Berger Formula," Fast Company, February 11, 2013, accessed September 6th, 2013, http://www.fastcompany.com/3005679/why-ideas-and-products-become-contagious-jonah-berger-formula.

[27] Comediva, "G-Male," Uploaded on YouTube August 28th, 2011, accessed September 6th, 2013, http://www.youtube.com/watch?v=dx-cX7W03RI.

[1] Daniel Goodall, "Owned, Bought, Earned Media," March 2nd, 2009, accessed September 9th, 2013, http://danielgoodall.com/2009/03/02/owned-bought-and-earned-media/.

[2] Sean Corcoran, "Defining Earned, Owned and Paid Media," Forrester Research, December 16, 2009, accessed September 9th, 2013, http://blogs.forrester.com/interactive_marketing/2009/12/defining-earned-owned-and-paid-media.html.

[3] Research Measures Effectiveness of Packaging Brand Messages as Newsworthy Video, Synaptic Digital and Kantar Video, June 21st, 2011, accessed September 9th, 2013, http://www.synapticdigital.com/2011/06/21/research-measures-effectiveness-of-packaging-brand-messages-as-newsworthy-video/#sthash.qCoRloeD.dpuf.

[4] Shea Bennett, "Paid, Owned, Earned: A Strategic Business Model For Effective Social Media Marketing [INFOGRAPHIC]," The Brian Strom Group," February 14, 2013, accessed September 9th, 2013, http://www.mediabistro.com/alltwitter/files/2013/02/social-media-party.jpg.

[5] Rebecca Lieb and Jeremiah Owyang, "The Converged Media Imperative: How Brands Must Combine Paid, Owned & Earned Media," Altimeter Group Network, uploaded on SlideShare on July 18th, 2012, accessed December 9th, 2013, http://www.slideshare.net/Altimeter/the-converged-media-imperative.

[6] Lieb, "Converged Media."

[7] Nancy Bhagat, "The Blending of Media," Intel, June 22nd, 2012, accessed December 9th, 2013, http://blogs.intel.com/marketeer-musings/2012/06/22/the-blending-of-media/.

[8] "The Giants Drive Fan Engagement with Year-round Social Strategies," Mass Relevance, December 2011, accessed December 9th, 2013, http://lp.massrelevance.com/rs/massrelevance/images/Case_Study_Giants_Mass_Relevance.pdf?mkt_tok=3RkMMJWWfF9wsRonvanPZKXonjHpfsX56uokWKe2lMl%2F0ER3fOvrPUfGjl4ATsJll%2BSLDwEYGJlv6SgFSLjBMa5m3rgJXxl%3D.

[9] Carolyn Heller Baird and Gautam Parasnis, "From Social Media to Social CRM," IBM Institute for Business Value, June, 2011, accessed December 10th, 2013, https://www.ibm.com/midmarket/uk/en/att/pdf/social_media_Part_Executive_Report.pdf.

[10] "Customer Relationship Management," accessed December 10th, 2013, http://en.wikipedia.org/wiki/Customer_Relationship_Management.

[11] Guide to Understanding Social CRM," Chess Media Group, uploaded to SlideShare on Feb 20, 2011, accessed December 10th, 2013, http://www.slideshare.net/fred.zimny/chess-media-group-guide-to-social-crm-2010.

[12] Paul Greenberg, "CRM at the Speed of Light, Forth Edition: Social CRM Strategies, Tools and Techniques for Engaging Customers," New York: McGraw Hill, 2010.

[13] "Measurement and Social CRM: Top Priorities for CMOs," iStrategy, October 9th, 2013, accessed December 10th, 2013, http://www.womma.org/posts/2013/10/measurement-and-social-crm-top-priorities-for-cmos.

[14] "2011 Customer Experience Impact Report."

[15] Domenico Azzarello and Mark Kovac, "Can communications services providers earn their customers' love?" Bain and Company, August 11, 2011, accessed December 10th, 2013, http://www.bain.com/publications/articles/can-communications-service-providers-earn-customers-love.aspx.

[16] "50 Facts about Customer Experience," October 26th, 2010, accessed December 10th, 2013, http://returnonbehavior.com/2010/10/50-facts-about-customer-experience-for-2011/.

[17] "Customer Service Lessons Learned," accessed December 10th, 2013, http://www.crmsearch.com/service.php.

[18] Anant Jhingran, "Making the Shift from Big to Broad Data," Apigee, May 4th, 2012, accessed December 10th, 2013, https://blog.apigee.com/detail/making_the_shift_from_big_to_broad_data.

[19] Robert Moran, "The Futures of Marketing Research," StrategyOne US, accessed December 10th, 2013, http://www.sagepub.com/upm-data/43895_Epilogue.pdf.

[20] Moran, "The Futures of Marketing Research."

[21] Ray Poynter, "Putting why in the picture. Is market research ready for Big Data?" Vision Critical, March 12th, 2012, accessed December 10th, 2013, http://www.visioncritical.com/blog/market-research-ready-big-data.

[22] Lauren Drell, "Inbound Marketing vs. Outbound Marketing [INFOGRAPHIC]," Voltier Digital, October 30th, 2011, accessed December 10th, 2013, http://mashable.com/2011/10/30/inbound-outbound-marketing/.

[23] "Inbound Methodology," HubSpot, accessed December 10th, 2013, http://www.hubspot.com/inbound-marketing.

[24] "Inbound Methodology."

[25] Drell, "Inbound Marketing."

[26] Drell, "Inbound Marketing."

[27] Drell, "Inbound Marketing."

[28] "2013 State of Inbound Marketing," HubSpot, accessed December 30th, 2013, http://offers.hubspot.com/2013-state-of-inbound-marketing.

CHAPTER 6

[1] "Integrated Marketing Communications," Wikipedia, accessed December 30th, 2013, http://en.wikipedia.org/wiki/Integrated_marketing_communications#cite_note-2.

[2] "Integrated Marketing Communications."

[3] Brian Bennett and Bill Kresse, "It's Time to Redefine Integrated Marketing," Stirology, April 16th 2013, accessed December 30th, 2013, http://blog.stirstuff.com/2013/04/16/time-to-redefine-integrated-marketing.

[4] David Moth, "Only 12% of businesses take an integrated approach to all marketing activities," Econsultancy, December 19th, 2013, accessed December 30th, 2013, http://econsultancy.com/blog/64029-only-12-of-businesses-take-an-integrated-approach-to-all-marketing-activities.

[5] "Integrated Marketing Survey," Ignition One, 2013, accessed December 30th, 2013, http://pages.ignitionone.com/integrated-marketing-survey.

[6] "Full Integrated Digital Marketing Campaign Case Study with Lexus," Soul Digit, July 2nd, 2012, accessed November 10th, 2013, https://www.youtube.com/watch?v=cHKjXm6SblU.

[7] "The Integrated Marketing Playbook," Ignition One, 2013, accessed November 28th, 2013, http://pages.ignitionone.com/integratedmarketing.

[8] Kip Knight, "Brand Workshop," Knightvision, April 2012, accessed and amended November 20th, 2013, private document.

CHAPTER 7

[1] Robert Mills, "Finding Your Tone of Voice," Smashing Magazine, August 21st, 2012, accessed December 18th, 2013, http://uxdesign.smashingmagazine.com/2012/08/21/finding-tone-voice/.

[2] Aarron Walter, "Designing Personas," accessed December 18th, 2013, http://aarronwalter.com/design-personas/.

[3] Rebecca Churt, "SEO – The Past, Present, and Future," HubSpot, accessed December 18th, 2013, http://offers.hubspot.com/search-engine-optimization-past-present-future.

[4] Elizabeth Komar, "How Consumers Found Websites in 2012," Forrester Research, July 19th, 2013, accessed December 18th, 2013, http://www.forrester.com/How+Consumers+Found+Websites+In+2012/fulltext/-/E-RES92661.

[5] Benjamin Kabin, "Social Media May Soon Drive More Traffic to Your Website Than Search Engines," Entrepreneur, June 25, 2013, accessed December 20th, 2013, http://www.entrepreneur.com/article/227178#ixzz2ojwDNz4B.

[6] Scott Gillum, "The Stanley Cup of B-to-B Social Media," Online Media Daily, June 12, 2013, accessed December 20th, 2013, http://www.mediapost.com/publications/article/202199/the-stanley-cup-of-b-to-b-social-media.html?edition=61062#axzz2W0Z8vkhW.

[7] Nora Ganim Barnes, Ava M. Lescault, and Stephanie Wright, "2013 Fortune 500 Are Bullish on Social Media," University of Massachusetts Dartmouth Center for Marketing Research, accessed December 18th, 2013, http://www.umassd.edu/media/umassdartmouth/cmr/studiesandresearch/2013_Fortune_500.pdf.

[8] Maeve Duggan and Aaron Smith, "Social Media Update 2013," Pew Internet and American Life Project, December 30, 2013, accessed January 2nd, 2014, http://www.pewinternet.org/Reports/2013/Social-Media-Update/Main-Findings.aspx.

[9] Duggan, "Update 2013."

[10] Duggan, "Update 2013."

[11] "Facebook Statistics," Statistic Brain, January 1st, 2014, accessed June 13th, 2014, http://www.statisticbrain.com/facebook-statistics/.

[12] Mantas, "Social Media."

[13] Copper Smith, "Statistics About Facebook Users That Reveal Why It's Such A Powerful Marketing Platform," Business Insider Report, November 16th, 2013, accessed December 20th, 2013, http://www.businessinsider.com/a-primer-on-facebook-demographics-2013-10.

[14] "Twitter Usage," Twitter, accessed June 13th, 2014, https://about.twitter.com/company.

[15] Mantas, "Social Media."

[16] "Twitter Usage."

[17] Mantas, "Social Media."

[18] Mantas, "Social Media."

[19] Nate Smitha, "Despite a Rocky Road, 59% of Top Brands Are Now Active on Instagram," Simply Measured, February 19th, 2013, accessed December 20th, 2013, http://simplymeasured.com/blog/2014/01/07/simply-measureds-top-tweeters-of-2013/.

[20] "About LinkedIn," LinkedIn, accessed June 13th, 2014, http://press.linkedin.com/about.

[21] "About LinkedIn."

[22] "About LinkedIn."

[23] "Instagram Press News," Instagram, accessed June 13th, 2014, http://instagram.com/press/.

[24] Mantas, "Social Media."

[25] "Instagram Press News."

[26] Mantas, "Social Media."

[27] Mantas, "Social Media."

[28] Mantas, "Social Media."

[29] Mantas, "Social Media."

[30] Mantas, "Social Media."

[31] Mantas, "Social Media."

CHAPTER 8

[1] "A Day in the Life of Web Content," Chartbeat, November 4th, 2013, accessed January 2nd, 2014, http://www.slideshare.net/chartbeat/mockup-infographicv4-27900399.

[1] "A Day in the Life of Web Content," Chartbeat, November 4th, 2013, accessed January 2nd, 2014, http://www.slideshare.net/chartbeat/mockup-infographicv4-27900399.

[2] Joe Pulizzi, "What is the Essence of Content Marketing?" Content Marketing Institute, accessed November 2nd, 2013, http://contentmarketinginstitute.com/author/joepulizzi/.

[3] "2013 State of Inbound Marketing," Hubspot, accessed November 2nd, 2013, http://offers.hubspot.com/2013-state-of-inbound-marketing.

[4] "B2C Content Marketing 2014 Benchmarks, Budgets, and Trends – North America" Content Marketing Institute & MarketingProfs, accessed November 2nd, 2013, http://contentmarketinginstitute.com/wp-content/uploads/2013/10/B2C_Research_2014-withlinks.pdf.

[5] "Content Marketing Survey Report," Econsultancy, October 2012, accessed November 2nd, 2013, http://econsultancy.com/reports/content-marketing-survey-report.

[6] Ted Karczewski,"Could a Content Marketing Platform Help Marketers Engage?" The Content Standard, September 24th, 2013, accessed November 2nd, 2013, http://www.contentstandard.com/contentmarketing/could-a-content-marketing-platform-help-marketers-engage-study/.

[7] Alyssa Adkins, "How to Run Your Social Media Marketing Like a Newsroom," July 23rd, 2013, accessed November 2nd, 2013, http://engage.synecoretech.com/marketing-technology-for-growth/bid/183982/How-to-Run-Your-Social-Media-Marketing-Like-a-Newsroom%5d.

[8] Jeff Denenholz, "Online Consumers Fed Up with Irrelevant Content on Favorite Websites, According to Janrain Study," Harris Interactive on behalf of Janrain, July 31st, 2013, accessed November 2nd, 2013, http://janrain.com/about/newsroom/press-releases/online-consumers-fed-up-with-irrelevant-content-on-favorite-websites-according-to-janrain-study/.

[9] Jeff Denenholz, "Online Consumers Fed Up with Irrelevant Content on Favorite Websites, According to Janrain Study," Harris Interactive on behalf of Janrain, July 31st, 2013, accessed November 2nd, 2013, http://janrain.com/about/newsroom/press-releases/online-consumers-fed-up-with-irrelevant-content-on-favorite-websites-according-to-janrain-study/.

[10] Denenholz, "Online Consumers."

[11] Denenholz, "Online Consumers."

[12] Joe Pulizzi, "2014 B2B Content Marketing Research: Strategy is Key to Effectiveness," Content Marketing Institute, October 1st, 2013, accessed November 2nd, 2013, http://contentmarketinginstitute.com/2013/10/2014-b2b-content-marketing-research/.

[13] Chris Abraham, "Building Social Media Communities" Huffington Post, November 5th 2012, accessed November 8th, 2013, http://www.huffingtonpost.com/chris-abraham/building-social-media-com_b_2073864.html.

[14] Lee Odden, "Break Free of Old SEO & Become the Best Answer for Prospects, Customers & The Media," Top Rank Blog, 2013, accessed November 28th, 2013, http://www.toprankblog.com/2013/07/break-free-old-seo/.

[15] "Link to your Google+ profile using rel="author"," Google Webmaster Tools, accessed November 28th, 2013, https://support.google.com/webmasters/answer/2539557?hl=en.

[16] Aleh Barysevich, "10 Alternatives to Google AdWords," PPC Hero, August 9th, 2013, accessed November 28th, 2013, http://www.ppchero.com/10-alternatives-to-google-adword/.

[17] "How Retargeting Works," AdRoll, accessed November 28th 2013, https://www.adroll.com/retargeting.

CHAPTER 9

[1] Kathryn Zickuhr, "Location-Based Services," Pew Internet, September 12th, 2013, accessed November 28th, 2013, http://pewinternet.org/Reports/2013/Location/Overview.aspx.

[2] Zickuhr, "Location-Based Services.

[3] Zickuhr, "Location-Based Services.

[4] Jason Spero, "The Mobile Playbook, 2nd edition," Google, October 2013, accessed November 29th, 2013, http://www.themobileplaybook.com/en-us/#/chapter4_2.

[5] "Across Industries, Mobile Ad Spend Increases Dramatically,"eMarketer, January 2nd, 2014, accessed January 6th, 2014, http://www.emarketer.com/Article/Across-Industries-Mobile-Ad-Spend-Increases-Dramatically/1010499#zZHj6VwAZk2LJexH.99.

[6] Graham Charlton, "10 mind-blowing mobile infographics," Econsultancy, June 24th, 2011, accessed November 29th, 2013, http://econsultancy.com/blog/7697-10-mind-blowing-mobile-infographics.

[7] "15 Mind-Blowing Stats about Mobile Advertising," CMO.com, January 22nd, 2014, accessed March 5th, 2014, http://m.cmo.com/content/cmo-m/home/articles/2014/1/22/15_Stats_Mobile_Advertising.html.

[8] "PAA Internet Jargon Buster," accessed November 29th, 2013, http://www.silas.com.au/jargonbuster.html.

[9] Ashley Verrill, "Compare Customer Relationship Management Software Solutions," Software Advice, January 9th, 2014, accessed January 10th, 2014, http://www.softwareadvice.com/crm/.

[10] Geeta Rohra and Mridul Sharma, "Social CRM – Possibilities and Challenges," Tata Consulting Services, accessed January 6th, 2014, http://www.tcs.com/SiteCollectionDocuments/White%20Papers/ConnectedMarketing_Whitepaper_Social_CRM%E2%80%93Possibilities_Challenges_0912-1.pdf.

[11] Rohra, "Social CRM."

[12] Verrill, "Compare Customer Relationship."

[13] Verrill, "Compare Customer Relationship."

CHAPTER 10

[1] "An Introduction to Inbound Marketing Analytics," Hubspot, accessed January 6th, 2014, http://offers.hubspot.com/intro-to-inbound-marketing-analytics.

[2] "Inbound Marketing Analytics."

[3] "Inbound Marketing Analytics."

[4] Kayden Kelly, "What is Bounce Rate? Avoid Common Pitfalls," Blast, February 12th, 2012, accessed January 4th, 2014, http://www.blastam.com/blog/index.php/2012/02/what-is-bounce-rate/.

[5] Kelly, "Bounce Rate."

[6] "Inbound Marketing Analytics."

[7] "Inbound Marketing Analytics."

[8] Luke Chitwood, "5 social media metrics that your business should be tracking," The Next Web, October 29th, 2013, accessed January 4th, 2014, http://thenextweb.com/socialmedia/2013/10/29/5-social-media-metrics-business-tracking/#!sbh7a.

[9] Chitwood, "5 social media metrics."

[10] Chitwood, "5 social media metrics."

[11] Meghan Keaney Anderson, "The 5 Social Media Metrics Your CEO Actually Cares About," Hubspot Inbound Marketing, May 29, 2013, accessed January 4th, 2014, http://blog.hubspot.com/marketing/social-media-metrics-ceos-cares-about.

[12] Jasmine Jaume "What Do Marketers Think About Social Media Monitoring?" Brandwatch, April 22nd 2013, accessed January 4th, 2014, http://www.brandwatch.com/2013/04/what-do-marketers-think-about-social-media-monitoring-infographic/.

[13] Jaume "Social Media Monitoring."

[14] Kashmir Hill, " 'Google Alerts' Are Broken," Forbes, July 30th, 2013, accessed January 4th, 2014, http://www.forbes.com/sites/kashmirhill/2013/07/30/google-alerts-are-broken/.

[15] "Social Media Management," TrustRadius, accessed January 5th, 2014, http://www.trustradius.com/categories/social-media-management.

CHAPTER 11

[1] Sora Park, "Dimensions of digital media literacy and the relationship to social exclusion," Academia.edu, February 2012, accessed September 24th, 2013, https://www.academia.edu/2125068/Dimensions_of_digital_media_literacy_and_the_relationship_to_social_exclusion.

[2] Roland Deiser and Sylvain Newton, "Six social-media skills every leader needs," McKinsey Quarterly, February 2013, accessed September 24th, 2013, http://www.mckinsey.com/insights/high_tech_telecoms_internet/six_social-media_skills_every_leader_needs.

[3] "Leading Through Connections," IBM Institute for Business Value 2012 Global CEO Study, 2012, accessed September 24th, 2013, http://www.ihrim.org/Pubonline/Wire/Sept12/LeadingThruConnections.PDF.

[4] Deiser, "Six social-media skills."

[5] Sandra Sieber, "Three Steps Towards Developing a Digital Mindset (video)," IESE Business School, July 25th 2013, accessed September 24th, 2013, http://www.youtube.com/watch?v=Kxfl38ndNdE.

[6] Deiser, "Six social-media skills."

[7] Deiser, "Six social-media skills."

[8] Avi Dan, "Just How Does Coca-Cola Reinvent Itself In A Changed World?" Forbes, October 7th, 2013, accessed October 28th, 2013, http://www.forbes.com/sites/avidan/2013/10/07/just-how-does-coca-cola-reinvent-itself-in-a-changed-world/.

[9] Debra Zahay-Blatz, "Secrets of Innovation and Data Management from Kayak," Data Driven Digital Marketing, November 16th, 2013, accessed November 28th, 2013, http://datadrivendigitalmarketing.blogspot.com/2013/11/secrets-of-innovation-and-data.html.

[10] Zahay-Blatz, "Secrets of Innovation."

[11] Zahay-Blatz, "Secrets of Innovation."

[12] Andrea Goldberg, "Aligning Social Business and Organizational Culture," Digital Culture Consulting, September 10th, 2013, http://www.digitalcultureconsulting.com/aligning-social-business-and-organizational-culture.

[13] Avinoam Nowogrodski, "How Do We Prepare for Generation Collaboration?" July 2nd, 2013, accessed November 28th, 2013, http://www.wired.com/insights/2013/07/how-do-we-prepare-for-generation-collaboration/?inf_contact_key=2a2a765f501b76632b46d4d32347da9d6cb64d899e2acc696f42f93b6f7962c9.

[14] "The Integrated Marketing Playbook," Ignition One, 2013, accessed November 28th, 2013, http://pages.ignitionone.com/integratedmarketing.

[15] Giselle Abramovich, "Inside Taco Bell's Social Media Strategy," CMO EXCLUSIVES, CMO.com, September 18th, 2013, accessed November 28th, 2013, http://www.cmo.com/content/cmo-com/home/articles/2013/9/6/inside_taco_bell_s_s.html.

[16] Robert Safian, "The Secrets of Generation Flux," Fast Company, October 15th, 2012, accessed November 28th, 2013, http://www.fastcompany.com/3001734/secrets-generation-flux.

[17] Brad Brown, Johnson Sikes, and Paul Willmott, "Bullish on digital: McKinsey Global Survey results," McKinsey Quarterly, August 2013, accessed November 28th, 2013, http://www.mckinsey.com/insights/business_technology/bullish_on_digital_mckinsey_global_survey_results?cid=other-eml-nsl-mip-mck-oth-1309.

[18] Katie Smith, "Why leadership is crucial for driving digital transformation," Cogapp, March 14th, 2013, accessed November 29th, 2013, http://www.theguardian.com/voluntary-sector-network/2013/mar/14/leadership-driving-digital-transformation.

[19] Deiser, "Six social-media skills."

[1] Tom French, Laura LaBerge, and Paul Magill, "We're all Marketers Now," McKinsey Quarterly, July 2011, accessed December 8th, 2013, http://www.mckinsey.com/insights/marketing_sales/were_all_marketers_now.

[2] John Kotter, "Hierarchy and Network: Two Structures, One Organization," HBR Blog Network, May 23th, 2011, accessed December 8th, 2013, http://blogs.hbr.org/2011/05/two-structures-one-organizatio/.

[3] "Minding your Digital Business: McKinsey Global Survey results," McKinsey & Company, May 2012, accessed December 8th, 2013, http://www.mckinsey.com/insights/business_technology/minding_your_digital_business_mckinsey_global_survey_results.

[4] Safian, "Generation Flux."

[5] Neil Smith, "To Build Your Business, Smash Your Silos," Fast Company, June 5th, 2012, accessed December 8th, 2013, http://www.fastcompany.com/1839317/build-your-business-smash-your-silos.

[6] Kotter, "Hierarchy."

[7] Kotter, "Hierarchy."

[8] John Kotter, "Hierarchy and Network: Two Structures, One Organization (video)," Kotter International, 2011, accessed December 8th, 2013, http://vimeo.com/24629683.

[9] Joseph Bradley and Shari Slate, "Enterprise Collaboration: Top 10 Insights," Cisco IBSG Horizons, 2012, accessed December 8th, 2013, http://www.cisco.com/web/about/ac79/docs/re/Enterprise-Collaboration_Top-10.pdf.

[10] Safian, "Generation Flux."

[11] Michael Cuthrell and Bert Sandie, "Managing Beyond the Organizational Hierarchy with Communities and Social Networks at Electronic Arts," Management Innovation eXchange, December 19, 2011, accessed December 8th, 2013, http://www.managementexchange.com/story/managing-beyond-organizational-hierarchy-communities-and-social-networks-electronic-arts.

[12] Krish Krishnakanthan, "Getting into your customers' heads: An interview with the COO of Electronic Arts Labels," McKinsey & Company, January 2013, accessed December 8th, 2013, http://www.mckinsey.com/insights/business_technology/getting_into_your_customers_heads_an_interview_with_the_coo_of_electronic_arts_labels.

[13] Solis, "Business 2013."

[14] Brian Solis and Charlene Li, "The State of Social Business 2013: The Maturing of Social Media into Social Business," Altimeter Group, October 14th, 2013, accessed December 9th, 2013, http://www.slideshare.net/Altimeter/report-the-state-of-social-business-2013-the-maturing-of-social-media-into-social-business.

[15] Aaron Shapiro, "Skunkworks, Reorganization, and other Tactics to Excel in the Digital Age," Fast Company, February 22nd, 2012, accessed December 9th, 2013, http://www.fastcompany.com/1817130/skunkworks-reorganization-and-other-tactics-excel-digital-age.

[16] Jason Mogus, Michael Silberman, and Christopher Roy, "Four Models for Managing Digital at Your Organization," Stanford Social Innovation Review, October 13th, 2011, accessed December 9th, 2013, http://www.ssireview.org/blog/entry/four_models_for_organizing_digital_work_part_two.

[17] Laura McLellan, "By 2017 the CMO will Spend More on IT Than the CIO," Gartner Webinars, January 3rd, 2012, accessed December 9th, 2013, http://my.gartner.com/portal/server.pt?open=512&objID=202&mode=2&PageID=5553&resId=1871515&ref=Webinar-Calendar.

[18] Laura Ramos,"B2B CMOs Must Evolve or Move On," Forrester Research, July 3rd, 2013, accessed December 9th, 2013, http://solutions.forrester.com/Global/FileLib/Reports/B2B_CMOs_Must_Evolve_Or_Move_On.pdf.

[19] "From Stretched to Strengthened," IBM Institute for Business Value, 2011, accessed December 9th, 2013, http://public.dhe.ibm.com/common/ssi/ecm/en/gbe03433usen/GBE03433USEN.PDF.

[20] Kenneth Corbin, "Gartner Says CIOs and CMOs Must Learn to Collaborate on Digital Marketing," CIO.com, October 18th, 2013, accessed December 9th, 2013, http://www.cio.com/article/741623/Gartner_Says_CIOs_and_CMOs_Must_Learn_to_Collaborate_on_Digital_Marketing.

[21] French, "Marketers Now."

[22] Jeff Pundyk, "Collaboration Is the Path To Digital Connection," CMO.com Exclusive, September 26th, 2012, accessed December 9th, 2013, http://www.cmo.com/content/cmo-com/home/articles/2012/9/26/collaboration-is-the-path-to-digital-connection.html.

[23] Laura Montini, "Jack Dorsey: Be Totally Transparent With Employees," Inc. Magazine, November 5th, 2013, accessed December 9th, 2013, http://www.inc.com/laura-montini/why-600-employees-know-everything-about-square-at-all-times.html.

[24] Ryan Holmes, "The $1.3 Trillion Price of not Tweeting at Work," Fast Company, August 30, 2012, accessed December 9th, 2013, http://www.fastcompany.com/3000908/13-trillion-price-not-tweeting-work.

[25] Russell Herder, "Social Media: Embracing the Opportunities, Averting the Risks," Ethos Business Law, August 2009, accessed December 9th, 2013, http://www.nasba.org/files/2011/03/Social_Media_Policy_Article_Presentation-Aug09.pdf.

[26] Jennifer Amanda Jones, "10 Tips for Creating a Social Media Policy for Your Business," Social Media Examiner, February 9th, 2012, accessed December 19th, 2013, http://www.socialmediaexaminer.com/10-tips-for-creating-a-social-media-policy-for-your-business/.

[27] Ed Catmull, "How Pixar Fosters Collective Creativity," Harvard Business Review, September 2008, accessed December 19th, 2013, http://hbr.org/2008/09/how-pixar-fosters-collective-creativity/ar/1.

[28] Greg Satell, "Rethinking Marketing Strategy For The Digital Age," Digital Tonto, April 3rd, 2013, accessed December 19th, 2013, http://www.digitaltonto.com/2013/rethinking-marketing-strategy-for-the-digital-age/.

CHAPTER 13

[1] IStrategy, "Measurement and Social CRM: Top Priorities for CMOs," Word of Mouth Marketing Organization, October 9th, 2013, accessed December 21st, 2013, http://www.womma.org/posts/2013/10/measurement-and-social-crm-top-priorities-for-cmos.

[2] "Online Measurement and Strategy Report 2013," Econsultancy, July 2013, accessed December 21st, 2013, http://econsultancy.com/reports/online-measurement-and-strategy-report.

[3] Angela Jeffrey, Social Media Measurement: Putting it All Together, AMEC (International Association for Measurement and Evaluation of Communication), 2011, accessed December 21st, 2013, http://amecorg.com/wp-content/uploads/2012/10/Social-Media-Measurement-Putting-it-all-Together-2012.pdf.

[4] Elizabeth Lupfer, "The State of Social Media Marketing," Awareness Software, January 4th, 2012, accessed December 21st, 2013, http://www.slideshare.net/PingElizabeth/the-state-of-social-media-marketing-report-awarenessinc.

[5] "Leading Through Connections," IBM Institute for Business Value, 2012, accessed December 22nd, 2013, http://public.dhe.ibm.com/common/ssi/ecm/en/gbe03486usen/GBE03486USEN.PDF.

[6] John Lovett, "Building a Culture of Measurement," Webtrends, accessed December 22nd, 2013, http://webtrends.com/files/whitepaper/Whitepaper-BuildingACultureOfMeasurement-Webtrends.pdf

[7] Avinash Kaushik, "Digital Marketing and Measurement Model," Occam's Razor, accessed December 22nd, 2013, http://www.kaushik.net/avinash/digital-marketing-and-measurement-model/.

[8] Mike Ricci, "Using Metrics to Fuel Social Media ROI," Webtrends, Dec 1st, 2012, accessed December 22nd, 2013, http://www.slideshare.net/MRicci1234/using-metrics-to-fuel-social-media-roi.

[9] Ricci, "Using Metrics."

[10] Kaushik, "Measurement Model."

[11] John Koetsier, "Superheroes of marketing automation: The VentureBeat top 10," December 16th, 2013, accessed December 22nd, 2013, http://venturebeat.com/2013/12/16/superheroes-of-marketing-automation-the-venturebeat-top-10/view-all/.

[12] Ricci, "Using Metrics."

[13] Baird, "Social CRM."

[14] "Return on marketing investment," Wikipedia, November 23rd, 2013, accessed December 22nd, 2013, http://en.wikipedia.org/wiki/Return_on_marketing_investment.

[15] "From Stretched to Strengthened."

[16] "Real ROI from social in 5 steps," bazaarvoice, April 2nd, 2012, accessed December 22nd, 2013, http://www.bazaarvoice.com/research-and-insight/white-papers/Real-ROI-from-social.html.

[17] Meghan Keaney Anderson, "20 Stats That Explain Why Marketers Still Struggle to Measure Social Media ROI," Hubspot, October 11th, 2012, accessed December 22nd, 2013, http://blog.hubspot.com/blog/tabid/6307/bid/33672/20-Stats-That-Explain-Why-Marketers-Still-Struggle-to-Measure-Social-Media-ROI-Data.aspx.

[18] "Why marketers aren't giving social the credit it deserves," Adobe Digital Index Report, 2012, accessed December 22nd, 2013, http://success.adobe.com/assets/en/downloads/whitepaper/18011_201205_Digital_Index_Social_Report.pdf.

[19] Jennifer Beese," Social Networks Influence 74% of Consumers' Buying Decisions," SproutSocial, November 16th, 2011, accessed December 22nd, 2013, http://sproutsocial.com/insights/social-networks-influence-buying-decisions/.

[20] Peter Schoewe, "Measuring your Return on Investment in Multichannel Fundraising Campaigns," Mal Warwick | Donordigital, accessed December 22nd, 2013, http://donordigital.com/publications/Donordigital_Measuring-Your-Return-on-Investment_Dec2012.pdf.

[21] "Social Brands 100: The Report 2013."

CHAPTER 14

[1] John Elkington, "Towards the Sustainable Corporation: Win-Win-Win Business Strategies for Sustainable Development." California Management Review; 36, no. 2 (1994): 90–100.

[2] Timothy F. Slaper and Tanya J. Hall, "The Triple Bottom Line: What Is It and How Does It Work?" Indiana Business Review; 86, no. 1 (2011): 4-8, accessed September 22nd, 2013, http://www.ibrc.indiana.edu/ibr/2011/spring/article2.html#ftn1.

[3] "Social Corporate Responsibility," Wikipedia, accessed September 22nd, 2013, http://en.wikipedia.org/wiki/Corporate_social_responsibility.

[4] Philip Kotler, Hermawan Kartajaya, and Iwan Setiawan, "Marketing 3.0: From Products to Customers to the Human Spirit," New Jersey: Wiley, 2010.

[5] "Philip Kotler talks to Techronicle about 'Values-based Business,'" Techronicle, accessed September 22nd, 2013, http://www.avanzasolutions.com/Techronicle/philip-kotler-interview.

[6] Kotler, Kartajaya, and Setiawan, Marketing 3.0, 42.

[7] "Frequently asked Questions," S.C. Johnson Company, accessed September 24th, 2013, http://www.scjohnson.com/en/company/faqs.aspx.

[8] Kotler, Kartajaya, and Setiawan, Marketing 3.0, 43.

[9] John Browne and Robin Nuttall, "Beyond corporate social responsibility: Integrated external engagement," McKinsey & Company, March 2013, accessed September 24th, 2013, http://www.mckinsey.com/insights/strategy/beyond_corporate_social_responsibility_integrated_external_engagement.

[10] Michael E. Porter and Mark R. Kramer, "Creating Shared Value," Harvard Business Review, January 2011, accessed September 24th, 2013, http://hbr.org/2011/01/the-big-idea-creating-shared-value.

[11] "Nestlé in society: Creating Shared Value and meeting our commitments," Nestlé Corporation, accessed September 24th, 2013. http://www.Nestlé.com/csv.

[12] Aman Singh, "Is Nestlé Waters really creating 'shared value'?" Greenbiz.com, August 8th, 2013, accessed September 24th, 2013, http://www.greenbiz.com/blog/2013/08/08/Nestlé-waters-really-creating-shared-value.

[13] "Nestlé in society."

[14] Singh, "Is Nestlé Waters."

[15] Stacy Mitchell, "Walmart's Greenwash: How the company's much-publicized sustainability campaign falls short, while its relentless growth devastates the environment." Institute for Local Self-Reliance, March 2012, accessed September 25th, 2013, http://www.ilsr.org/wp-content/uploads/2012/03/walmart-greenwash-report.pdf.

[16] "Nestlé in society."

[17] Stuart I. Hart, "Sustainable Value," accessed September 25th, 2013, http://www.stuartlhart.com/sustainablevalue.html.

[18] Browne and Nuttall, "Integrated external engagement."

[19] Jenny Carless, "John Chambers Plays Leading Role in Discussing Global Prosperity and Security at World Economic Forum," Cisco Newsroom, January 21st, 2004, accessed September 26th, 2013, http://newsroom.cisco.com/dlls/2004/ts_012104.html?CMP=AF17154&vs_f=News@Cisco:+EMEA+Public+Policy+News&vs_p=News@Cisco:+EMEA+Public+Policy+News&vs_k=1.

[20] Browne and Nuttall, "Integrated external engagement."

[21] Browne and Nuttall, "Integrated external engagement."

[22] Michelle Lee Stallard, "What are Sustainable Values?" E Pluribus Partners, May 17th, 2010, accessed September 26th, 2013, http://www.michaelleestallard.com/what-are-sustainable-values.

[23] Stallard, "Sustainable Values."

[24] Daniel Saks, "The War for Tech Talent: Genius is Not Enough," Guest Post for Forbes, February 23rd, 2012, accessed September 26th, 2013, http://www.forbes.com/sites/ciocentral/2012/02/23/the-war-for-tech-talent-genius-is-not-enough/.

[23] Stallard, "Sustainable Values."

[24] Daniel Saks, "The War for Tech Talent: Genius is Not Enough," Guest Post for Forbes, February 23rd, 2012, accessed September 26th, 2013, http://www.forbes.com/sites/ciocentral/2012/02/23/the-war-for-tech-talent-genius-is-not-enough/.

[25] Günter K. Stahl, Ingmar Björkman, Elaine Farndale, Shad S. Morris, Jaap Paauwe, Philip Stiles, Jonathan Trevor, and Patrick Wright, "Six Principles of Effective Global Talent Management," MIT Sloan Management Review, March 2012, accessed September 26th, 2013, http://sloanreview.mit.edu/article/six-principles-of-effective-global-talent-management/.

[26] 2013 Millennial Impact Report, The Case Foundation, July 2013, accessed September 26th, 2013, http://www.themillennialimpact.com/2013Research.

[1] "What is Social Business?" Yunus Social Business, accessed September 4th, 2013, http://www.yunussb.com/social-business/.

[2] Charlene Li and Brian Solis, "The Evolution of Social Business: Six Stages of Social Business Transformation," Altimeter Group, March 6th, 2013, accessed September 14th, 2013, http://www.altimetergroup.com/research/reports/evolution-social-business.

[3] Li, "Social Business."

[4] Solis, "Business 2013."

[5] Solis, "Business 2013."

[6] "Why social business works," IBM Social Business Unit, accessed September 14th, 2013, http://www-07.ibm.com/innovation/in/social-business/index.html.

[7] Michael Fitzgerald, "Making Social Business Work in Organizations (Video)," MIT Sloan Management Review, November 13th, 2013, accessed November 24th, 2013, http://sloanreview.mit.edu/article/video-making-social-business-work-in-organizations/.

[8] Stuart Elliott, "Apple Passes Coca-Cola as Most Valuable Brand," NY Times, September 29th, 2013, accessed November 24th, 2013, http://www.nytimes.com/2013/09/30/business/media/apple-passes-coca-cola-as-most-valuable-brand.html?_r=2&.

[9] Elliott, "Apple Passes."

[10] Fitzgerald, "Making Social."

[11] Louis Columbus, "Social Business Beyond Kumbaya: How Enterasys Networks Strengthened Their Serve," Forbes, December 28th, 2012, accessed November 24th, 2013, http://www.forbes.com/sites/louiscolumbus/2012/12/28/social-business-beyond-kumbaya-how-enterasys-networks-strengthened-their-serve/.

[12] Fitzgerald, "Making Social."

[13] Solis, "Business 2013."

[14] Solis, "Business 2013."

[15] Michael Chui, James Manyika, Jacques Bughin, Richard Dobbs, Charles Roxburgh, Hugo Sarrazin, Geoffrey Sands, and Magdalena

Westergren, "The social economy: Unlocking value and productivity through social technologies," McKinsey Global Institute, July 2012, accessed November 24th, 2013, http://www.mckinsey.com/insights/high_tech_telecoms_internet/the_social_economy.

[16] "IBM Study: Investments in Social Technologies Climb, While Management Struggles with Uptick," IBM, November 13th 2012, accessed November 24th, 2013, http://www- 03.ibm.com/press/uk/en/pressrelease/39472.wss.

[17] "Case Study: T.M. Lewin," accessed November 24th, 2013, http://www.figarodigital.co.uk/case-study/tm-lewin-email.aspx.

[18] Brian Solis, "The Gap Between Social Media and Business Impact: 6 stages of social business transformation," Brian Solis Blog, March 12th, 2013, accessed November 24th, 2013, http://www.briansolis.com/2013/03/the-gap-between-social-media-and-business-impact-introducing-the-6-stages-of-social-business-transformation/.

[19] Solis, "Business 2013."

[20] Nina Kruschwitz and Knut Haanaes, "First Look: Highlights from the Third Annual Sustainability Global Executive Survey," September 21st, 2011, accessed November 24th, 2013, http://sloanreview.mit.edu/article/first-look-highlights-from-the-third-annual-sustainability-global-executive-survey/.

[21] French, "Marketers Now."

[22] Jean-Baptiste Coumau, "Engaging boards on the future of marketing," McKinsey Quarterly, February 2013, accessed November 24th, 2013, http://www.mckinsey.com/insights/marketing_sales/engaging_boards_on_the_future_of_marketing.

[23] "From Leading Through Connections."

[24] Kruschwitz, " First Look:

[25] Kruschwitz, " First Look:

[26] "What's a Social Enterprise?" Social Enterprise Alliance," accessed December 13th, 2013, https://www.se-alliance.org/why#whatsasocialenterprise.

[27] "What are B Corps?" B Certified Corporation, accessed December 13th, 2013, http://www.bcorporation.net/.

[28] Marc Pfitzer, Valerie Bockstette, and Mike Stamp, "Innovating for Shared Value," Harvard Business Review, September 2013, accessed December 13th 2013, http://hbr.org/2013/09/innovating-for-shared-value/ar/1.

[29] "Leading Through Connections."

GLOSSARY

Our goal with this glossary is to facilitate digital literacy and provide a vocabulary that executives, managers, students, and entrepreneurs can easily understand. Throughout the book, we have provided brief definitions of digital marketing terminology. We have aggregated and summarized the majority of these definitions in the following glossary. It also contains a number of terms common to marketing in general and digital marketing in particular. For any terms cited in the book but excluded from this glossary, further explanation can be found in the related links referenced in the chapter endnotes.

DIGITAL MARKETING GLOSSARY

Ad Retargeting tracks the users who visit your site and displays your retargeted ads to them when they visit other sites online.

Alerts provide instant knowledge of any webpage, newsfeed, blog, or discussion containing the keywords you designate for monitoring. Given their ease of set up and use, alerts are one of the simplest tools for online "listening."

Anticipatory Recommendations (aka Anticipatory Recommendation Engine, Anticipatory Computing) refers to a subset of predictive intelligence technologies that are able to access Internet, social, mobile, and geolocational data (aka proactive information discovery), and then filter, categorize, and contextualize it to deliver real-time information, content, and search results. These technologies also utilize complex predictive modeling algorithms to "anticipate" what information users will likely require in the future, and then proactively serve it up.

Benefit Corporation (B-Corp) is a corporate entitiy type designed for for-profit entities that want to consider society and the environment in addition to profit in their decision-making process. The main goal of a benefit corporation is to create general public benefit, which is defined as a materially positive impact on society and the environment. The B-Corp offers a positive vision of a better way to do business by voluntarily meeting higher standards of transparency, accountability, and performance.

Big Data refers to the collection of data sets (diverse sources in aggregated fragments of small and contextually related data points) so large and complex that it becomes difficult to process using on-hand database management tools or traditional data processing applications.

Blog is a website or web page on which an individual or organization publishes written, auditory, or visual content, often on a regular, chronological basis. The term is a truncation of the expression "web log."

Brand Blueprint is a framework to help your organization shape various aspects of its brand message and ensure each aligns with your values and goals.

Brand Essence is an encapsulation of an organization's fundamental qualities and characteristics, a concise articulation of its unique identity, or the few words that serve as the consistent touchstone for all of its marketing efforts.

Brand Message is the sum of an organization's communication with the outside world. A well-crafted brand message uses a unified brand voice to articulate an organization's brand essence and brand promises.

Brand Promise is the value an organization brings to its consumers. It should reflect the things a brand guarantees or the problems/pain points it solves.

Brand Voice is a brand's personality; it reflects the consistent identity or execution of its essence.

Brand Website is the cornerstone of an organization's online marketing efforts. Brand websites have become the primary go-to source of information for prospects and consumers, supporting, replacing, and in some cases improving upon, many of the business functions of their bricks-and-mortar counterparts.

Branded Content (aka Native Advertising or Advertorials) is a novel approach to content marketing in which the brand attempts to connect with the end user by providing customized content designed to naturally and contextually "fit in" with the content that it appears alongside. Branded content can take on virtually any form, such as videos, news articles, social media posts, even television shows. Examples of branded content in social media include Facebook's Sponsored Stories, Twitter's Promoted Tweets, and YouTube's TrueView Ads.

Broad Data reflects the shift from a small number of organizationally controlled data sources (e.g. bricks-and-mortar stores, websites, and customer data warehouses) to myriad data sources of varying nature and size. Broad data refers to the collection and analysis of real-time or near-real-time customer experience data to inform marketing strategies and tactics.

Call-to-Action (CTA) is a banner, button, or some other graphic or text on a web page, social platform, or email message directing the user to take a specific action, such as "click here," "download," "submit," or "purchase." CTAs work in tandem with landing pages to promote online (web, social, or mobile) content offers.

Chief Information Officer (CIO) is the C-suite executive responsible for overseeing the IT and computer systems of the organization. The CIO anticipates technological trends in the marketplace and navigates these trends through expert guidance and strategic IT planning that is aligned to organizational strategy.

Chief Marketing Officer (CMO) is the C-suite executive responsible for the marketing activities of the organization. Traditionally, the CMO has directed a siloed effort to get attention in the marketplace, which may include brand building, increasing the effectiveness of advertising initiatives, and market research. In recent years, this role is expanding to include managing the customer experience, building new digital marketing capabilities throughout the enterprise, collaborating on digital transformation, and overseeing customer engagement throughout the organization.

Cloud Computing is a model for enabling convenient, on-demand network access to a shared pool of configurable computing resources (e.g. networks, servers, storage, applications, and services) that can be rapidly provisioned and released with minimal management effort or service provider interaction. For the average end-user, it refers to the storing and accessing of data and programs over the Internet instead of on your computer's hard drive.

Connected Digital Experience (CDE) integrates various digital technologies, including video commenting, augmented reality, and marketing automation, to revolutionize user engagement with print and digital media. The CDE transforms static media into dynamic, interactive, rich content that generates measurable data in real time.

Consumer Decision Journey encapsulates the touch points and key buying factors resulting from the explosion of product choices and influence from digital channels that affect the consumer's decision-making process and post-purchase behavior.

Content Management System (CMS) is a computer program for website design that supports content publishing and editing as well as workflow management.

Converged Media integrates paid, earned, and owned media to support an organization's goals. It reflects the customer's seamless journey between devices, channels, and media.

Converged Social Business is a strategic business process whereby social merges with digital to create holistic customer experiences and form a social culture.

Core Values are the beliefs an organization holds important and meaningful. Clarifying and defining core values is necessary to building an authentic and transparent brand.

Corporate Social Responsibility (CSR) addresses four levels of responsibility: economic (make profits), legal (obligation to comply with laws), ethical (do the right thing because its right) and philanthropic (go above and beyond to give back to the community).

Creating Shared Value (CSV) measures economic and social value or new benefits that exceed the costs for the business and society to engage the scale and innovation of companies to advance social progress. It is an internally generated measure not confined to financial budgets.

Cross-Functional Team includes representatives from diverse functional departments within an organization in which each team member has a stake and role in the launch and outcome of the project or initiative.

Crowdsourcing taps into interconnecting networks of people to more efficiently address challenges and solve complex problems.

C-Suite refers to a corporation's most important senior executives whose titles tend to start with the letter C, for "Chief," as in Chief Executive Officer (CEO), Chief Financial Officer (CFO), etc.

Culture is the cumulative deposit of knowledge, experience, beliefs, attitudes, meanings, and hierarchies of a particular society or group.

Customer Experience (CX) is the sum of all experiences a customer has with a supplier of goods (products) or services over the duration of their relationship with that supplier. CX includes all customer touch points as they interact during the buying, using, owning, servicing, and recommending of any given product or service.

Customer Relationship Management (CRM) leverages digital technologies to organize, automate, and synchronize sales, marketing, customer service, and technical support. CRM software is primarily used by organizations to manage interactions with current and future customers.

Demand-Side Platforms (DSPs) are similar to Google AdWords in that they are buying platforms on which to create ad campaigns. However, DSPs go beyond AdWords in that they are often designed around building display ad campaigns within a vendor-neutral, real-time-bidding environment.

Digital Alien is a term referring to an individual schooled before the existence of digital technology, but who has managed to develop a basic skill set with computers and the Internet. C-suite digital aliens are often slow to acknowledge the relevance of digital for business and routinely block its adoption within the organization. Holding traditional and hierarchical values, they are seldom conditioned to rely on the voices of their employees or consumers, and are largely closed to open dialogue or collaboration. Characteristically, the digital alien has a hard time accepting that digital can have a profound impact on the organization's bottom line.

Digital Alignment is the harmonizing of the organization's core values and business goals with its digital marketing strategies and tactics, infrastructure, and information systems. It reflects a new method of doing business where technology, people, and processes are seamlessly integrated.

Digital Culture represents a specific set of core values and fundamental attributes (see page 13) that, when taken together, are reflective of a nascent global culture. The digital culture transcends geographical proximity; it knows no physical boundaries; it recognizes no socio-economic, racial, or ethnic hierarchies or divisions. It is a virtual culture open to anyone with access to a computing device and an Internet connection.

Digital Diagnostics are tools for self-reflection included in the book to help practitioners and executives ask the right questions as they work through the challenges of digital integration and transformation. Digital diagnostics allow the reader to take an accurate snapshot of where their organization is on the *Path to Digital Integration*.

Digital DNA represents a collective set of fundamental characteristics that enable an organization to leverage technology to operate and excel in today's rapidly changing business environment.

Digital Evolution is not merely comprised of the next hot social media tool. Rather, it is an all-encompassing paradigm shift, and as such demands a fundamental shift in thinking.

Digital Footprint is the data trail left by users when they interact with the brand online. Alerts, analytics, and social mentions provide real-time insight into an organization's digital footprint.

Digital Immigrant is an individual who recognizes the value of digital marketing but needs to learn more about the strategies, tactics, and tools necessary for its effective implementation. The digital immigrant needs guidance in order to fully adopt a digital mindset and seamlessly integrate digital throughout the organization.

Digital Insight is the ability of an organization to anticipate and measure how various digital marketing drivers and trends will impact the organization, both now and in the future. Digital insight is a vital tool for achieving competitive advantage.

Digitally Integrated Organization (DIO) is an entity that combines digital technologies and digital marketing strategy with core human values to generate abundance for all stakeholders – its employees, shareholders, customers, and community.

Digital Integration is the leveraging of the broad capabilities and vast efficiencies of digital technology and media by organizations to provide customers relevance and value, thereby enhancing the customer experience.

Digital Involvement Cycle reflects the existing customer decision process with an organization's product, service, or brand. The customer interacts with networks of touch points as they move through each stage of the *Cycle*, from the pre-decision process to Commitment and from Commitment through the post-decision process to Champion. At this point, a second *Cycle* begins to grow as the "loyal customer" shares their customer experience with their social communities advocating, and ultimately championing, the brand.

Digital Marketing is any marketing action that is reliant on a digital medium to execute its specific function or complete its intended action.

Digital Marketing Evaluation Model is a five-step model that builds upon each previous step to provide an actionable organizational framework for measurement and evaluation.

Digital Marketing Resource Center is *Digital Marketing's* companion website (www.dmresourcecenter.org), where the reader can access the most current information, case studies, and best practices on digital marketing and digital transformation, and subscribe to receive updates on requested topics via email.

Digital Mindset reflects the extent of an individual or organization's integration into the digital culture. On a business level, digital mindset provides the organization a strategic context to process the challenges and opportunities presented by the rapidly changing digital marketplace.

Digital Native is an individual who has an organic relationship with digital technology, using digital media as a primary means of social interaction, entertainment, and information discovery. The challenge for many digital natives is to learn how to translate their proficiency with digital technologies into viable business strategies.

Digital Personas are profiles of online user behavior, which might include digital attributes, digital body language, up and downstream click-stream data, sales funnel position, and device preferences.

Digital Return On Investment (DROI) helps brands analyze the performance of traditional and digital tools to achieve company goals. An expansion of ROI, DROI considers the impact of digital technologies on brand engagement and customer relationships and advocacy, in addition to traditional ROI metrics of exposure, sales, and profit.

Digital Transformation is part of a continuous process of change within an organization that reveals new possibilities daily as relationships, data, and markets expand. Digital transformation alters existing communications structures, influence flow, and access to critical data, encouraging collaboration and joint decision-making. It requires all members of an organization to adopt a digital mindset and integrate it into how they communicate and serve their employees, consumers, and the greater community. Organization-wide adoption of a digital mindset fuels digital transformation, encouraging democratic participation in the enterprise's strategic decision making, continuous innovation in the design and implementation of products and services, and deeper connection with existing and future customers.

Digital Trend Analysis is the process of analyzing and prioritizing different trends to determine which ones are the best fit to explore for an organization.

Earned Media represents any form of positive brand messaging that is produced and diffused by unpaid influencers. It often comes in the form of user-generated content that is shared by brand advocates.

Editorial Calendar is a monthly or weekly schedule of all content to be published for that time period. It usually contains all of the information needed to produce each content piece, such as the topic, author, keywords, links to resources, draft and publication due dates. Most editorial calendars are organized by author, content type, or campaign.

Engagement Pyramid concentrates an organization's sales efforts on the five percent of customers who really care about and have affinity with the brand; customers who are most likely to use their networks to advocate for the brand.

Generation Collaboration is a term that reflects the need to find bridges that engage and inspire everyone within an organization.

Geofencing is a virtual perimeter established around any physical space, such as a bar or restaurant, a retail location, an airport, or a stadium, that sends text notifications on an opt-in basis to mobile devices within its sphere.

Geotagging is the process of adding geographical location information to media. It's used to pinpoint the exact location mobile device users, often through social media apps.

Google Authorship allows individuals, if accepted as a trusted author, to have their name posted next to all of their published content appearing on Google's search engine results pages.

Graph Search is Facebook's internal semantic seach engine that combines data from its over 1 billion users with external data to deliver user-specific search results.

Houzz is social media site similar to Pinterest but specific to the home remodeling and construction industry.

HTTPS/SSL Encryption or Hypertext Transfer Protocol Secure (HTTPS) is a communications protocol for secure communication over a computer network, with especially wide deployment on the Internet.

Inbound Links (aka referral traffic, back links) are incoming links to your website or specific webpage.

Inbound Marketing is a holistic, data-driven strategy that helps organizations attract and convert visitors into customers by providing personalized, relevant information and content instead of interruptive messages.

Influence Marketing builds relationships with individuals who have influence over a target audience of buyers.

Infographic is a graphic visual representation of information, data, or knowledge intended to present complex information quickly and clearly.

Infrastructure as a Service (IaaS) provides cloud computing infrastructure (servers, storage, network and operating systems) as a fully outsourced, on-demand service.

Integrated Digital Marketing a comprehensive marketing strategy that merges multiple digital channels, platforms, and media to help organizations achieve their goals by providing value for and building sustainable relationships with their target audience.

Integrated External Engagement takes a unified approach to managing the organization's engagement with the external world (e.g. employees, consumers, regulators, potential users, social media activists, and legislators). Decisions made at all levels of the organization must be integrated consistently with its core values, as they affect the relationships with the external world and impact its shared value.

The Internet of Things (aka The Internet of Everything) is the world where virtually every thing (humans included) is imbued with one or more tiny computers or smart sensors, all transmitting an unending flow of data onto the Internet.

Key Performance Indicators (KPIs) are metrics that help an organization gauge performance in relation to objectives.

Landing Page is a webpage that allows brands to capture visitor information through a customized lead form. Landing pages work in tandem with CTAs to promote online (web, social, or mobile) content offers.

Lead Nurturing is an ongoing *IDM* tactic that allows organizations to leverage content to more deeply connect with their target audience, and in doing so more efficiently convert leads into customers and brand advocates.

Marketing 2.0 is a marketing model that completely integrated traditional print media with online marketing in ways that were more effective and efficient. As a result, the concept of integrated marketing communications developed.

Marketing 3.0 is human-centric marketing, or looking at prospects and customers holistically – as multi-dimensional, values-driven, global human beings whose needs go far beyond the direct consumption or experience of a brand's product or service, to encompass higher emotional, intellectual, and spiritual desires. In marketing 3.0, end users serve multiple roles as participants in product and brand creation, consumers, and advocates.

Marketing Automation refers to any number of integrated software applications designed to help organizations manage their digital marketing efforts. Organizations use marketing automation to drive web traffic, manage search-engine optimized web and social content, create CTAs and landing pages to turn web traffic into viable leads, build customized, segmented email campaigns that engage prospects as they proceed through the *Digital Involvement Cycle,* and measure results.

Market Segmentation is a marketing strategy that involves dividing a broad target market into one or more subgroups, each of which has common wants and needs, and then designing and implementing strategies to target these wants and needs using media channels and other touch points that are considered most likely to reach each subgroup.

Measurement is the yardstick by which organizations are judged. Nurturing a culture of measurement allows businesses both large and small to leverage data to accomplish their goals. When this use of data becomes rooted within the culture of an organization, the benefits of making data-driven decisions become immediately apparent.

Massive Open Online Courses (MOOCs) are free or low-cost online courses aimed at unlimited participation and access via the web. MOOCs encourage transparent interaction and information exchange, recognizing that the power is ultimately in the hands of the students, not the institutions.

Mobile Apps are software applications designed to run on smartphones, tablets, and other mobile devices. Native apps need to be connected to the Internet, as they are specific to the mobile device on which they operate; mobile web apps run on a mobile device's Internet browser, like a mobile website; hybrid mobile apps operate as native apps with embedded HTML technology that pulls updates from the web.

Near-Field Communication (NFC) is a short-range, wireless RFID technology which supports data transfer over minimal distances to encourage shoppers to purchase in-store merchandise online with the wave of their smartphone or mobile device.

New Marketing Normal is values-driven marketing for the digital age which incorporates the six P's of marketing (product, price, place, promotion, participation, and principles) to grow customer loyalty and advocacy, with sustainable outcomes for all stakeholders.

Newsjacking is the practice of an organization "hijacking" a popular news story and using it as content for its brand.

Omni-Channel is a technology driven, multi-channel approach to retailing which is focused on creating seamless consumer experiences by incorporating all available shopping channels, such as mobile Internet devices, computers, bricks-and-mortar, television, radio, direct mail, catalog, etc.

Organic Search is a search engine query initiated by a person without any preconceived intent to visit a specific brand's website or engage with its online content.

Organizational Structure reflects the way decisions are made, communications are sent and received, innovations are processed, rewards are dispensed, and ultimately, the speed and extent of digital integration.

Owned Media is any kind of content or media outlets created and owned by the brand.

Path to Digital Integration is the five-step process outlined throughout the book (mindset, model, strategy, implementation, sustainability) that has been designed to help organizations achieve digital integration.

Paid Media is any form of media where an organization pays the media owner to insert its message.

Platform-as-a-Service (PaaS) provides a platform for the creation of software delivered over the web.

Premium Content is any type of content marketing collateral that offers more expansive or in-depth information than a single content piece such as a blog post. Examples include webinars, SlideShare presentations, ebooks, and whitepapers.

QR (Quick Response) Code is a machine-readable code consisting of an array of black and white squares, typically used for storing URLs or other information that can be scanned with a smartphone.

Reddit is a social news and entertainment site which has become the highest supplier of news among social networks.

Return on Marketing Investment (ROMI) is the contribution attributable to marketing (net of marketing spending), divided by the marketing "invested" or risked.

Reverse Mentoring is the process of connecting digitally-savvy millennials with senior-level business leaders to discuss the latest digital technologies and social buzz. It exposes leaders to the digital mindset, encourages experimentation, and fosters relationships with future managers.

Sales Funnel is a sales model for leveraging various channels and tools (e.g. sales staff, email, call centers, website) to shepherd prospects through (down) various stages of the sales cycle to action.

Search Engine Optimization (SEO) is the process of affecting the visibility of a website or a web page in a search engine's "natural" or un-paid ("organic") search results. Digital marketers and professional SEOs try to optimize web-based content for keyword-initiated search queries (e.g. the words the user places in the search bar) and then carefully track the results of their efforts.

SERP (Search Engine Results Page) is the list of results returned by a search engine (i.e. Google, Bing, Yahoo!, etc.) in response to a keyword query.

Semantic Search a technique in which a search engine seeks to determine the intent and contextual meaning of the words and phrases used in a search query.

SERVAS Digital Analysis is a tool that uses six benchmarks to evaluate the potential effectiveness of an organization's digital marketing efforts.

Skunkworks Project creates a new, small and nimble division placed outside of the existing organizational structure that reports directly to a C-level executive and is tasked with creating cutting-edge products and solutions that support user and business needs.

Smart Content is content that adapts, or personalizes, based on the preferences of the user who is consuming it.

Short Message Service (SMS) is a text messaging service component of phone, Web, or mobile communication systems that uses standardized communications protocols to allow fixed line or mobile phone devices to exchange short text messages.

SMS Payments is a popular method of paying for goods and services via mobile, whereby the user sends an SMS text to a short code, and the stipulated charges are applied to their phone bill. When payment is made, the seller is informed of the transaction.

SMS Text Marketing is the use of text messaging via mobile devices to promote an organization's products or services.

SnapChat is a photo messaging mobile app used to send disappearing images that last less than ten seconds on the receiver's device.

Software-as-a-Service (SaaS) is software that is deployed over the Internet by a cloud hosting provider and managed from a central location, where the client has access to it via the web. With SaaS, the hosting provider often licenses the software to the client on a subscription basis.

Social Business (aka Social Enterprise) is a non-dividend company created to solve a social problem. Like a non-governmental organization it has a social mission, but like a business, it generates its own revenues to cover its costs and is financially sustainable (definition from Professor Muhammad Yunus).

Social Business is an organization that deeply integrates social media and social methodologies across the entire organization to drive business impact internally and externally (definition from Altimeter Group).

Social Brand is an interactive platform or open brand ecosystem that regularly interacts with fans and followers to co-produce the compelling experiences that keep consumers engaged.

Social Check-In is a feature that enables social media users to broadcast where they are, or "check-in," at any given time on their chosen network, sharing their location with followers. Social platforms such as Swarm (Foursquare), Yelp, Google Plus, and Facebook all have social check-in features.

Social Curation is collaborative sharing of Web content organized around one or more particular themes or topics; social curation sites include Digg, Reddit, Delicious, and Pinterest.

Social Customer Relationship Management (SCRM) integrates social data into CRM systems to help organizations better serve their customers, employing digital media to increase engagement and enhance the customer experience.

Social Media Marketing is the process of gaining traffic (e.g. website, landing pages, etc.) or attention through social media sites, networks, and sharing.

Social Marketing seeks to develop and integrate marketing concepts with other approaches to influence behaviors that benefit individuals and communities for the greater social good.

Social Media Literate Leadership is the interplay of leadership skills and related organizational design to create compelling, engaging multimedia content; excel at cocreation and collaboration; understand the nature of different social media tools and the unruly forces they can unleash; and cultivate a new, technologically linked social infrastructure that by design promotes constant interaction across physical and geographical boundaries.

SoLoMo reflects the convergence of social media, local proximity, and mobile devices. It represents the growing marketing trend of targeting mobile consumers based on their current location with content or promotions designed to be shared via social networks.

Sustainable Values (or Universal Values) are beliefs and behaviors that produce an inspiring identity, human value, and knowledge flow in groups, and help people thrive individually and collectively.

Structural Integration is the redesign of siloed departments to facilitate open communication, collaboration, and innovation. It utilizes digital technologies to realize optimal solutions.

StumbleUpon is a discovery engine that finds and recommends web content to its users.

SWOT Analysis is a framework to analyze an organization's Strengths and Weaknesses, and to examine Opportunities and Threats.

Triple Bottom Line (TBL) is a framework to measure sustainability performance that goes beyond optimizing short-term profits, return-on-investment, and shareholder value to consider comprehensive environmental and social impact. TBL introduced the concept of the 3P's: profits, people, and planet.

Tumblr is a social networking site that allows users to easily post multimedia and other content to a short-form blog.

User-Generated Content (UGC) refers to various types of online content produced by the general public rather than by paid professionals and experts. User-generated content comes in many forms, including blogs, wikis, forums, podcasts, product/service reviews, and news and informational articles.

Values-Driven Marketing explores how brands impact societal challenges (e.g. public health, environment) as well as shareholders and stakeholders (e.g. consumers, employees, channel partners).

Value Proposition articulates in one sentence why people should buy an organization's products or services. It should address four key questions: What does the brand provide?; Who is its target audience?; Why is its offering unique?; and What are the expected results?

Vine is a mobile video sharing app with a maximum clip length of six seconds.

Virtual Cards are essentially digital versions of the traditional gift card located inside of an app. When customers pay via a virtual card, the app issues a barcode which can be scanned to complete the purchase.

Vlogging is video blogging.

Vusay is a point-in-time video commenting solution that increases engagement and social discovery for publishers, brands, and other sites. Vusay's video commenting technology has been integrated with Zappar's augmented reality mobile app to transform *Digital Marketing* into a truly *Connected Digital Experience (CDE)*.

Zappar is an augemented reality app that allows you to add digital layers onto the world around you through your mobile's camera view. It connects the physical world with digital devices displaying video, photo, sounds, animations, and more. The Zappar augmented reality experience has been integrated with Vusay's video commenting technology to transform *Digital Marketing* into a truly *Connected Digital Experience (CDE)*.

INDEX